Governance, Development, and Social Inclusion in Latin America

Series Editors
Rebecka Villanueva Ulfgard
International Studies
Instituto Mora
Mexico City, Mexico

César Villanueva Rivas
Department of International Studies
Universidad Iberoamericana
Mexico City, Mexico

This series seeks to go beyond a traditional focus on the virtues of intra-regional and inter-regional trade agreements, liberal economic policies, and a narrow security agenda in Latin America. Instead, titles deal with a broad range of topics related to international cooperation, global and regional governance, sustainable development and environmental cooperation, internal displacement, and social inclusion in the context of the Post-2015 Development Agenda — as well as their repercussions for public policy across the region. Moreover, the series principally focuses on new international cooperation dynamics such as South-South and triangular cooperation, knowledge sharing as a current practice, and the role of the private sector in financing international cooperation and development in Latin America. The series also includes topics that fall outside the traditional scope of studying cooperation and development, in this case, (in)security and forced internal displacement, cultural cooperation, and *Buen Vivir* among indigenous peoples and farmers in Latin America. Finally, this series welcomes titles which explore the tensions and dialogue around how to manage the imbalance between state, markets, and society with a view to re-articulating cooperation and governance dynamics in the 21st century.

More information about this series at
http://www.palgrave.com/series/15135

Roberto Zepeda

The Decline of Labor Unions in Mexico during the Neoliberal Period

palgrave
macmillan

Roberto Zepeda
Universidad Nacional Autónoma de México
Mexico City, Mexico

Governance, Development, and Social Inclusion in Latin America
ISBN 978-3-030-65709-3 ISBN 978-3-030-65710-9 (eBook)
https://doi.org/10.1007/978-3-030-65710-9

This Palgrave Macmillan imprint is published by the registered company Springer Nature Switzerland AG
The registered company address is: Gewerbestrasse 11, 6330 Cham, Switzerland

Interviews

Alcalde, A. (September, 2007). Labor lawyer and advisor of independent labor unions (FAT, UNT and others), Mexico City.
Amezcua, F. (November, 2007). Secretary of external affairs, SME, Mexico City.
Barba, H. (December, 2007). Union advisor (STRM and UNT), Mexico City.
Bouzas, A. (September, 2007). Labor lawyer and academic scholar, UNAM, Mexico City.
Bizberg, I. (October, 2007). Academic scholar, el Colegio de Mexico, Mexico City.
Gimenez-Cacho, L. (November, 2007). Academic scholar and director of NEXOS magazine, Mexico City.
Confidential interview. (November, 2007b). Retired worker (CTM), Mexico City.
De Buen, N. (September, 2007). Labor lawyer and union advisor (SNTMM and others), Mexico City.
De la Garza, E. (October, 2007). Academic scholar, Universidad Autonoma Metropolitana, Mexico City.
Esparza, M. (November, 2007). Secretary-general of SME, Mexico City.
Farina, F. (October, 2007). Union advisor (SME and INEGI union), Mexico City.

Galindo, C. (November, 2007). Secretary of external affairs of STUNAM, Mexico City.
González, I. (October, 2007). Academic scholar and union organizer, Friedrich Ebert foundation, Mexico City.
Guerra, T. (October, 2007). Academic scholar and labor lawyer, Universidad Autonoma de Sinaloa.
Ibarra, G. (October, 2007). Academic scholar, Universidad Autonoma de Sinaloa.
Meléndez, M. (2007). Union leader (CTM). Mazatlán, Sinaloa, México.
Meyer, L. (February, 2006). Academic scholar, El Colegio de Mexico, Mexico City.
Miron, L. (November, 2007). Ministry of labor, government of Distrito Federal, Mexico City.
Merced, J. (February, 2007). Union organizer and director of CEMPROS, Mexico City.
Robles, J. (September, 2007). Union leader (FAT and UNT), Mexico City.
Sánchez, A. (February, 2006). Secretary of external affairs, SME, Mexico City.
Zapata, F. (October, 2007). Academic scholar, el Colegio de Mexico, Mexico City.

Contents

Abbreviations

AFL-CIO	American Federation of Labor and Congress of Industrial Organizations
ASPA	Asociación Sindical de Pilotos Aviadores
ASSA	Asociación Sindical de Sobrecargos de Aviación
ATM	Alianza de Tranviarios de México
BLS	Bureau of Labor Statistics
CFE	Comisión Federal de Electricidad
CGT	Confederación General de Trabajadores
CIA	Central Intelligence Agency
CIOSL	Confederación Internacional de Organizaciones Sindicales
CIPM	Coordinadora Intersindical Primero de Mayo
CLC	Commission for Labor Cooperation
CLyFC	Compañía Luz y Fuerza del Centro
CNOP	Confederación Nacional de Organizaciones Populares
CNT	Cámara Nacional del Trabajo
CNTE	Coordinadora Nacional de Trabajadores de la Educación
COCM	Confederación de Obreros y Campesinos de México
CONAPO	Consejo Nacional de Población
CPN	Confederación Proletaria Nacional
CROC	Confederación Revolucionaria de Obreros y Campesinos
CROM	Confederación Regional Obrera Mexicana
CT	Congreso del Trabajo
CTM	Confederación de Trabajadores de México
CUT	Confederación Única de Trabajadores
DF	Distrito Federal
EAP	Economically Active Population

ENIGH	Encuesta Nacional de Ingresos y Gastos de los Hogares
ENOE	Encuesta Nacional de Ocupación y Empleo
EPI	Economic Policy Institute
EU	European Union
EZLN	Ejercito Zapatista de Liberación Nacional
FAO	Federación de Agrupaciones Obreras
FAT	Frente Auténtico del Trabajo
FDI	Foreign Direct Investment
FEDESSP	Federación Democrática de Sindicatos de Servidores Públicos
FENASIB	Federación Nacional de Sindicatos Bancarios
FESEBS	Federación de Sindicatos de Empresas de Bienes y Servicios
FNSU	Federación Nacional de Sindicatos Universitarios
FONACOT	Fondo Nacional para el Consumo de los Trabajadores
FSM	Frente Sindical Mexicano
FSTSE	Federación de Sindicatos de Trabajadores al Servicio del Estado
GATT	General Agreement on Tariffs and Trade
GDP	Gross Domestic Product
IFE	Instituto Federal Electoral
ILO	International Labor Organization
IMF	International Monetary Fund
IMSS	Instituto Mexicano de Seguridad Social
INEGI	Instituto Nacional de Estadística, Geografía e Informática
INFONAVIT	Instituto del Fondo Nacional de la Vivienda para los Trabajadores
ISSSTE	Instituto de Seguridad y Servicios Sociales de los Trabajadores del Estado
JFCA	Junta Federal de Conciliación y Arbitraje
JLCA	Junta Local de Conciliación y Arbitraje
LFT	Ley Federal del Trabajo
LFTSE	Ley Federal de los Trabajadores al Servicio del Estado
MNC	Multi National Corporations
MW	Minimum Wages
NAALC	North American Agreement on Labor Cooperation
NAFTA	North American Free Trade Agreement
OECD	Organization for Economic Cooperation and Development
OIT	Organización Internacional del Trabajo
OP	Occupied Population
PAN	Partido Acción Nacional
PEMEX	Petróleos Mexicanos
PRD	Partido de la Revolución Democrática
PRI	Partido Revolucionario Institucional
PRM	Partido de la Revolución Mexicana

SITUAM	Sindicato de Trabajadores de la Universidad Autónoma Metropolitana
SME	Sindicato Mexicano de Electricistas
SNTE	Sindicato Nacional de Trabajadores de la Educación
SNTMM	El Sindicato Nacional de Trabajadores Mineros y Metalúrgicos
SNTSS	Sindicato Nacional de Trabajadores del Seguro Social
STFRM	Sindicato de Trabajadores Ferrocarrileros de la República Mexicana
STPS	Secretaría del Trabajo y Previsión Social
STRM	Sindicato de Telefonistas de la República Mexicana
STUNAM	Sindicato de Trabajadores de la UNAM
SUTERM	Sindicato Único de Trabajadores Electricistas de la República Mexicana
SUTGDF	Sindicato Único de Trabajadores del Gobierno del Distrito Federal
SUTIN	Sindicato Único de Trabajadores de la Industria Nuclear
TELMEX	Teléfonos de Mexico
UGOCM	Unión General de Obreros y Campesinos de México
UK	United Kingdom
UNAM	Universidad Nacional Autónoma de México
UNT	Unión Nacional de Trabajadores
US	United States
US DOL	United States Department of Labor
WB	World Bank
WFTU	World Federation of Trade Unions
WTO	World Trade Organization

List of Figures

List of Tables

CHAPTER 1

Introduction

The Decline of Labor Unions

Since the last quarter of the twentieth century, labor unions around the world faced numerous difficulties in overcoming the challenges caused by economic and political transformations which have reshaped the world of labor.[1] For example, labor unions lost ground as major actors in the political and labor realms, compared with their privileged position over the post-war period. Similarly, union representation within the employed labor force has declined concurrently with the deterioration of real wages, fringe benefits, and social provisions. Collective labor contracts were dismantled during the *flexibilization* of labor. Furthermore, organized labor has seen its influence reduced in the political sphere, which has created an unfavorable context for workers. The collective bargaining power of labor unions before employers has also eroded because of the ease with which capital can relocate production. In sum, organized labor has seen its position reduced in various spheres and has faced a crisis.

Significant academic research has demonstrated the decline of labor unions in the last decades. In a wide study covering 92 countries, the International Labor Organization (ILO) (1998) demonstrated that during the 1980s and 1990s the share of unionized workers with respect to the labor force diminished in most of these countries. The Organization for Economic Cooperation and Development (OECD) has found

R. Zepeda, *The Decline of Labor Unions in Mexico during the Neoliberal Period*, Governance, Development, and Social Inclusion in Latin America, https://doi.org/10.1007/978-3-030-65710-9_1

out that the expansion of union density in the employed labor force is the exception, not the rule, in the majority of the countries of this organization (OECD, 2004).

Although there is a consensus in academia that labor unions and workers have seen a detrimental panorama in recent decades, this is not the case regarding the factors explaining the weakening of labor unions which appear divergent in each country and typically depend on national institutions, making necessary the study of individual cases. There are different explanations for union density decline. For instance, changes in employment composition; such as the decline of industry and the rise of services; the new labor force largely consisting of youth and females who do not trust on labor unions; the role of the state, employers and corporations, among others. In addition, economic and social policies and the dismantling of corporatist structures are also important in this regard. In view of that multiplicity of factors, it is crucial to establish those most relevant to the decline of labor union density. Obviously, factors relating to the decline of unions are heterogeneous and merit proper classification as well as an explanation of their relevance in specific cases.

In the case of Mexico, this study focusses on the main factors accounting for the decline of labor unions. In this sense, it observes the transitions in the political and economic spheres taking place during the neoliberal period and their impact on labor unions and workers. Since the 1980s, three developments have coincided. First, there has been a consolidation of a paradigm in economic policy known as neoliberalism; second, the most recent wave of democratization has extended and remained in various regions of the world. Third, there has been a decline of labor union representation and power in the majority of countries from both the developed and developing world. This study explores the connections among these developments, especially in the case of Mexico.

Aims of the Study

As mentioned above, the general purpose of this study is to determine the factors triggering the decline of labor unions in relation to their position in the labor and political spheres during the neoliberal period. This period is particularly relevant because neoliberal policies expanded during this time in Mexico within a political context of a democratic transition.

Union density is regarded as the main variable accounting for the decline of unions, but other aspects are also determinant to measure the importance of labor unions. In other words, the analysis of union density is conducted along with other characteristics of the labor system, such as employment composition, the political regime, among others. In this way, we can assess the decline of labor unions, considering not only the variations of union density rates but also the role and representation of labor unions in the political arena and their influence on policymaking process. The economic policies associated with neoliberalism are explored in order to identify their effects on the labor sphere since the 1980s, but also the political system and the institutional context in which these policies were implemented.

On the other hand, relying on official data, fluctuations of union density rates are calculated and analyzed, including the aggregate and disaggregated union density by industry, occupation, region, age, labor organization, among others. The analysis of statistical data does not mean that other relevant developments are neglected; for instance, the transition from an authoritarian towards a more democratic political system that stimulated the emergence or revival of an independent labor movement in recent years. This research comprises the period from 1980 to 2018, since in this period the decline of trade unions intensified in many countries. In the case of Mexico, economic crises were recurrent, and the conditions of the working class deteriorated drastically concurrently with union membership.

Assessing these developments helps identify the factors behind the adverse landscape faced by labor unions and possible solutions to such obstacles. Regarding the effects of neoliberal policies on labor unions, it is significant to highlight not only the main features of these processes but also the context in which neoliberalization took effect; that is, the characteristics of political institutions and the diverse economic policies supported by domestic governments.

This study therefore focusses on features of the most relevant transformations in the economy and politics over the last three decades before assessing the impact of such developments on the labor sphere with the purpose of explaining the decline of labor unions. It concentrates on the case of Mexico, hence a single country case study that allows for a deeper analysis, while it should also provide elements suitable for undertaking a comparison with other countries and regions of the world.

Labor Unions

Labor unions are organized groups of working people, usually but not invariably in industrial and commercial rather than agricultural concerns (Robertson, 2004: 481). They are permanent associations of waged workers, committed to defending or to improving labor conditions in the workplace. The historical origins of labor unions can be attributed to industrialization. "In the industrialized economy workers were organized into unions as a form of protection against possible or real exploitation by employers and sought to establish acceptable wages and conditions for their members", as observed by Bosworth and Dawkins (1996: 346). The UK and Germany have the oldest trade union organizations of a legal nature, though in both countries the fight for legal recognition was prolonged. According to Western (1993), the essential role of labor unions is to defend workers' salaries and labor conditions, but unions are viewed also as a key power resource of class actors that affect, for example, economic growth, industrial conflict and development of the welfare state. He also contends that different types of unions imply different types of membership, different sizes, and different objectives. Unions are not homogeneous, have different objectives and use different ways of exerting their influence on labor market outcomes (Western, 1993).

The decline of labor union density constitutes the central theme of this study. Union density, which is represented by the percentage obtained from the number of unionized workers among the total labor force, was selected as the indicator to be considered as one of the main variables to demonstrate labor union power. As will be discussed in more detail, a significant number of researchers have focused on union density as an important indicator of labor union presence in the employed labor force and as a figure of power and influence (Schnabel, 2003; Scruggs & Lange, 2002; Visser, 2006). Similarly, labor union strength has been considered in relation to the number of union leaders as members of the legislative branch, as well as the union representation in labor-related institutions (Wallerstein & Western, 2000; Western, 1997). In Mexico, the sources of influence of labor unions stem from the relationship with the state. Reliable data and statistics on union membership are also quite ambiguous.

Recently, studies conducted by scholars explaining union density fluctuations in developed countries have shown that the trends of unionization rates do not show a convergence. Moreover, specific factors have been found to be more relevant in some countries as determinants of union density variations (Ebbinghaus & Visser, 1999; Schnabel, 2003; Scruggs & Lange, 2002; Visser, 2006). In the case of Latin America, the landscape is also diverse, although we can observe a decline of unionization in some countries of the region, such as Mexico, Argentina and Colombia (Cardoso & Gindin, 2009: 22; Smith, 2005).

As noted, statistical reports show an overwhelming decline of union density through a wide group of industries and sectors in most countries in the last two decades of the twentieth century (OECD 1997, 2009; ILO, 1998). The exceptions represent a minority, for example, Sweden, Finland, Iceland, Belgium, Spain, and Chile. In terms of unionization among the labor force, one of the most striking declines took place in the United States, from 22% to 13% in the period 1980–2000. The United Kingdom, France, and Japan also suffered drastic declines in union representation. In Japan, it fell from 35.1% in 1970 to 19.7% in 2003, while in the United Kingdom, it fell from 44.8% to 29.3%. In France, union density decreased from 21.7% to 8.3% in the same period (Visser, 2006: 45). In contrast, there was a diverse landscape both in terms of union representation and the factors accounting for these trends.

Nonetheless, despite the negative trends of unionization, the role of labor unions is still relevant in many countries. In short, labor unions have not disappeared and still occupy a relative significant position, despite their reduced presence in the employed labor force. Regardless of its considerable decline, organized labor remains a substantial social, economic and political presence (Gamble, Ludlam, Taylor & Wood, 2007).

On the other hand, in countries with specific features in the political system, the power of labor unions stems from their relationship with political parties or with the state through political alliances or corporatist arrangements. In other cases, labor union power derives from their capacity of mobilization. Union density is around 10% in Mexico and France. However, labor organizations in France mobilized in the streets in alliance with other social groups to prevent the reform of labor legislation. In Mexico, during the 1980–2018 period, labor confederations negotiated with the state the no-modification of the labor code, despite their reduced level of union affiliation during this period.

The Case of Mexico

The case of labor unions in Mexico is pertinent for various reasons. On the one hand, it is a country where a peculiar authoritarian political system flourished after a social revolution (1910–1920) but more clearly since the 1930s and prevailed during most of the past century. Since the late 1980s political transition intensified and produced the democratization of the country in 2000 (Hagopian & Mainwaring, 2005) when the PRI (*Partido Revolucionario Institucional*, Institutional Revolutionary Party) was defeated in the presidential elections and removed from the highest political position in the country. However, other studies suggest that Mexico had become democratic during the administration of Ernesto Zedillo between 1994 and 2000 (UNDP, 2004: 80; Woldenberg, 2002). During the 2000s, many analysts observed that significant components of the former PRI authoritarian regime still prevailed in the country. Although the country became democratic in 2000, at the regional level, authoritarian features in the political regime persist (Ackerman, 2015; Aguayo, 2010; Middlebrook, 2004).

Two elements in the political system of Mexico are crucial for understanding the role of trade unions. First, the hegemonic party system incorporated labor unions as one of its crucial partners. Second, the unique corporatist framework regulating the relation of the state with organized actors, among them, labor unions. In this way, during most of twentieth century Mexico had an authoritarian political system, characterized by the existence of one dominant political party and a corporatist framework that fueled the operation of such a system. There are certainly other relevant elements, but I regard these two components of the political machinery in Mexico with the most influence on organized labor. The main national labor organizations, such as the CTM (*Confederación de Trabajadores de Mexico*), CROM (*Confederación Regional Obrera Mexicana*), CROC (*Confederación Revolucionaria de Obreros y Campesinos*) and the CT (*Congreso del Trabajo*), which affiliated most unionized workers in the PRI era, were part of the system as members of the official party and thus were identified as the official unions. In contrast, independent labor unions and other social movements were restrained by the state and marginalized from political power and various social benefits.

In such a context, the peculiarities of the corporatist system define the relationship between trade unions and the state in Mexico and are essential in understanding the role and operation of trade unions as components of this framework. Corporatism is understood as the political and institutional framework that regulates and delineates the relations between the state and organized groups in society such as trade unions and other interest groups. This framework has two distinct features. First, it integrates both formal and informal elements. In other words, it includes elements enshrined in national labor legislation, but also informal arrangements between the state and organized groups. For instance, one of the corporatist elements is the labor legislation (*Ley Federal del Trabajo*, LFT) of 1931, since it enables the state to control the creation and operation of labor unions. Second, it implies an exchange of loyalty between the state and organized sectors in society, which is known as *clientelism*. An important component in this regard is the access of official union leaders to the governmental bureaucracy and political spaces in exchange of political support. These conditions were sustained during most of the PRI rule, but since the 1980s the political democratization and economic liberalization have triggered a process of deterioration of the corporatist structure.

On the other hand, neoliberal reforms have been implemented widely since the 1980s in such a way that Mexico is regarded as one of the countries where the conversion into a free-market oriented economy was achieved more rapidly than in other developing countries. In approximately a decade, Mexico became a neoliberal state and integrated into international trade and financial markets. In this way, Mexico's economy relied on exports mainly directed to the United States, and on the attraction of foreign investment to boost its economy and productive activities. The economic model, in this way, complicated the position of traditional labor unions, which began losing ground. Additionally, independent unions faced limitations in expanding their perspectives within a corporatist structure in labor legislation.

The largest official labor organizations, the Confederation of Mexican Workers (CTM) and the umbrella organization, the Congress of Labor (CT), played a key role in the corporatist relationship between the government and workers during PRI rule. As a result of the integration of labor organizations, emerging after the Mexican Revolution, the CTM was founded in 1936, which, with the support of the government, became the main labor confederation in the country. The CT was created in 1966 to generate an official body to bring together the main PRI-affiliated labor organizations such as the CTM, the CROM and the CROC and to control the labor movement, preventing the consolidation of real independent unions. These labor confederations were determinant in sealing the corporatist alliance between labor, capital, and the state, in which these official labor organizations represented the overall working class, and thus were able to coordinate policies with the government.

However, the political regime that sustained these institutional arrangements initiated a process of deterioration from the 1980s onwards as a result of economic and political liberalization. The corporatist arrangements were adapted to the new circumstances, and the government reduced the support to labor organizations. A decline of union membership took place in the period 1989–1996 during the Salinas and Zedillo administrations. Similarly, the decline of union influence can also be seen in labor representation in the Congress (legislative branch) and other political positions.

Consequently, democratization (or more clearly political liberalization) led to labor fragmentation and, as a result, new independent labor organizations emerged in the labor sphere during the 1990s, mainly the FESEBES, CIPM, among others, but the most relevant were the National Union of Workers (*Unión Nacional de Trabajadores*, UNT) and the Mexican Union Front (*Frente Sindical Mexicano*, FSM). Most of the power of the official unions relied on the hegemony of the PRI regime. As the PRI became weaker, official labor also lost power and suffered division. Political liberalization reduced the political spaces occupied by the official party and its sectors (including the labor sector). The former powerful labor organizations became more fragmented, facilitating the organization of new independent labor organizations. These organizations have reshaped the landscape of labor union leadership in the country and have become an opposition movement to neoliberal reforms and the dominance of the official unions.

The Analytical Framework

As mentioned above, there is considerable research on union density, especially concentrated on developed countries. A significant number of these studies attempt to detect the factors that have influenced union density patterns in a specific period either in a single country or in different countries. These factors are classified within the cyclical, structural and institutional approaches. Within the cyclical approach, some scholars have considered various factors such as inflation, unemployment, and economic performance. In the structural approach, diverse factors are examined, including employment composition (industrial and service jobs within the employed labor force), socio-demographic characteristics of workers (sex, age and education), the share of jobs in the informal and formal sectors, and the overall number of jobs within the public and private sectors.

In the political-institutional approach, the specific factors are more abundant. It includes labor-related legislation, the Ghent system or any other scheme in which workers obtain certain benefits through labor unions. The number of strikes (strike petitions are also considered in the case of Mexico), which are regulated by labor legislation, is also considered in this category in terms of its relation to unionization levels. In the same way, the centralization of collective bargaining or the specific level of negotiation between labor unions and employers (company, industry, and national levels).

Following this approach, this study emphasizes the role of corporatism since it is relevant and applicable to the case of Mexico. Corporatism has been discussed within the institutional scheme by different authors (Ebbinghaus & Visser, 1999; Sano & Williamson, 2008) as a strong determinant of union density, especially among OECD members. In Chapter Four, the specific form of corporatism developed in Mexico will be assessed and its implications for organized labor. Government partisanship, either right or left wing, is also included and, finally, the composition of the legislative power such as the total number of deputies and senators by party affiliation. Table 1.1 shows the classification of the factors accounting for union density decline.

The Dual Transition

Two processes help explain the situation faced by workers and their organizations in the last two decades of the twentieth century in Latin America. The conversion to a neoliberal economic model and the transition of the political system towards a more democratic system of government (also known as 'democratization') have reshaped labor markets and political institutions. These two processes, seldom simultaneous but usually sequential and therefore referred as 'dual-transition' (Cook, 2002; González, 2008),[2] have impacted on the labor sphere and contributed to modify the position of labor unions in many regions of the world. For instance, in a relatively short period of two decades neoliberal

Table 1.1 Factors explaining union decline

Political-institutional factors	
Neo-liberal policies against unions	*Limited government regulation of labour markets* *Privatisation of main sectors* Flexibilization *of labour markets*
Weak alliance between unions and political parties	Political parties do not rely on unionized workers to win elections. Trade unions are not key political allies and increasingly, their presence in the political arena has diminished
Divided labour movement	Reduced strength of labour movement to oppose anti-union agenda
Legislation	Unfavourable legislation to organise workers hinders union growth
Decline of corporatism	Governments set rules of labour issues without unions' participation
Obstacles to union affiliation	Bureaucratic procedures block the creation and recognition of labour unions (e.g., Mexico)
Structural factors	
Industrial composition	Reduction or stagnation of industrial, male, full-time, public sector, and formal jobs while there has been an expansion of services, female, part- time and informal jobs
Globalization and trans-nationalization of production	Trans-national corporations (TNC) move to low-paid countries This reallocation of production throughout the world decreases the power of labour unions *vis-a-vis* the employers Productive systems beyond national frontiers extend the *army of reserve*
Economic model	Keynesianism and Import Substitution Industrialization (1940–1980): Labour unions as relevant organisations in labour systems Neoliberalism (1980-): Labor unions are regarded as outdated organisations that hinder productivity at workplaces
Cyclical factors	

(continued)

Table 1.1 (continued)

Political-institutional factors	
Neo-liberal policies against unions	*Limited government regulation of labour markets* *Privatisation of main sectors* Flexibilization *of labour markets*
Employment	Employment growth is conducive to union organizing, while the opposite complicates union affiliation
Unemployment	The higher the unemployment rate, the lower the union density and lower influence of trade unions in the collective bargaining process
Economic Performance	Low economic growth tends to reduce employment and union density affiliation (and vice versa)

Source Elaborated by the Author

reforms have restructured the industrial sectors, the composition of the labor force but also molded the political institutions and the interactions among political and social actors. Such transformations are pertinent in understanding the situation faced by workers and labor unions.

In this manner, the main dimensions of this study rely on three major interconnected themes. The first dimension explores democratization or political transition and its consequences on labor-state relations, the role of unions in the structure of the official party and governmental bureaucracy. The second deals with the effects of neoliberal policies on labor markets and trade unions. The third assesses the representation of trade unions in the employed labor force as well as their presence in labor and political realms. In the case of Mexico, between the 1930s and 1980s the rise of labor unionism took place within a protectionist economic model of Import Substitution Industrialization (ISI) and an authoritarian political system characterized by a hegemonic party and a robust corporatist structure sealed with an alliance between organized labor and the state through the official party. During the dual transition, which took place between the 1980s and 2000s, a group of determinant factors altered the characteristics in the two spheres mentioned above and at the same time impacted how labor unions functioned.

In Latin America, "the state is often the chief architect of economic reform as well as of legal and institutional changes in industrial relations", observes Cook (1998: 313). Considering the features of the political system in Mexico, the PRI governments played a decisive role in the implementation of neoliberal policies and in the political liberalization process. The administrations of de la Madrid and Salinas were able to implement, at least without major difficulty, the neoliberal agenda and to lead a gradual democratization process, which has been identified more precisely as political liberalization (Loaeza, 1994: 107–108; Middlebrook, 1986).[3] This is a feature of the Mexican political regime.

The dual transition triggered a crisis of the organized labor movement in Latin America. In the political sphere, this was mainly because the largest labor organizations were key members of dominant political parties or were linked to the state through corporatist alliances. In this sense, it is noteworthy that the party systems in Brazil, Mexico, Argentina, Chile, Peru, Bolivia, and Venezuela were regarded as labor-based parties because they were mass-based, labor-mobilizing populist or leftist parties with a commitment to redistributive social reforms (Roberts, 2007: 118). On the other hand, in the economic realm, labor unions received the state support to sustain an Import Substitution Industrialization (ISI) model of development, especially in the largest economies of the region: Mexico, Brazil, and Argentina. Collier (2000: 94) notes that major economic models based on the creation of national industrial capacity and national markets (models rooted in Keynesianism, ISI or central planning) could potentially provide the material base for majoritarian political coalitions that included labor movements as a core constituency. As noted by Thomas (1995: 6), in Mexico, Brazil, India, among others, the labor movement could reap considerable benefits if the ISI strategy provided protection and predictability in domestic markets. In this manner, Roberts (2007: 117) identified an elective affinity between strong developmentalist states, mass party organizations, and dense trade unions movements.

Democratization means the replacement of an authoritarian government by another that was democratically elected (Huntington, 1991: 9) but also involves the removal of authoritarian social practices (Grugel, 2002: 31). A democratic regime implies free and fair elections, protection of civil liberties, the opportunity for most of the adult population to vote in elections with no interference from the military or other actors (Hagopian & Mainwaring, 2005: 3). The kind of democracy determines the characteristics of political institutions and the possibilities of organization and operation of social groups like labor unions. In the case of Mexico, democratization was a gradual process.

Regardless of the posture of organized labor, the crucial role it played in the evolution of the political system and the form of government is clear, either as a promoter of democracy or as a crucial ally of authoritarian regimes to obstruct the political democratization process. As has been demonstrated, in some cases unions have promoted democracy and have been one of the social groups that have advanced their position within a democratic regime. Although some of the labor unions have championed democracy and have consolidated their position within a democratic environment, it is also notable that "in Latin America the relationship between labor strength and democracy has generally been weak, and during some periods it may have been negative" (Levitsky & Mainwaring, 2006: 38). In many countries with corporatist structures, including Mexico, where labor unions were part of the dominant parties, the political democratization process meant the reduction of their privileged position. Thus, labor unions, especially the official wing, opposed the wave of democratization.

Neoliberalism

The embrace of the neoliberal economic model in the 1980s brought significant consequences for labor. Neoliberalism is generally understood as a set of economic policies implemented by national governments during the last four decades. They comprise the retreat of the state from the regulation of the economy and other prescriptions, leading to the formation of a free-market economy. The implications of these processes are examined in Chapter 3. To an extent, it is evident that the outcomes of the neoliberal economy shaped a new scenario for trade unions in several countries. Thus, not only does the conversion of the economic model need to be considered but also the role of national governments as decisive in fostering a new and unparalleled scenario for trade unions.

Neoliberalism refers to a revival of economic liberalism beginning in the mid-1970s (in Chile, for instance) but more clearly since the 1980s when the major economies of the world (for instance the USA and the UK) turned to these prescriptions to resolve substantial economic failures, such as chronic inflation and slow economic growth. Neoliberalism aims to halt, and if possible, reverse, the trends towards 'big' government and state intervention that had characterized much of the twentieth century

(Heywood, 2003: 54–55). In the same way, the advent of a neoliberal consensus during the 1980s and 1990s, favoring economic liberalism and the free market, has transformed the character of the Latin American state which had evolved alongside industrialization, and reconfigured the relative power of interest groups such as business organizations and trade unions (O'Toole, 2007: 441).

A variety of policy prescriptions, which are essential in understanding this economic doctrine, was summarized by Williamson (2000)[4] in the late 1980s, now identified as the Washington Consensus. Among the ten points listed in this Consensus are the harmonization of macroeconomic indicators, especially inflation and reduction of public deficits but also fiscal discipline, tax reform, liberalization of trade and foreign investment, privatization, and deregulation. These policies have completely transformed the role of the state in the economy and correspondingly the instruments of public policy for economic development but also, crucial for labor unions, they reshaped the relations between the state and organized social actors.

As noted above, neoliberalism refers to many aspects of political economy, but the crucial point is that it marks a watershed in the economic model implemented by many countries during the decades between 1930 and 1980. The analysis of neoliberalism is focused essentially on three perspectives. First, neoliberalism implies a reduction of state intervention in the economy, encouraging the privatization of state corporations. This has affected the position of trade unions as they were especially strong in the public sector. The privatization of firms tends to lead to a more flexible labor system in order to increase productivity rates by lowering employment levels and reducing the wide array of fringe benefits for workers. This also includes the dismantling of national collective agreements and the offensive on trade unions by neoliberal and conservative governments. Thus, privatization was used in many cases to reduce the power of trade unions. While public enterprises were privatized, union membership eroded drastically, since the most important unions in terms of membership and political influence were in this sector. In Mexico, the privatization process was significant in dismantling nationwide collective agreements and weakening trade unions. During the period 1982–1994, around 80% of total state enterprises were privatized (MacLeod, 2005: 42–45). In this process, union membership in sectors such as mining, steel, railway, among others, was eroded drastically (see Chapters 4 and 6).

As mentioned above, neoliberal policies comprise the stabilization of macroeconomic indicators, particularly the control and reduction of inflation rates and public deficits. While the reduction of inflation was one of the priorities of the Mexican government, other aspects, such as the stimulation of employment, were relegated, impacting negatively on the creation of formal jobs, particularly in the public sector. In this way, as noted by prominent economists, in Mexico the achievement of this goal was attained successfully, although it comprised the containment of wages and prices, which eroded the overall real wages of workers. On the other hand, the lowering of public deficits led to cutbacks in social spending including subsidies to foodstuffs and other social benefits, which were especially harmful to the living standards of the working class in the first phase of reforms in the 1980s. In the Keynesian economic model or in the ISI model, the state relied on organized labor to contain inflation, whereas in the neoliberal model, the cutbacks in public spending became more crucial in this regard.

Second, the deregulation of the economy has led to labor reform in the form of more flexible legislation. This aspect is also crucial for the working class as it usually decreased some of the previous benefits obtained by workers and labor unions. In this way, neoliberal policies include the deregulation of the economy, for instance, the *flexibilization* of labor markets, discarding trade unions as major actors in the productive system. This *flexibilization* is portrayed by employers to deregulate labor and, supposedly, increase productivity, but in reality, it is used as a tool to remove the benefits workers achieved during the Keynesian period (1930s–1970s). This process has generated different effects, for instance, the fall of real wages and the undermining of trade unions, creating labor markets characterized by employment insecurity (Palley, 2005: 23). Neoliberalism contributed to the restructuring of capitalism, providing the essential means by which capital started to remove many of the compromises that had been set during the Keynesian era; for instance, governments' commitment to full employment policy, which had increased the power of trade unions (Gamble, 2001: 131). In the case of Mexico, during the 1980–2010 period *flexibilization* did not result in the reform of the labor code, partly due to the opposition of the official labor confederations (Cook, 2007), which can be considered as an evidence of their political influence.

Finally, neoliberal principles stimulated policies to increase economic integration among countries. Economic globalization represents the increasing integration of economies around the world, particularly through free trade and financial flows (IMF, 2002). Latin American countries, in order to foster economic performance, favored export-led growth over Import Substitution Industrialization, which was one of the elements that sustained the existence of strong labor movements.

Neoliberal policies, according to the perspectives mentioned above, have defined Mexico's economy over the last decades, but they have also become crucial for the evolution of trade unions. As a result of the economic collapse generated by the debt crisis of 1982, Latin American countries (including Mexico) required external assistance to overcome domestic problems, mainly the payment of foreign debt. International financial institutions, particularly the World Bank and the International Monetary Fund (IMF), set as a condition for the financial loans, the implementation of neoliberal policies, creating pressure to open their economies (Stiglitz, 2002: 37–38), which generated a major economic transformation.

In this context, Mexico became a member of the General Agreement on Tariffs and Trade (GATT) in 1986, NAFTA and the OECD in 1994, and the World Trade Organization (WTO) in 1995. In fact, by 2007 it had signed 12 free trade agreements which involved more than 40 countries, for example, the European Union in 1999, Japan in 2004, among others. Indeed, Mexico's inclusion into the NAFTA agreement in 1994, with the United States and Canada, created one of the largest free trade regions in the world. This has made its economy more dependent on and linked to the economy of the United States. By 2006, around 85% of Mexico's exports, which accounted for US$ 212 billion, were directed to the United States (US-Embassy, 2008).

Nonetheless, despite the economic transformation in harmony with neoliberal prescriptions, based on a transnational productive model focused on external markets, Mexico's economy has not had a remarkable performance and labor markets have become more precarious. Overall, economic growth has been modest and inadequate in creating formal jobs for an ever-increasing labor force, triggering informal employment. The unemployment rate, according to official statistics, remains relatively low; however, it is not a suitable indicator in assessing labor market conditions in Mexico, as a large share of the workforce, which is located within the informal sector, is not considered as unemployed. It is estimated that around 50% of the Economically Active Population (EPA) is employed in the informal sector.

Consequently, migration to the United States (in most cases illegal) of Mexican workers increased significantly in the period 1990–2010. Although NAFTA allows for the free trade of goods and services, it does not allow for the free movement of labor such as exists in the original multi-national trading bloc, the European Union. Mexican migrants seeking higher living standards across the border face deportation and criminalization. More than 1,600 Mexicans died trying to cross the border between 1998 and 2004 (Livingstone, 2009). The remittances sent by migrants in the US to their families in Mexico represent one of the main sources of incomes in the country, only exceeded by oil revenues. Therefore, the model of economic development has failed to reactivate the economy and create decent work,[5] making Mexico more dependent on external factors, as can be demonstrated by various economic and labor indicators. Furthermore, the formulation of an adequate industrial policy to generate employment in Mexico has been relegated by government officials (Dussel, 2003).

In the midst of these conditions, labor unions faced difficulties in organizing new members, as there has not been a significant economic growth and the number of jobs in the formal sector, which constitutes potential union membership, has not expanded substantially since the 1980s.

The effects of neoliberal policies have triggered wide opposition in the Latin American sub-continent since the late 1980s. Social movements have appeared in many countries as a result of the increased inequality in income distribution and poverty in the last decades. For instance, in Latin America, significant mobilizations have taken place against the neoliberal agenda. The role of labor unions in some countries has become significant in this opposition movement whereas their role has been marginal in other counties.

Methodology

In the case of Mexico, it is important to analyze the characteristics of the political system as well as the relationship between labor unions and political parties. These dynamics impact the access that labor unions have to political officials and resources, which, in turn, influences the strength of the unions. The majority of previous studies emphasizes the restrictions of labor unions imposed by the political system. Generally, they highlight different aspects of the PRI-regime and identify a corporatist system that determines the position of labor unions in Mexico.

In this study, a broader approach is utilized, focusing on not only the political system but also the characteristics of labor markets (employment composition) and macroeconomic indicators. Therefore, the interrelation between political actors, economic performance, and labor markets was examined.

On the other hand, the presentation of original data on union membership is one of the main contributions of this study. Previous research, although it incorporates union density in the analysis, has not been presented in a single study along with complete and detailed statistical data on union membership in Mexico over a number of years and, more importantly, relying on the same source and method to estimate the figures and presenting total union membership along with other categories of the labor force, which could be used as useful material for further research.

Outline of the Study

The study is divided into two major sections. The first section outlines the role of labor unions in the labor sphere and the political system. It also identifies and classifies the main factors accounting for union density fluctuations in selected countries. In this section, democratization and neoliberalism are defined with respect to their outcomes on labor markets and labor unions. It identifies the levels of union membership in the employed labor force during the decades of 1980, 1990 and 2000, especially in OECD countries with the purpose of contrasting trends and levels of unionization as well as the position of Mexico in the international arena.

While the first section analyzes the general context in which the main arguments are developed, the second includes the chapters concentrated on the case of Mexico. It focuses on the examination of labor unions in Mexico to identify the main factors behind the weakening of labor unions. Chapters 4, 5 and 6 examine the political context and economic performance, in order to determine the factors explaining the decline in union density in Mexico, which is demonstrated in detail in Chapter 7.

Chapter 7 describes the most important dimensions of union membership in the country, specifically aggregated and disaggregated union density in the period of neoliberal reforms and political democratization. Drawing on previous research, original figures are produced based on the

ENIGH survey micro-data, using schemes A and B. This chapter demonstrates the decline of trade unionism from 1989 to 1996, the increase during the second half of the 1980s, the stability of union density rates between 1996 and 2006, in view of overall unionization rates.

Finally, the conclusions are presented and discussed in Chapter 8, considering the former sections in an integrated approach. The chapter examines the relevance of the factors accounting for union density decline in Mexico as well as the perspectives of organized labor. In the last section, I discuss the final conclusions and suggestions for further research.

Notes

1. For example, these transformations were strongly influenced by the neoliberal economic policies promoted by Margaret Thatcher in the United Kingdom and by Ronald Reagan in the United States during the 1980s.
2. For instance, these authors use the term 'dual transition' to identify both the neoliberalization and democratization processes in Latin America. Cook analyzed especially the impacts of the dual transition on labor legislation in Argentina, Brazil and Chile, whereas González refers to the cases of Chile and Mexico as authoritarian political systems in which neoliberal reforms occurred before democratization. See Maria Lorena Cook (2002); and also, Francisco González (2008).
3. The evolution of the political system in Mexico during the 1980s and early 1990s has not been regarded as democratization, but rather as political liberalisation (Loaeza, 1994). See Chapters 3 and 4.
4. For a detailed description of the prescriptions of the Washington Consensus, see Williamson (2000).
5. Decent work is considered as "opportunities for women and men to obtain decent and productive work in conditions of freedom, equity, security and human dignity". See ILO (1998).

Bibliography

Ackerman, J. (2015). *El mito de la transición democrática: Nuevas coordenadas para la transformación del régimen mexicano*. Spain: Grupo Planeta.

Aguayo, S. (2010). Vuelta en U: Guía para entender y reactivar la democracia estancada. Santillana ediciones Generales.

Bosworth, D., & Dawkins, P. (1996). *The economics of the labor market*. Harlow: Longman.

Cardoso, A., & Gindin, J. (2009). *Industrial relations and collective bargaining: Argentina, Brazil and Mexico compared*. Working Paper No. 5, Geneva:

Industrial and Employment Relations Department International Labour Office.

Collier, R. B. (2000). The transformation of labor-based one-partyism at the end of the 20th century: The case of Mexico. In J. Hollifield & C. Jillson (Eds.), *Pathways to democracy: The political economy of democratic transitions*. London: Routledge.

Cook, M. L. (1998). Toward flexible industrial relations? Neo-liberalism, democracy, and labor reform in Latin America. *Industrial Relations, 37*(3), 311–336.

Cook, M. L. (2002). Labor reform and dual transitions in Brazil and the Southern cone. *Latin American Politics and Society, 44*(1), 1–34.

Cook, M. L. (2007). *The politics of labor reform in Latin America: Between flexibility and rights*. University Park: Pennsylvania State University Press.

Dussel, P. E. (2003). Industrial policy, regional trends, and structural change in Mexico's manufacturing sector, In K. Middlebrook & E. Zepeda (Eds.), *Confronting development: Assessing Mexico's economic and social policy challenges*. Stanford University Press (pp. 241–274).

Ebbinghaus, B., & Visser, J. (1999). When institutions matter: Union growth and decline in Western Europe, 1950–1995. *European Sociological Review, 15*, 135–158.

Gamble, A. (2001). Neo-liberalism. *Capital and Class, 75*, 127–134.

Gamble, A., Ludlam, S., Taylor, A., & Wood, S. (2007). Labour, the state, social movements and the challenge of neo-liberal globalization, Manchester University Press.

González, F. E. (2008). *Dual transitions from authoritarian rule: Institutionalized regimes in Chile and Mexico, 1970–2000*. Baltimore: Johns Hopkins University Press.

Grugel, J. (2002). *Democratisation: A critical introduction*. Basingstoke: Palgrave.

Hagopian, F., & Mainwaring, S. (Eds.). (2005). *The third wave of democratization in Latin America: Advances and setbacks*. Cambridge: Cambridge University Press.

Heywood, A. (2003). *Political ideologies: An introduction*. Basingstoke, UK: Palgrave Macmillan.

Huntington, S. P. (1991). *The third wave: Democratisation in the late twentieth century*. Norman: University of Oklahoma Press.

IMF. (2002). Globalisation: Threat or Opportunity, Accessed June 2008 from https://www.imf.org/external/np/exr/ib/2000/041200to.html

International, Labor, & Organisation. (1998). *World labor report 1997–1998*. Geneva: ILO.

Levitsky, S., & Mainwaring, S. (2006). Organised labor and democracy in Latin America. *Comparative Politics, 39*(1), 21–42.

Livingstone, G. (2009). *America's backyard: The United States and Latin America from the Monroe Doctrine to the war on terror*. London: Palgrave Macmillan.

Loaeza, S. (1994). Political liberalisation and uncertainty in Mexico. In M. L. Cook, K. Middlebrook & J. Molinar (Eds.), *The Politics of economic restructuring*. La Jolla, San Diego: Center for US- Mexican Studies, University of California.

MacLeod, D. (2005). Privatization and the limits of state autonomy in Mexico. Rethinking the orthodox paradox. *Latin American Perspectives, 32*(4), 36–64.

Middlebrook, K., et al. (1986). Political liberalization in an authoritarian regime: The case of Mexico. In G. O'Donnell (Ed.), *Transitions from authoritarian rule: Latin America* (pp. 123–147). Baltimore: Johns Hopkins University Press.

Middlebrook, K. (2004). *Dilemmas of political change in Mexico, London: Institute of Latin American Studies*. San Diego, CA: Center for U.-Mexican Studies, University of California.

O'Toole, G. (2007). *Politics: Latin America*. Harlow, England: Pearson Longman.

OECD. (2009). *Society at a glance 2009—OECD Social Indicators*. Statistical annexe, trade union members.

OECD. (1997). *OECD Employment outlook*. Paris: OECD.

OECD. (2004). *OECD Employment outlook*. Paris: OECD.

Palley, T. (2005). From Keynesianism to Neoliberalism: Shifting Paradigms in Economics. In A. Saad-Filho (Ed.), *Neoliberalism: A critical reader* (pp. 20–29). London: Pluto press.

Roberts, K. M. (2007). The crisis of labor politics in Latin America: Parties and labor movements during the transition to neoliberalism. *International Labor and Working-Class History, 72*(1), 116–133.

Robertson, D. (2004). *The Routledge dictionary of politics*. London: Routledge.

Sano, J., & Williamson, J. B. (2008). Factors affecting union decline in 18 OECD countries. *International Journal of Comparative Sociology, 49*(6), 479–500.

Schnabel, C. (2003). Determinants of trade union membership. In J. Addison & C. Schnabel (Eds.), *The international handbook of trade unions* (pp. 13–43). Cheltenham: Edward Elgar.

Scruggs, L., & Lange, P. (2002). Where have all the members gone? Globalization, institutions, and union density. *the Journal of Politics, 64*(1), 126–153.

Smith, P. H. (2005). Democracy in Latin America: political change in comparative perspective. Oxford University Press.

Stiglitz, J. (2002). *Globalization and its discontents*. New York: W.W. Norton.

Thomas, K. (1995). *Globalisation and third world trade unions: The challenge of rapid economic change*. London: Zed Books.
United Nations Development Programme (UNDP). (2004). Democracy in Latin America. *Towards a citizens' democracy*, Vol. 2, Alfaguara.
US-Embassy in Mexico. (2008). Available online: https://mexico.usembassy.gov/eng/eataglance_trade.pdf, consulted in May, 2008.
Visser, J. (2006). Union membership statistics in 24 countries. *Monthly Labor Review, 129*(1), 38–49.
Wallerstein, M., & Western, B. (2000). Unions In decline? What has changed and why. *Annual Review of Political Science, 3*, 355–377.
Western, B. (1993). Postwar unionisation in eighteen advanced capitalist countries. *American Sociological Review, 58*(2), 266–282.
Western, B. (1997). *Between class and market: Postwar unionisation in the capitalist democracies*. Princeton, NJ: Princeton University Press.
Williamson, O. (2000). What should the World Bank think about the Washington consensus? *World Bank Research Observer, 15*(2), 251–264.
Woldenberg, J. (2002). La construcción de la democracia. Plaza & Janes.

CHAPTER 2

The Decline of Labor Unions

Why Labor Unions Matter

Labor unions are workers' organizations which defend labor rights before employers, negotiate social benefits and a favorable relationship with the state. Labor unions efforts were crucial in the enactment of a legislative framework that guarantees basic rights for workers, such as the right of union organization, collective bargaining, strike action as well as access to a wide range of fringe benefits. This process developed throughout the twentieth century in the majority of capitalist democracies. In Mexico, for instance, the constitution enacted in 1917 protects freedom of association, the right to organize unions and to strike. The labor–related legislation in this country sets a group of conditions for workers, such as a minimum wage, an 8-hour working day, distribution of profits, housing, and social security, among others (Loyzaga de la Cueva, 2002).

Freeman and Meddoff (1984) contend that the main advantages of union organization are that it provides a direct channel of communication between workers and management, as well as improvements in specific workers' training and labor conditions. According to Freeman, union organization is fundamental since it provides workers a mechanism to express their discontent without leaving corporations. Unions give management direct information on workers' aspirations and the kind of labor conditions they prefer, which hardly could be obtained

R. Zepeda, *The Decline of Labor Unions in Mexico during the Neoliberal Period*, Governance, Development, and Social Inclusion in Latin America, https://doi.org/10.1007/978-3-030-65710-9_2

in non-unionized workplaces. In addition, unions reduce the number of voluntary retirements, leaves of absence or other types of behavior that generate instability in the workplace (Freeman, 1994).

Ebbinghaus and Visser (2000) define labor unions as one of the most important institutions in contemporary industrial societies. They observe that it is revealing to examine their evolution during the last half of the twentieth century, since these organizations are increasingly facing pressures considering social, economic, and political changes at national and global levels. Furthermore, labor unions are one of the essential organizations within democratic societies. According to the ILO (2004), freedom of association and union organization are fundamental human rights in the workplace and represent central elements of democracy. They constitute the base of civil freedoms and a guarantee of protection against discrimination, maltreatment and harassment. Union organization may foster productivity and induce the distribution of benefits of economic growth.

Collier (1999, as cited in Haerpfer et al., 2009) suggested that the role of the working class–although not so important in the nineteenth and early twentieth century transitions in Western Europe as was suggested by Rueschemeyer et al. (1992)–was crucial in the most recent wave of democratization in Southern Europe and South America. While there is enough evidence to support the former argument in the regions just mentioned, it has not entirely been the case in a group of countries (for instance in Tunisia and Egypt) where labor unions have supported the perpetuity of authoritarian governments rather than fighting for democracy. Similarly, organized labor in Mexico obstructed the democratization process at different moments during the second half of the past century (Bellin, 2000: 199–203).

In this way, the participation of labor unions in the evolution of society and the configuration of the political system has proved to be crucial. In other words, both authoritarian and democratic political regimes have required labor organizations for the preservation of their political regime. In the same way that unions have promoted democracy and forged alliances with the state in democratic environments it has also been demonstrated that authoritarian regimes have used labor unions to gain legitimacy and preserve political power. In Mexico, the post-revolutionary regime strengthened its ties with organized labor to gain legitimacy and obtain a robust political support during most of the twentieth century (Middlebrook, 1995: 73–74).

Union Density

Union density is one of the most common measures to assess the strength of labor unions. It is taken as the fraction of all wage earners and salaried employees in employment, net of retired, unemployed or self-employed union members. If it is defined and analyzed in comparative perspective, it is useful to describe how the situation of trade unions has changed over time in different countries, industries, and sectors. The fluctuations of union density rates suggest changes in the social, legal, political, and economic context and the performance of trade unions (Visser, 2006). Similarly, the influence of unions has been measured according to the number of political seats in the legislative branches and the positions in the labor-related official institutions, occupied by union members and leaders (Wallerstein and Western, 2000; Western, 1997). The spaces of labor unions in the official bureaucracy are also relevant in this regard.

It has been argued that union density by itself does not embody union strength. The case of trade unions in France is a good example. French unionism is perceived as a unionism of activists that shares something of its ideological foundations with the Italian union movement; these considerations challenge the significance of membership (Vernon, 2006: 191). Furthermore, labor unions may have strength outside the arena of routinized industrial relations to which density relates; French unions, despite their weakness in membership and joint regulation, do indeed have a political role, though not in routinized concertation (Vernon, 2006: 203).

Another aspect to consider is that the union density measure may overstate the level of unionization because non-paying and retired members are frequently kept on union registers, although this upward bias may be offset if unions underreport membership to reduce payments to a central confederation (Bain & Price 1980: 5). In contrast, in some countries in which labor organizations are sections of political parties, they amplify their membership to expand their political influence in parties and official bureaucracy.

In the case of Mexico, union density alone is not a robust indicator to explain the strength and influence of labor unions. Cook (2007: 21) considers union density as a "common measure of labor strength, but a problematic one", since "high density in some countries, such as Mexico, may reflect involuntary or compulsory union membership and is therefore less meaningful as an indication of member commitment or mobilization capacity". In this context, it is necessary to analyze other dimensions and sources of power such as the relations of labor unions with both the state and political parties and the access of labor organizations to policy making.

Union density, however, is one of the most relevant indicators in the academic sphere, as can be seen in the scholarship of this subject in the United States, Canada, and other European and Asian countries. In addition, union density is employed by international bodies, such as the OECD and ILO in order to measure the presence of labor unions in the employed labor force but also to generate revealing comparative analysis.

The implications of the levels of union density are relevant for the working class as they influence wages and contribute to reducing inequality. According to Toke (2003), union density rates are closely related to the living standards of workers. Union members and other workers covered by collective agreements in industrial and developing countries obtain higher average salaries than workers who are not trade union members. The wage gap is larger in the United States (15%) than in most other industrial countries (5% to 10%). At the macroeconomic level, high unionization rates lead to lower inequality of earnings and can improve economic performance in the form of lower unemployment and inflation, higher productivity, and speedier adjustment to shocks.

Depending on the economic, institutional, and political environment in which unions and employers interact; collective bargaining, as opposed to individual contracting, can contribute negatively or positively to the economic performance of firms and to the well-being of workers. In addition, union membership reduces wage differences between skilled and unskilled workers as well as between female workers and male workers. Fringe benefits are more commonly found among unionized workers than among non-unionized ones. Furthermore, unionized workers tend to receive more training than their non-unionized counterparts, especially company-related training (Toke, 2003). Therefore, union density is relevant not only for workers since it means better wages and fringe benefits, but also for enterprises, providing more productivity.

In the United States, unionized workers earn higher wages and benefits compared to non-unionized workers. Unionized workers are 28.2% more likely to be covered by employer-provided health insurance. The growth of wage inequality in the United States is attributed to several factors, including significant changes in the labor market, such as the weakening of labor unions and the severe decline in the real value of the minimum wage (Mishel et al., 2012).

Marshall (2006) observes that the levels, trends, and determinants of unionization have not been systematically researched in Mexico and other Latin American states. The relative underdevelopment of this field of research in Latin America contrasts not only with the proliferation of studies in Europe, the United States, Canada and Australia, where more complete and accurate information exists on this topic, but also with the vast literature on the relation between labor unions and the state in the Latin American countries (2006).

Research focused on union density fluctuations in Latin America is limited due to many factors. First, the scarcity of statistical information regarding aggregated and disaggregated union membership, in contrast to developed countries, where the availability of union membership figures facilitates the comparison among several countries throughout different periods using statistical analysis. Second, the focal point of previous research has concentrated on the relation between labor unions and political actors, especially because most countries in this region were not democratic or were in the transition to democracy. Although some researchers have employed a comparative approach to examine labor unionism in Latin America, the majority of this scholarship has focused on the relation between labor unions and the state, their presence in party structure and bureaucratic positions, and on the study of several labor organizations or national unions in specific sectors and how they have reacted to the implementation of neoliberal policies or how organized labor has contributed to the consolidation of democracy (Bensusán, 2000; Burgess, 2004; Murillo, 2001; Patroni, 2001; Zapata, 1993). However, most of this academic scholarship has not deeply examined the fluctuations of union density in the region either in a single country or in a group of countries in recent decades.

The Decline of Organized Labor

During the post-second world war period, labor unions experienced their heydays reaching the pinnacle in the mid-1950s. In this period, the position of labor organizations throughout the world became more stable since they achieved the recognition of government and employers. This situation facilitated the recruitment and affiliation of workers to trade unions across most sectors and industries (Boeri, Brugiavini & Calmfors,

2001). Nevertheless, the constant expansion of union membership ended in the 1980s, which marked the starting point of a negative trend for labor organizations in comparison with the post-war period, in almost all OECD countries (Visser, 1991).

Towards the end of the twentieth century, there was a reduced labor movement in the world with lower leverage on policymaking, diminished relation with political parties and low representation in the employed labor force. The rapid expansion of labor union organization in all but a few industrialized market economies ended in the 1980s, sharply contrasting with what had in Europe been the main trend in preceding decades. Ebbinghaus and Visser (1999) observed that "economic, political and labor market changes in the period after the 'Golden Age of Capitalism' (1950–1973) have taxed the mobilizing capacity of European union movements; in all countries trade unions faced a less friendly climate".

In the World Labor Report of 1997–1998 prepared by the ILO (1998), a trend towards declining unionization was documented for most of the union movements in developing countries. However, there were some remarkable exceptions related to a return to democracy and improved union rights: South Africa and Chile were two notable cases. Union density was less than 10% in 19 countries, and in 54 countries it was lower than 25%. In other 19 countries unions organize more than half of the labor force. On the other hand, the report analyzed the unionization trends during the 1980s and 1990s. Union density levels decreased in 47 of the 66 countries in different regions of the world, but it was more or less stable in seven and increased in twelve countries (outside Europe these were South Africa, Zimbabwe, Chile, El Salvador, Hong Kong, Philippines and Taiwan) (Visser, 2000).

In the case of Latin America, a decline of labor union density can be seen in many countries from the mid-1980s to mid-1990s. Two of the main economies in the region, Argentina and Mexico, suffered the most notorious declines in unionization in that period. Also, the decline was evident in Venezuela, Uruguay and Costa Rica. In contrast, Chile was the only case in the region in which there was an increase of union density over this period. In North America, the United States saw a drastic drop of unionization rates between 1985 and 1995, whereas in Canada the unionization levels remained stable.

According to the World Labor Report (ILO, 1998), union density expanded only in some countries, particularly in South Africa, where the total number of unionized workers grew 130.8%, but also in the Philippines (84.9%), Spain (62.1%), Malta (35.8%), and Finland (16.1%). In this same report, the countries in which the majority of the employed labor force is unionized represent a minority: only in 14 out of 92 countries, where union density is known (calculated by considering non-agricultural labor force), it was more than 50% in 1995, but in the majority, 48 countries, unionization was lower than 20%.

In a wide analysis on labor union density, the OECD (2004) shows that only four out of twenty countries saw an increase in union density rates between 1970 and 2004: Belgium, Denmark, Finland and Sweden, the four countries with the "Ghent system" described later. Another Nordic country where density has increased in recent decades is Iceland, while union density improved in Spain, but stayed at rather low levels. In Finland, Iceland, and Sweden, more than three out of four salaried workers were unionized around 2004, while the figure is one in eight or less in France, Korea, and the United States.

Some even steeper declines are evident from the Table 2.1. Union density decreased by more than half in Portugal and New Zealand (where the 1991 Employment Contracts Act represented the end of a century of state protection of trade union organization), while it fell by over one-third in seven countries (Australia, France, Ireland, the Netherlands, Switzerland, the United Kingdom, and the United States). In absolute numbers, density fell 46 percentage points in New Zealand, 37 points in Portugal, and 23 points in Australia. In most countries where rates have fallen, membership levels fell as well, despite expanding employment. Finally, the data presented allow the generalization that density rates in European countries are, as a rule, above those from OECD countries in North America, Oceania, and Asia (OECD, 2004: 145).

Regarding the explanatory factors of the unionization levels, the OECD (2004: 144) contends that the extent of union membership can be influenced immensely by certain regulatory features. For instance, most OECD countries regulate their labor relations by means of one or several laws that determine the underlying conditions for employee representation, trade union formation, collective bargaining, and industrial conflict, among others. Legislation influences potential market power of trade unions and employers by setting and modifying statutory provisions that may tip a precarious balance in favor of one or the other side (OECD, 1997). Similarly, the decline of manufacturing and the growth of services,

Table 2.1 Trade union density in OECD countries, 1970–2018

	1970	*1980*	*1990*	*2000*	*2010*	*2018*	*2000–2018*
Australia	44	48	40	25	18	14	30
Austria	63	57	47	37	28	26	37
Belgium	41	54	54	56	51	50	+9
Canada	32	35	33	28	27	26	6
Czech Republic	–	–	46	27	17	12	34
Denmark	60	79	75	74	68	67	+7
Finland	51	69	72	76	70	60	+9
France	22	18	10	10	8	9	13
Germany	32	35	31	25	19	17	15
Greece	–	39	32	27	25	20	19
Hungary	–	–	63	20	17	8	55
Iceland	–	75	88	84	79	91	+3
Ireland	53	57	51	38	33	24	29
Italy	37	50	39	35	35	34	3
Japan	35	31	25	22	18	17	18
Korea	13	15	17	11	10	10	3
Luxembourg	47	52	50	34	37	32	15
Mexico	–	–	43	18	14	12	31
Netherlands	37	35	25	23	19	16	21
New Zealand	56	69	51	23	21	19	37
Norway	57	58	59	54	55	51	6
Poland	–	–	33	15	15	13	20
Portugal	–	61	32	24	19	15	46
Slovak Republic	–	–	57	36	17	11	46
Spain	–	7	11	15	16	14	+7
Sweden	68	80	80	79	68	65	3
Switzerland	29	31	24	18	17	15	14
Turkey	–	–	27	33	6	9	18
United Kingdom	45	51	39	31	26	23	22
United States	27	22	15	13	11	10	17

- Data not available

- 1971 for New Zealand

- 1981 for Luxembourg and Spain, 1982 for Australia and Portugal, 1983 for Iceland and 1984 for Canada

- 1987 for Luxembourg, 1991 for Mexico, 1993 for Iceland and 1995 for the Czech Republic, Hungary, Poland and the Slovak Republic

- 1997 for Mexico and Portugal, 1998 for Greece and Spain, 2001 for the Czech Republic, Hungary, Luxembourg, Poland and Switzerland and 2002 for the Slovak Republic

Source Elaborated by the author with statistical data from OECD, 2004 and 2012, 2020

the size and expansion of the public sector, the spread of flexible contracts and the extent of unemployment have also influenced union membership.

The reduction of union representation occurred both in Europe and the United States during the period 1960–2000. Union density climbed from 37% to 43% in Europe during the period 1960–1980, but then it declined to 33% by 1997 (Boeri, Brugiavini & Calmfors, 2001: 15). Waddington (2005) points out that union density has diminished in most European countries since 1980. His estimations suggest that the overall unionization level in the European Union countries (EU-25) has reduced from 33% in 1995 to 26% in 2001. Indeed, the reduction is more apparent among the new members of the EU, where unionization passed from 43% in 1995 to 20% by 2001. In the EU-15, it declined from 31% to 27% in the same period. Furthermore, the proportion of unionized workers had never been as low since 1950. On the other hand, in the Scandinavian countries (Denmark, Finland, and Sweden) and Belgium, the dimension of the decline has been almost imperceptible due to the existence of the 'Ghent system', which allows trade unions to manage welfare and unemployment benefits. The situation for labor unions in the United States was even more dramatic; union density decreased from 32% to 22% between 1960 and 1980, the decline persisted in the following decades to 13.9% by the year 2000 (Boeri, Brugiavini, & Calmfors, 2001: 15).

Considering the levels of union density, labor unions have successfully adapted to the conditions imposed by neoliberal globalization in a small group of countries over the last quarter of the twentieth century. For instance, Finland, Spain, and Belgium have seen a pattern of growth in union density rates in the period 1980–2006 (Visser, 2006). However, in most OECD countries, including Mexico, labor unions have witnessed a notable decline during the 1980s and 1990s as a result of several factors. In this way, the trends of union density during the neoliberal period display expansion of labor unions in a few countries and overwhelming decline in most.

Union Density in 30 OECD Countries

The decline of labor unions can be corroborated in most recent statistics presented by the OECD where the overall unionization rate has decreased in the countries of this organization. There is a noticeable decline of labor union representation in the employed labor force in the majority of capitalist democracies in the last two decades of the twentieth century, whereas in the early decades of the twenty-first century the decline persists although to a lesser extent (see Table 2.1).

Table 2.1 illustrates union density in thirty OECD countries in the 1980–2018 period. It reveals that the trends of the thirty countries are divergent and do not present similar levels of unionization. However, it can be highlighted that twenty-five out of thirty countries experienced a negative trend during the neoliberal period between 1980 and 2018. Only five countries saw an expansion in terms of unionization: Belgium, Denmark, Finland, Iceland, and Spain. As we can observe, the period 1980–2000 was more detrimental for labor unions regarding their representation in the labor force, comparing with other periods or decades.

Unionization rates increased in the countries just mentioned above mainly as a result of political-institutional factors; for instance the "Ghent scheme" in the cases of Belgium, Iceland, and Finland, whereas the case of Spain is mostly attributable to the democratization process after the decline of the authoritarian regime headed by Franco (1939–1975).

Union Density Trends in Latin America

Unionization trends in Latin America present diverse trends and dynamics (Cardoso, 2004; Cardoso & Gindin, 2009; Celhay, 2007; Smith, 2005; Visser, 2003). As can be seen in Table 2.2, by the mid-2000s, Argentina was the most unionized country in the region with around 25% of unionized workers in the employed labor force, which was higher than Brazil (17%), Chile (16%), and Mexico (10%). Mexico was ranked among the countries with the lowest levels of union affiliation in the region with only 10% of union density. In this mixed panorama, political regimes, employment composition, trade unions, and labor legislation have played a relevant part in the landscape of union representation in every country.

In Argentina, Colombia and Peru, union density has fallen dramatically as part of a labor *flexibilization* process in the context of trade liberalization. During the 1990s, rates of unionization fell in several Latin American countries, continuing a trend that had already started in the 1980s and that is also observed in industrial countries. A large part of the reduction in unionization is explained by the reduction in public sector

Table 2.2 Union density as a percentage of non-Agricultural labor force in Latin America, 1986–2010

	1986–1990	*1991–1995*	*2000–2005 (b)*	*2010 (c)*
Argentina	48.7	25.4	25	32
Bolivia	.	16.4		27
Brazil	.	32.1	17	18
Chile	11.6	15.9	16	12
Colombia	11.2	7		7
Ecuador	.	10		2
Mexico (a)	14	11	10	10
Venezuela	25.9	15		13
Uruguay	19.9	12		25
Paraguay	.	9.3		10
Peru		8		6

Source OIT, 1998. (a) Aguilar, 2008. (b) Data of Argentina and Brazil 2000–2005, Cardoso and Gindin, 2009. Data of 2000–2005, Chile, Celhay, 2007. (c) Confederación Sindical de las América (CSA) (2010), ponencia "Sindicalización y Densidad Sindical en las Américas", *Curso: Formación Sindical sobre Empleo, Salarios y Piso básico de Protección Social*, Cancún–México, November 4–9, 2010

employment. However, there has also been a sharp reduction in union affiliation in the private sector (Saavedra, 2003: 245–246).

In the case of Mexico, there was also a clear decline of union density, from 14% to 10% between 1985 and 2005, according to official data. It, however, should be noted that unionization rates calculated in Chapter 7 differ of the estimations of international bodies, such as the OECD and ILO.

In 2005, Mexico was the country with the lowest levels of unionization among the largest economies in Latin America (see Table 2.2). In the second half of the 1990s, Colombia and Peru were the countries with the less unionized workforce (in the group of eleven countries examined here), with 7% and 8% of union representation, respectively, according to the OIT (2003: 65). Mexico is less unionized than Brazil, Argentina, and Chile. As mentioned above, these countries were under the control of military regimes between 1964 and 1990 in which labor rights were largely restricted and unions faced difficulties to operate freely. The military governments in South America employed the systematic extermination, incarceration, disappearance, and torture of union members and left-wing party leaders and their activists (O'Donnell, 1973, as quoted by

Magaloni, 2006: 10; Stepan, 1971). In Brazil, the military government remained from 1964 to 1985, in Argentina it was from 1976 to 1983 and in Chile from 1973 to 1990. That is to say, workers in these countries suffered constraints with regard to union organization which was not the case of Mexico, as the political regime permitted, although with certain restrictions, the operation of labor unions during the second half of the twentieth century.

By 2005, Argentina was the country with the highest level of union density rates with 25% (O'Toole, 2007). Indeed, in the early 1990s, the unionization rate was at 37% on average. The decline of union representation is mainly attributed to neoliberal reforms during the Menem government in the 1990s (Murillo, 2000). Since the 1950s, Argentina has been at the top in terms of union density in Latin America, as a result of the political pact between state and unions promoted by Domingo Peron. During the periods under the influence of Peron (1943–1946 as minister of labor and 1946–1955 as president) workers were integrated into the political structure. The levels of unionization in Argentina fluctuated between 40% and 30% in the period 1960–1980 (Torre, 1972; Zapata, 1976). On the other hand, union density in Chile declined from 19% in 1990 to 15% in 2000, mainly attributed to the neoliberal environment created in this country during and after the military regime of Pinochet.

The number of jobs in the service sector in the national economies of Latin America increased notably during the 1990s. The expansion of services explains more than 95% of new net job creation in Latin America between 1990 and 1997. The service sector is highly heterogeneous, but two general situations can be identified. First, commerce, restaurants, and hotels, together with social, communal, and personal services, accounted for 74% of all jobs created in the region. Second, financial services, insurance, real estate, and business services experienced even faster growth (Stallings & Peres, 2000: 198). As mentioned in this chapter, the proliferation of jobs in this sector is one of the structural factors of union density decline due to the fact that this sector is more difficult to organize, which constraints the expansion of union membership. On the other hand, the industrial sector is considered as the greatest bastion of trade unionism; however, in the majority of the countries in Latin America this sector has presented a descendant tendency (UNDP, 2004).

Approaches to Examine Union Density Variations

Ebbinghaus and Visser utilized an analytical framework (1999) to examine union density fluctuations among different countries in specific periods.[1] According to this structure, union density fluctuations are explained considering three different kinds of factors, these are: cyclical factors (politico-economic changes), structural factors (social change), and configurational factors (institutional context). The cyclical approach is advocated essentially by historians and economists; they claim that both the booms and crises of labor union movements depend upon periods of prosperity and economic depression. It also comprises the political cycle which means the political changes of government from the pro-union left or the anti-union right, and the main policies directing the economy (Keynesian vs. neo-liberal macro-economic policies). The structural approach assesses trade union growth and decline in light of the changes in the employment composition; the number of jobs either in services and industrial or public and private sectors; socio-demographic characteristics of workers; flexibility of labor market; temporary or part-time jobs. The configurational approach considers the institutional context and is focused on the welfare functions of unions and their role at the workplace as well as the employer strategies.

The Cyclical Factors

In the early twentieth century, academic research focused on the relation between economic performance and union membership levels. It was identified as the cyclical approach. It suggests that union membership would be more likely to increase in periods of economic expansion encouraging greater ability for employers to give concessions, and greater pressure for the workers to demand better salaries and benefits. On the other hand, in the periods of economic crisis, union density is highly probable to decline exactly by the opposite causes. Consequently, employers would be less likely to grant concessions, and workers would be less inclined to pressure for improvements in salaries and labor conditions. In some cases, the crises in the economic activity also would lead to political unrest, since labor demands could be obtained through political activity (Price, 1991: 39–41). According to Galenson (1994: 13), economic growth should be a plus for unionization since a growing economy offers more scope than a stagnant one for improving wages and other working conditions. In addition, rising profits may cause employers to look with less disfavor on organization among their employees. With employment opportunities rising, employees are less fearful of losing their jobs if they join unions. With increasing incomes, workers are more able to pay union fees regularly (Ibid).

However, a weak relationship between movements in union density and macroeconomic performance was found in the OECD countries, specifically during the period 1970–1994 (Blanchflower, 1996). Galenson (1994: 14–15) analyzed the variations of union density in the 1980s and early 1990s in a group of 25 countries, including 13 developed and 12 developing countries.[2] Galenson found no significant relationship between economic performance and union density variations during the 1980s, especially in developed countries, whereas a marginal level of significance was detected in developing countries.

On the other hand, high unemployment rates are claimed to negatively affect union affiliation because unemployment reflects the relative bargaining power of unions and employers. Employers oppose unions during periods of high unemployment because the cost of industrial action is relatively small in times of reduced aggregated demand. However, employer opposition to unions decreases when labor markets are featured by low unemployment. For workers, the cost of union membership is absurdly high and its benefits too few during spells of unemployment (Bain & Elsheikh 1976, quoted by Western, 1993). A negative effect of unemployment on unionization was found in Australia, Sweden, the United Kingdom, and the United States (Western, 1993). Visser (2000) suggests that a return to lower unemployment may eliminate one factor which has worked in the direction of lower unionization. Visser (2000) contends that the downward trend in unionization during the period 1985–1998 is related to the rise in unemployment but also to other factors such as structural changes in labor market and employment.

Workers' bargaining power reduces when unemployment and informal employment rates are relatively high, since this means that employed workers can be more easily replaced by what Marx called 'the reserve army' (that is, the wide layer of unemployed around the world). Over the last decades, neoliberal globalization has brought an integration of labor markets through the world by the reduction of constraints to international trade and investment. For workers in high-wage countries, such as the United States, this means that the 'reserve army' is expanded worldwide to include unemployed workers in poor countries (Pollin, 2003:

13). Even though workers from rich countries seem to be losing ground during the neoliberal globalization era, this does not mean that workers from poor countries are gaining better positions in collective bargaining, due to fact that the power of unions in these countries and the average wages for the working class has also eroded (ILO, 1998).

Golden et al. (2002) investigated union density fluctuations in 12 countries. They found that the lack of a uniform pattern of union density decline by virtually any available measure, which causes one to be skeptical of all general explanations for why unions are declining. General explanations seem to explain too much. Only in terms of recent membership trends is union decline widespread, and here the evidence points as much to mass unemployment as to domestic and international structural changes as the underlying cause. The current weakness of unions appears, in most countries, to be more of a product of sustained unemployment (and occasionally political assault) than an instance of institutional decay.[3]

Nevertheless, in the case of countries where labor unions manage the unemployment insurance (the Ghent system), it has been demonstrated that unemployment rates generate positive effects on labor unions. That is, higher rates of unemployment stimulate union affiliation, since workers have access to these benefits through labor organizations. In this category, I found countries like Sweden, Belgium, and Finland, which are the most unionized countries in the world. On the other hand, consumer price inflation increases unionization because workers organize to protect their real wages, and employers have an incentive to recognize unions to avoid interruptions in production during economic boom periods. Western (1993) contends that many studies show that inflation had strong positive effects on unionization in Sweden, the United Kingdom, and the United States.

The former section has underlined the relevance and influence of economic performance, unemployment, and inflation on the levels of union membership in the employed labor force. Nevertheless, the existing literature coincides in the fact that although the factors considered in this approach are significant, they are not determinant by themselves; rather they have to be analyzed along with other multiple factors within the structural and political-institutional spheres.

The Structural Factors

The structural composition of the labor force comprises factors such as the significant increase of services jobs and the decrease of industrial jobs during the second half of the twentieth century. This impacted negatively union density since the industrial workers are more likely to be unionized and the service employees are more difficult to organize. This relation was more striking in the United States. Visser (2000) argued that structural changes associated with industrial and demographic change and rising participation rates (in most countries from rather low levels) are likely to continue to exert downward pressure on rates of unionization. On the other hand, public sector workers have a higher probability of membership than private sector workers, as do manufacturing workers compared with those in private services (Blanchflower, 1996; Galenson, 1994).

Scruggs and Lange (2002) detected in a group of 16 OECD countries that the expansion in public employment is strongly and positively associated with union density growth. The effect is larger in Ghent and high-access countries than in non-Ghent and low-access countries, but it is lower in highly centralized or corporatist countries (and in countries with a high combined institutional score) than in decentralized or pluralist cases.[4]

Various academic research and reports (Blanchflower, 2007; ILO, 1998; Visser, 2006) have demonstrated that the levels of unionization have remained higher in the public sector than in the private sector. For instance, among the public sector employees, in 2007 union density in Canada was 72%, in the United Kingdom, 59%; the United States, 35.9%, and Spain, 18.6%.[5] In Mexico and other Latin American countries there was no consistent statistical data but unionization was considerably higher in the public sector. In Latin America, according to Saavedra (2003: 246), a large part of the decline in unionization is explained by the reduction in public-sector employment; however, there has also been a sharp reduction in union affiliation in the private sector. For Blanchflower (2007: 17), it was evident that labor unions had been more successful in the public sector than in the private: public-sector densities in many countries were more than 20 percentage points higher.

According to the Bureau of Labor Statistics, BLS (2008),[6] union density rates in the public sector have remained stable in the United States but have slightly increased since 1983. In 2007, the public sector registered a union density rate four times more than that of the private sector

(35.9% compared with 7.5%). On the other hand, union membership in the private sector decreased by around a half during the same period. In that year, union density for government workers was around 36% and for private industry workers it was almost 8%.

Visser (2006)[7] found that the decline in unionization is concentrated very strongly in the market or private sector of the economy, with rates of unionization in the public or government sector remaining very high in most countries. "Unionization in manufacturing, together with public-sector unions, still represent the vertebrate of today's labor unions and federations" in the majority of countries surveyed (2006: 47).

On the other hand, Visser (2000) found that the downward trend in unionization during the period 1985–1998 is related partly to structural changes in labor market participation and employment, bringing in groups with a lower propensity to unionize (service workers, workers finding employment in small firms) and groups that go into non-standard employment, like part-timers and workers on temporary contracts, or informal and undeclared workers.

Portes and Hoffman (2003: 55) observed four trends in the employment in Latin America. First, a consistent decline of public sector workers was observable in every country of the region. Second, a parallel decline of the formal proletariat as a whole in every country took place with the exception of Argentina. Third, a major trend was the rise of the class of minor entrepreneurs and fourth, the stagnation or increase of the informal proletariat.[8]

The presence of female workers in employment is considered to be a negative factor for union affiliation, since women are less likely to be union members. Notwithstanding, statistics demonstrate an expansion of female workers in union membership over the last 20 years, as is the case of both Canada and the United States (US DOL, 2008; Statistics Canada, 2004). Visser (2006) found that in several countries the female unionization rate is equal with (Canada, the United Kingdom, Ireland) or even higher (Sweden, Norway, Finland) than the male unionization rate. The rapid advance of female union membership and density, combined with the fall in male unionization, is probably the "biggest and most profound transformation in union membership" (2006: 46–47). Men are more likely to be members than women, but the gap appears to be narrowing over time, at least in the US and the UK (Blanchflower, 1996).

Similarly, the characteristics of individual workers appear to be determinant factors on union density. There are many similarities across countries in who belongs to unions. The probability of belonging to a union is age-related, maximizing at around 45 years (Blanchflower, 1996). The fact that fewer young workers have in recent years joined the unions implies that the average age of union members has increased. This in itself means that the recruitment task of unions has become more difficult. As a significant proportion of members will leave the unions in coming years, unions face a formidable challenge to make up their numbers with more and younger recruits.

Blanchflower (2007) shows that union membership follows an inverted U-shape (the author refers to a graph shape) in age across many countries with different density levels and trends. This feature was found in 27 out of the 30 members of the OECD. The only exceptions are Turkey, Korea, and Iceland. The same inverse U-shaped was detected in non-OECD countries such as Bangladesh, Chile, Bulgaria, Estonia, Israel, Norway, and Russia. The exceptions are Cyprus, Brazil, Latvia, and the Philippines (Ibid).

The declining levels of union density have occurred in most countries both within and outside the OECD in recent years. Evidence was also found that males had higher probabilities of being union members in the majority of countries examined, although there was some evidence that females had higher probabilities in the public sector. Similarly, some evidence suggested that education had a positive impact in the public sector and a negative impact in the private (Blanchflower, 2007).

The Political-Institutional Factors

The political-institutional approach observes the performance of political institutions: their position towards trade unions, employers and the kind of policies implemented. It is claimed that leftist governments have brought more advantages for workers and labor unions; in contrast, "conservative parties have actively resisted unions through labor legislation and in industrial relations" (Wallerstein & Western, 2000: 359).[9] According to this approach, labor legislation is regarded as a determinant of union density. In the United States, for instance, *Right to Work* regulation inhibits union affiliation in 22 states of the US (Goldfield, 1989).

Visser (2000) identified large cross-national differences in unionization levels and argued that these variations are the result of long-term developments, rooted in highly unique, national combinations of institutional and political conditions. He mentions three major institutional conditions conducive to union organization: union access to the workplace, union involvement in the provision and administration of unemployment insurance, and centralization of collective bargaining. He contends that where all three of these institutions are (or were) present (as in Northern Europe), unions are capable of protecting against the negative influence on membership growth caused by unemployment and structural change.

Western (1997: 193) asserts that "centralized labor markets and union-run unemployment insurance reformulated the logic of union growth", and he affirms that with "these institutions, union density withstood recessions and extended well beyond the core manufacturing industries". Visser (2006: 39) observes that comparative studies in Europe have demonstrated that unionization rates are 20–30 percentage points higher when unions, rather than the state, control unemployment insurance claims even where the insurance itself is fully subsidized and non-members have legally the same entitlements as members.

Domestic labor-related legislation allows actions against union organization, such as employers' opposition to the organization of new labor unions at workplaces in the US (AFL-CIO, 2006) or the state control on the official registration and recognition of new labor organizations in Mexico (Bensusán, 2000). Hence, the relationship between labor unions and political actors is important to analyze when evaluating the representation of workers' interests in the political arena. If unions have not forged political alliances, they will not be able to influence a favorable labor system.

In most of Latin America, as labor unions were or are still tied to the state and political parties in power, they have relied more on these relations than on their numerical presence in the employed labor force or the relations with employers. Cook (1998: 314) refers to "the politicization of labor" as an important characteristic in the Latin American region. Therefore, union density alone may not represent the most important indicator in the region to ponder the relative power and influence of labor unions. However, research reveals that the ties of organized labor and political actors in Latin America were the main explaining factor of the highest rates of unionization during the twentieth century, especially in Brazil, Argentina, and Mexico. In contrast, as noted later in this chapter, the strength of labor unions in Europe stem from their representation in the employed labor force, the capacity of organization at workplaces and the collective bargaining with employers. Therefore, such institutional conditions are more relevant for trade unions in Europe than in Latin America.

Golden et al. (2002: 224) confirmed that only the USA and the UK have witnessed union decline along multiple dimensions. These two cases both point to the importance of government policy. The United States and the UK are the only countries (the study included 12 countries) where conservative governments actively encouraged employers to engage in attacks on union power. The rapidity of union density decline in these two countries is a stark reminder of the vulnerability of unions to political attack, but it says little about the vulnerability of unions to occupational change or international economic transformations.

Regarding the relation between strikes and union density, Sano and Williamson (2008) found a positive effect of strike activity on union density, implying that as strike activity increases, so does union density. This effect was clearer among the countries with a medium level of Traditional Union Density.[10] However, they found a lack of a significant relationship for countries with a high Traditional Union Density level, mainly explained by the higher level of corporatism often present in these countries where unions may have more bargaining power and more avenues for negotiations than in the countries with lower traditional union densities. In the highly corporatist countries citizens may see strikes as drastic measures and interpret them as the unions taking their participation in government for granted, therefore making striking in these countries less effective. Furthermore, striking may be ineffective in countries with low levels of Traditional Union Density, such as the United States, where there may be less overall support for union activity and often more localized bargaining. On the other hand, Visser (2000) detected that there is no strong link between union density and worker militancy, since high rates of strike involvement, however measured, are found in countries with both high and low union membership.

Therefore, political-institutional factors, such as the labor legislation and the role of labor unions in the labor relations system explain the low or high levels of unionization. The low union density rates in the United States for instance are explained by aspects related to labor legislation, but also the high levels of union density in countries such as Sweden and Finland are explained for the Ghent system, which is an institution that permits labor unions to distribute unemployment benefits.

Corporatism

The neoliberal wave throughout the world swept up the corporatist pact in most capitalist democracies. The collaboration between the state and interest groups was a significant component of corporatism; the major decisions on domestic matters emerged from discussion between the government and top associations representing the major social partners: capital and labor (Hague & Harrop, 2007). In the neoliberal context, the policies adopted by many governments in Europe and Latin America were designed to remove the social pact among labor unions, employers, and the government, which prevailed during the second post-war period. As will be mentioned, Mexico experienced similar developments in this regard. However, in the case of Mexico the corporatist framework, although weakened, survived during the dual transition.

With the decline of union membership and large manufacturing companies, as well as the rise of pro-marketing ideals, traditional corporate arrangements have declined even in European countries, where they were once entrenched. However, widespread consultation persists among the organized groups and government. And some countries, including Ireland and the Netherlands, have even developed or revived social partnerships as a means to improved labor efficiency. Certainly, the political significance of peak associations continues to vary across the liberal democratic world, precluding any simple assumption of decline (Hague & Harrop, 2007: 211–212). Wiarda (1997) defines corporatism as a system of social and political organization in which major societal groups or interests (among them labor and business) are integrated into the governmental system, often on a monopolistic basis or under state guidance, tutelage, and control, to achieve coordinated national development.

Schmitter (1974) defines corporatism as "a system of interest representation"[11] and identifies two kinds of corporatism. First, he recognizes social corporatism, which predominates in democratic and liberal states such as Sweden and the Scandinavian countries. The other category is the state corporatism, which is characteristic of anti-liberal and authoritarian states, including some Latin American countries. As noted by Schmitter, corporatism is present in both authoritarian and democratic regimes. Corporatism, therefore, is compatible with different political regimes or systems of government. Moreover, there is not a clear connection between corporatism and democracy, whereas it is difficult to establish evident patterns of relationship among corporatist frameworks and political systems. The international landscape shows that both authoritarian and democratic states have relied on corporatist schemes to create a common governmental agenda with social partners, among them labor unions. This was true in authoritarian countries throughout different stages of the past century when corporatist mechanisms were used to control workers in different ways but also in democratic countries where corporatism was used as a system to set a common governmental agenda.

However, in some cases with authoritarian antecedents, corporatism adapted successfully to democratic political systems and cohabited with democratic institutions; this could be the case of Mexico.

According to Liphart and Crepaz (1991: 235), democratic corporatism can be identified by two distinct meanings. First, it implies a system composed by interest groups; such groups are organized in peak organizations that are national, specialized, hierarchical, and monopolistic. Second, it refers to the participation of such interest groups into the process of policy making and execution. Indeed, according to Schmitter, the second meaning has also been considered as 'concertation'; however, the two tend to occur together because corporatism in the narrow sense is almost a necessary condition for 'concertation'. Liphart and Crepaz created an indicator to define the relative presence of corporatism in a group of countries. They identify countries like Austria, Norway, and Sweden as the most corporatist states whereas countries such as the United States, Canada and New Zealand are the most plural states. Furthermore, middle and higher levels of union density are in the countries with the highest levels of corporatism and vice versa. In this sense, it can be said that corporatism is a strong determinant of the levels of union density in different countries (Table 2.3).

In a wide research, covering 16 European countries,[12] Ebbinghaus and Visser (1999) found out that those countries with highly corporatist systems had more stable union densities than countries with less or no existence of corporatism. In this sense, corporatism is a crucial component in creating a suitable political context to maintain a certain level of union membership in the employed labor force and union power in the political realm. In Europe, the clear examples of the just mentioned are Sweden, Denmark, and Austria. In contrast, among countries with low levels of union density, a general pattern of decentralization emerged and has remained substantially un-changed since the 1950s. In this manner, the lack of corporatism, along with the existence of more pluralist schemes

Table 2.3 Levels of corporatism and union density in 18 countries

Country	*Index of corporatism*	*Union density*
Austria	1.600	47
Norway	1.531	59
Sweden	1.396	80
Netherlands	1.006	25
Denmark	0.518	75
Switzerland	0.505	24
Germany	0.480	31
Finland	0.427	72
Belgium	0.258	54
Japan	0.053	25
Ireland	−0.528	51
France	−0.725	10
Italy	−0.851	39
UK	−0.862	39
Australia	−1.025	40
New Zealand	−1.106	51
Canada	−1.335	35
United States	−1.341	16

Source Adapted from Liphart and Crepaz (1991: 239, Table 1). Union density in 1990 (Visser, 2006)

in state-organized group relations, in countries like the United States and France were significant factors for union decline in the last two or three decades of the twentieth century.

The participation of labor unions in the political system is a determining factor for unionization. In the political–institutional configuration, corporatism is one of the main factors explaining the rise or decline of labor unions during the contemporary era in most capitalist countries. Strong labor movements depend to a great extent on the relations with the state. Those countries with corporatist systems are more unionized, especially in Europe but also in Latin America. Although corporatism in Latin America is particularly different regarding the European case, it can be seen the presence of solid corporatist frameworks in the region. For instance, corporatism played a significant role in the strongest labor movements of the region, especially in Brazil, Mexico, and Argentina and "reflected an effort to promote harmonious capital-labor relations through strong state mediation" (Cook, 1998: 314). In Mexico, the corporatist structure included a strong alliance between organized labor and the state. It was created after the Mexican Revolution

(1910–1920) and developed during the hegemonic party rule especially from the mid-1930s to the early 1980s; thereafter it underwent a process of deterioration.

In a cross-country research study, comprising 18 OECD countries, Sano and Williamson (2008: 496) detected that "the national recognition and influence of unions in corporatist nations allows for greater workplace access, better relationships with employers, and better bargaining arrangements". They found that the presence of corporatism is a positive significant predictor across all three levels of Traditional Union Density (high, middle, and low levels of union density). This finding suggests that "as a country becomes more corporatist, union density will increase. In a more corporatist nation organizations such as labor unions have a greater national presence and voice in legislation" (2008).

The participation of labor confederations in macroeconomic decision-making, through corporatist frameworks, enables labor unions to protect organized industries and occupations and to direct investment and subsequent employment to these or other sectors that can be unionized (Visser, 2000). In the case of Mexico, there is not a very important centralization in terms of labor—employer negotiations, since most of the collective bargaining is given in the enterprise level (Murillo, 2003).

Conclusions

In this chapter, union density fluctuations have been examined as an indicator of labor unions presence in the employed labor force. A substantial reduction of union density happened in most developed and developing capitalist countries during the last decades of the past century. Unionization levels reduced between 1980 and 2000 but they have remained relatively stable in the twenty-first century. It can be observed that both the trends and levels of union density differ significantly among the surveyed countries. This suggest that the factors accounting for union decline are also divergent across countries.

In general, union density remains higher in Europe than in the Americas. Specifically, the countries with higher union density rates (Belgium, Denmark, Finland, and Sweden) have special regulations in the institutional framework of labor relations. For instance, the 'Ghent' system, in which labor unions manage unemployment insurance in the labor system, has stimulated union organization. In Finland, Sweden, and Denmark three out of four workers are unionized, while in France and Mexico this proportion is one out of ten; in the United States the proportion is one in nine.

The analysis of disaggregated statistics on union membership and density permit to establish the major general patterns in the international sphere. Male workers are more likely to be unionized than their female counterparts. However, the gap has narrowed in the last two decades in such a way that the levels of unionization are very similar among males and females. Unionized workers are more likely to be found in the industrial sector than in service industries. The highest rates of unionization are in industrial sectors, especially in the manufacturing sector, and the lowest rates of union representation are in the services, especially in financial sectors. Union membership is higher among workers whose age oscillates between 30 and 50 years. The younger workers are less unionized than their older counterparts, however, the rate of affiliation starts to decline in workers older than 50 years. Workers are more unionized in the public sector than in the private due to the fact that labor legislation is more suitable for union organizing in the public sector but also because employers in the private sector have showed more opposition to labor organization.

In terms of unionization, Mexico is located among the lowest positions in the American continent but also within the OECD. The differences observed in the OECD countries in terms of union density levels and fluctuations is also detected in the Americas. Countries such as Argentina and Brazil are among the most unionized in the region whereas countries like Colombia, Peru, and Paraguay are among the least unionized.

It can be suggested that variations of union density rates in these regions are explained mainly by political-institutional factors, such as the domestic political systems and the institutions regulating labor relations between unions and employers. In the same way, structural factors were important, particularly the dominant sectors in the employed labor force. There was also a discernible negative effect of the expansion of the service sector as well as the growth of female, young and informal employment.

On the other hand, a positive relation between corporatism and union density was detected. Corporatism is one of the main factors explaining the rise or decline of labor unions. Strong labor unions depend on the existence of corporatist frameworks that regulates their relations with the state and employers. The most suitable examples of corporatist countries, with high levels of union density, are Austria, Norway, and Sweden. Even though corporatism in Latin America is very different from that in Europe, the presence of solid corporatist frameworks in the region and strong labor movements has persisted. For instance, Argentina, Brazil, and Mexico could be considered as suitable examples in this regard in Latin America.

Notes

1. An adaptation of this framework will be used here in order to analyse the factors accounting for union density variations.
2. Galenson include in his study countries like Australia, Canada, Denmark, France, Germany, Italy, Japan, New Zealand, Spain, the United Kingdom, and the United States, Norway and Sweden (developed countries) and Argentina, Brazil, Chile, Egypt, India, Kenya, Korea, Malaysia, Mexico, the Philippines, Taiwan, and Thailand (developing countries).
3. The countries included Austria, Canada, Denmark, Finland, France, Germany, Italy, Japan, Norway, Sweden, United Kingdom and the United States. See Miriam A. Golden, Michael Wallerstein and Peter Lange (2002).
4. The countries included in the study were: Sweden, Denmark, Austria, Norway, Australia, Belgium, UK, Netherlands, Switzerland, Germany, Finland, Japan, US, Canada, Italy, and France. See Scruggs and Lange (2002).
5. Data of Canada see Statistics Canada; for the United States see United States Department of Labor; in the case of the UK see Department for Business Enterprise and Regulatory Reform (2008), "Trade union membership 2007", National Statistics Publication: United Kingdom. In the case of Spain see: "Encuesta de Calidad de Vida en el Trabajo (ECVT)" (2008), Ministerio del Trabajo e Inmigración, Gobierno de España.
6. See United States Department of Labor (USDOL), available online: http://www.dol.gov/laborday/
7. The countries included in this study are: United States, Canada, Australia, New Zealand, Japan, Republic of Korea, Germany, France, Italy, United Kingdom, Ireland, Finland, Sweden, Norway, Denmark, Netherlands, Belgium, Spain, Switzerland, Austria, Hungary, Czech Republic, Slovak Republic and Poland.
8. According to Portes and Hoffman (2003: 45–50), the "petty bourgeoisie" is the group in possession of some monetary resources; some professional, technical, or artisanal skills; and the employment of a small number of workers supervised on a direct, face-to-face basis. The formal proletariat corresponds to workers in industry, services, and agriculture who are protected by existing labor laws and covered by legally mandated systems of health care, disability, and retirement. The informal proletariat

the sum total of own account workers (minus professionals and technicians), unpaid family workers, domestic servants, and waged workers without social security and other legal protections in industry, services, and agriculture.

9. The authors consider three categories of countries: "high density countries": Belgium, Denmark, Finland and Sweden. Middle density countries: Australia, Austria, Canada, Germany, Ireland, Italy, New Zealand, Norway and UK. Low density countries: France, Japan, Netherlands, Switzerland and US.
10. In this study, Sano and Williamson consider three categories of countries according to the levels of union density: Sweden, Finland, Denmark and Belgium are considered as High Union Density countries; Austria, Australia, Canada, Germany, Italy, New Zealand, Norway, UK are classified as Middle union Density countries; and France, Japan, Netherlands, Switzerland, Ireland and the US are in the category of Low union Density countries. For more details see Sano, J. and Williamson, J. B. (2008).
11. Corporatism will be analysed in Chapter Four with regard to the case of Mexico.
12. The countries included are: Sweden, Finland, Denmark, Norway, Ireland, Great Britain, Belgium, Austria, Germany, Switzerland, Netherlands, Italy, Portugal, Spain, France and Greece.

Bibliography

AFL-CIO. (2006). American federation of labor—Congress of Industrial Organizations. Available online: http://www.aflcio.org/ consulted in October, 2006.

Bain, G. S., & Price, R. (1980). *Profiles of union growth: A comparative statistical portrait of eight countries*. Basil: Blackwell.

Bellin, E. (2000). Contingent democrats: Industrialists, labor, and democratization in late developing Countries. *World Politics, 52*(2), 175–205.

Bensusán, G. (2000). *El modelo mexicano de regulación laboral*. Mexico: Plaza y Valdés-UAM-Flacso-FES.

Blanchflower, D. G. (1996). The role and influence of trade unions in the OECD. *CEP Discussion Papers 0310*. London: National Bureau of Economic Research and Centre for Economic Performance.

Blanchflower, D. (2007). International patterns of union membership. *British Journal of Industrial Relations, 45*(1), 1–28.

Boeri, T., Brugiavini, A., & Calmfors, L. (2001). *The role of unions in the twenty-first century: a report for the Fondazione Rodolfo Debenedetti*. Oxford University Press.

Bureau of Labor Statistics, BLS. (2008). Available online: https://www.bls.gov/. consulted in October, 2009.

Burgess, K. (2004). *Parties and unions in the new global economy*. Pittsburgh: University of Pittsburgh Press.

Cardoso, A. (2004). Industrial relations, social dialogue and employment in Argentina, Brazil and Mexico. *Employment Strategy Papers*.

Cardoso, A. & Gindin, J. (2009). *Industrial relations and collective bargaining: Argentina, Brazil and Mexico compared*. Working Paper No. 5, Geneva: Industrial and Employment Relations Department International Labor Office.

Celhay, P. (2007). *Sindicalización y negociación colectiva*. Chile: Informe de apoyo para consejo de trabajo y equidad.

Cook, M. L. (1998). Toward flexible industrial relations? Neo-liberalism, democracy, and labor reform in Latin America. *Industrial Relations, 37*(3), 311–336.

Cook, M. L. (2007). *The politics of labor reform in Latin America: between flexibility and rights*. University Park: Pennsylvania State University Press.

Ebbinghaus, B., & Visser, J. (1999). When institutions matter: union growth and decline in Western Europe, 1950–1995. *European Sociological Review, 15*, 135–158.

Ebbinghaus, B., & Visser, J. (2000). *Trade unions in Western Europe since 1945*. London, New York: MacMillan Reference, Grove's Dictionaries.

Freeman, R. (1994). *Mercados de trabajo en acción. Ensayos sobre economía empírica*. España: Ministerio de Trabajo y Seguridad Social.

Freeman, R., & Medoff, J. L. (1984). *What do labor unions do?*. New York: Basic Books.

Galenson, W. (1994). *Trade union growth and decline. An international study*. New York: Praeger.

Golden, M. A., Wallerstein, M. & Lange, P. (2002). Post-war trade union organization and industrial relations in twelve countries. In H. Kitschelt (Eds.), *Continuity and change in contemporary capitalism*. Cambridge University Press.

Goldfield, M. (1989). *The decline of organized labor in the United States*. Chicago: University of Chicago Press.

Haerpfer, Ch. W. et al. (edit) (2009). *Democratization*. Oxford University Press.

Hague, R., & Harrop, M. (2007). *Comparative government and politics* (7th ed.). London: MacMillan.

International Labor Organization. (1998). *World labor report 1997–1998*. Geneva: ILO.

International Labor Organization. (2004). *Declaration*. Geneva: ILO. Available on line http://www.ilo.org/declaration consulted in June, 2007.

Lijphart, A., & Crepaz, M. (1991). Corporatism and consensus democracy in eighteen countries: Conceptual and empirical linkages. *British Journal of Political Science, 21,* 235–246.

Loyzaga de la Cueva, O. (2002). *Neoliberalismo y flexibilización de los derechos laborales*. Mexico: UAM-Porrua.

Magaloni, B. (2006). *Voting for autocracy: Hegemonic party survival and its demise in Mexico.* Cambridge: Cambridge University Press.

Marshall, A. (2006). *Efectos de la regulación del trabajo sobre la afiliación sindical: estudio comparativo de Argentina.* Chile y México, Argentina: Cuadernos del Instituto de Desarrollo Económico y Social.

Middlebrook, K. (1995). *The paradox of revolution.* Baltimore and London: The John Hopkins University Press.

Mishel, L., Bivens, J., Gould, E. & Shierholz, H. (2012), *The State of Working America*, Cornell University Press.

Murillo, M. V. (2000). From populism to neoliberalism: Labor unions and market reforms in Latin America. *World Politics, 52,* 135–174.

Murillo, M. V. (2001). *Labor unions, partisan coalitions and market reforms in Latin America.* Cambridge: Cambridge University Press.

Murillo, M. V. (2003). Latin American labor. In J. I. Domínguez & M. Shifter (Eds.), *Democratic governance in Latin America and the Caribbean.* Johns Hopkins University Press.

O'Toole, G. (2007). *Politics: Latin America.* Harlow, England: Pearson Longman.

OECD. (1997). *OECD Employment outlook.* Paris: OECD.

OECD. (2004). *Trade union density and collective bargaining coverage* (p. 2004). Economic Outlook: OECD.

OECD. (2009). Society at a Glance 2009—OECD Social Indicators. Statistical annexe, trade union members.

OIT. (2003). *Panorama Laboral 2002. America Latina y El Caribe.* Lima, Peru: OIT.

Patroni, V. (2001). The decline and fall of corporatism? labor legislation reform in Mexico and Argentina during the 1990s. *Canadian Journal of Political Science XXXIV, 2,* 249–274.

Pollin, R. (2003). *Contours of descent. US economic fractures and the landscape of global austerity.* London and New York: Verso.

Portes, A., & Hoffman, K. (2003). Latin American class structures: Their composition and change during the neoliberal era. *Latin American Research Review, 38*(1), 41–82.

Price, R. (1991). The comparative analysis of union growth. In R. Adams (Ed.), *Comparative Industrial Relations. Contemporary Research and Theory* (pp. 37–55). Great Britain: Harper Collins Academic.

Rueschemeyer, D., Stephens, E. H., & Stephens, J. D. (1992). *Capitalist development and democracy*. University of Chicago Press.

Saavedra, J. (2003). Labor markets during the 1990s. In P. Kuczynski & J. Williamson (Eds.), *After the Washington Consensus: Restarting growth and reform in Latin America*. Washington, DC: Institute of International Economics.

Sano, J., & Williamson, J. B. (2008). Factors affecting union decline in 18 OECD countries. *International Journal of Comparative Sociology, 49*(6), 479–500.

Schmitter, P. C. (1974). Still the century of corporatism? *The Review of Politics, 36*, 85–131.

Scruggs, L., & Lange, P. (2002). Where have all the members gone? Globalization, institutions, and union density. *The Journal of Politics, 64*(1), 126–153.

Smith, P. H. (2005). *Democracy in Latin America: political change in comparative perspective*. Oxford University Press.

Stallings, B. & Peres, W. (2000). *Growth, employment and equity. The impact of the economic reforms in Latin American and Caribbean*, Economic Commission for Latin American and Caribbean, Washington: Brookings Institution Press.

Statistics Canada. (2004, 2005, 2006, 2007). Fact sheet on unionization. *Perspectives on labor and incomes*.

Stepan, A. C. (1971). *The military in politics*. Princeton University Press.

Toke, A. (2003). *Unions and collective bargaining, economic effects in a global environment*. Washington, DC: The World Bank.

Torre, J. (1972). *La tasa de sindicalización en Argentina*. Buenos Aires: Instituto Torcuato Di tella—Centro de Investigaciones Sociales.

United Nations Development Programme (UNDP). (2004). *Democracy in Latin America. Towards a citizens' democracy*, Vol. 2, Alfaguara.

US Bureau of Labor Statistics. (2008). Union Members 2007, 28 de enero, available at: https://www.bls.gov/news.release/archives/union2_01252008.pdf, consulted in January 2020.

Vernon, G. (2006). Does density matter? The significance of comparative historical variation in unionization. *European Journal of Industrial Relations, 12*(2), 189–210.

Visser, J. (1991). *Trends in trade union membership*. Paris: OECD Employment Outlook.

Visser, J. (2000). *Trends in unionization and collective bargaining*. Geneva: International Labor Office.

Visser, J. (2003). Unions and unionism around the world. In J. Addison & C. Schnabel (Eds.), *The international handbook of trade unions* (pp. 366–413). Cheltenham: Edward Elgar.

Visser, J. (2006). Union membership statistics in 24 countries. *Monthly Labor Review, 129*(1), 38–49.
Waddington, J. (2005). Trade union membership in Europe: the extent of the problem and the range of trade union responses. *ETUC/ ETUI—REHS top-level summer school*. Florence: ETUI—REHS Research Department.
Wallerstein, M., & Western, B. (2000). Unions in decline? What has changed and why. *Annual Review of Political Science, 3*, 355–377.
Western, B. (1993). Postwar unionization in eighteen advanced capitalist countries. *American Sociological Review, 58*(2), 266–282.
Western, B. (1997). *Between class and market: postwar unionization in the capitalist democracies*. Princeton, NJ: Princeton University Press.
Wiarda, H. J. (1997). *Corporatism and comparative politics: The other great "ism"*, Armonk, New York, London: M.E. Sharpe.
Zapata, F. (1976). Afiliación y organización sindical en México. In J. Reyna et al. (Ed.), *Tres estudios sobre el movimiento obrero en México*. El Colegio de México.
Zapata, F. (1993). *Autonomía y subordinación en el sindicalismo latinoamericano*. México: Fondo de Cultura Económica.

CHAPTER 3

Neoliberalism and Organized Labor

The Dual Transition

Neoliberalism is analyzed not only as process or model for governing public policies and economic life, but as a set of economic policies linked to cyclical (economic performance) and structural (employment composition) factors with specific effects on union density decline. Neoliberalism was integrated in the argument as a determinant of the labor sphere because its specific policies comprise, among others, the liberalization of trade, *flexibilization* of labor and privatization, which are other important factors linked to the decline of unionization. More importantly, neoliberal policies meant the ending of the Imports Substitution Industrialization (ISI) model in Latin America and Mexico, in which labor unions were strong institutions. This change was significant and thus plays a central part in the evaluation of the effects of neoliberalism on labor unions. However, the scope of influence of neoliberalism goes beyond the economic sphere as it has also been regarded as a political project. In this way, the implementation of neoliberal prescriptions was largely induced by domestic political actors. Therefore, the neoliberal model will be disaggregated for its assessment and integrated within the discussion of the analytical framework of this study.

On the other hand, democratization is taken here as a particular process linked to political-institutional factors with effects on labor union

R. Zepeda, *The Decline of Labor Unions in Mexico during the Neoliberal Period*, Governance, Development, and Social Inclusion in Latin America, https://doi.org/10.1007/978-3-030-65710-9_3

organization. The third wave of democratization that occurred in the Latin American countries is by no means a finished process since old undemocratic practices in several spheres co-exist with a general framework of democratic institutions.

During the last quarter of the twentieth century, Latin America experienced two processes that redefined fundamental aspects with regard to the economic model and the political regime: democratization and neoliberalism, also referred to as the dual transition.

[1]Despite the fact that the dual transition has enabled many regions to incorporate successfully into the international economy and advance the democratization extending wide political guarantees for citizenship, a condition of dissatisfaction still prevails among the population in many countries that have undergone these transitions.

Democratization facilitated the political transition from authoritarian rule to democratic regimes, but in many cases the progress has been confined to electoral democracy. Furthermore, it has neither extended to other pending issues such as the labor sphere nor has eliminated chronic problems in the region like corruption and weak political institutions (Grugel, 2002; O' Donnell, 1994; Phillips, 2003). On the other hand, neoliberal policies coincided with the low rates of economic growth and the expansion of informal employment, inequality, and the decline of union density rates (CEPAL, 2004; OIT, 2003; Rodrik, 2001). In this context, the dual transition has not resulted in an improvement for the majority of the working class, who saw their living conditions deteriorate, comparing with the beginning of neoliberal reforms or previously.

As mentioned before, labor unions became stronger in Latin America between 1940 and 1980, when diverse developmentalist states emerged in the region. In this period, labor unions were linked to these regimes mostly through the mediation of strong political parties that usually monopolized power. In addition, labor unions forged alliances with the state within corporatist frameworks. The alliance between the unions and the state was interrupted by the arrival of authoritarian military regimes in the 1960s and 1970s in several Latin American countries. The advance of democratization over the 1980s is crucial as it removed military regimes where labor unions had been restrained and often suppressed. Therefore, it was clear that organized labor supported the democratization process. Furthermore, labor unions became crucial in the struggle for democratic progress. The latter could be said of Argentina, Brazil, and Chile in the 1980s, but it was also the case in Spain in previous decades.

On the other hand, democratization undermined the former privileged position of unions by eroding authoritarian corporatist structures, especially in cases where labor-based political parties lost the monopoly of power. This can be certainly applied to the case of Mexico, which had a hegemonic party and a corporatist structure as defining features of its political system. In this case, organized labor rowed against the wave of democratization and became one of many other elements which delayed the arrival of democracy.

In Mexico, neoliberal reforms preceded democratization. Neoliberal reforms, especially of the first generation, were implemented within an authoritarian environment. Most of these reforms, in some cases, were endorsed by organized labor (Murillo, 2001, 2003), leaving labor organizations at a disadvantage vis-à-vis employers. In Mexico, economic liberalization strengthened employer groups relative to labor unions, and NAFTA tied the economy of this country more closely to that of the United States (Cook 2007). The dual transition in Mexico "has radically transformed the context in which the old corporatist trade unionism operated" and as a result they "have been forced to redefine themselves, to reassess their power resources and their strategies or to succumb to the new export-oriented economic model which gives unions little room to manoeuvre" (Bensusán, 2007: 75).

In general, the situation and perspectives faced by labor union organizations during the dual transition undermined their former position. Some unions adapted to this new scenario, but the vast majority experienced a decline in the number of union members. In this way, there is no doubt that organized labor weakened throughout most of Latin America during the 1980s and 1990s (Levitsky and Mainwaring, 2006).

Democratization and Organized Labor

What are the implications of a democratic system for organized labor? There is not a strong relation between unionization and democratization in the international sphere. For instance, countries or regions with the highest rates of unionization in the world are not always the most democratic countries. China and Russia, for instance, have the highest rates of unionization in the international sphere. By the year 2000, union density in Russia, Ukraine, and Belarus, considered as a region, accounted for 58% out of the labor force. During the same year, union density in

China was 42% of the total workforce; in Europe (comprising 33 countries) union density was 26%. In Latin America, it was 25%; in Africa, unionization stood at 16%, in North America, 13%, and the lowest rate was found in Asia with 10%. The average unionization rate in the world, across these regions, was 23% (Visser, 2003: 366).

On the other hand, strong labor movements prevailed in Latin America in different periods of the twentieth century along with authoritarian or semi-authoritarian regimes in Mexico, Brazil, Argentina, and other countries in the region. The majority of unions in Latin America, according to Wynia (1990), "secured their place under populist leaders or single-party governments that seldom lived by democratic rules". Indeed, "they learned early that what mattered most was not the form of government but the protection it gave to union organizations" (1990: 62–63).

Nevertheless, the poor and working classes, who often had no voice in authoritarian or military governments, acquired greater importance in democratic politics as a large voting population (Bruhn, 1996). Democratization opens new opportunities for social actors to participate in politics and to be represented (Shadlen, 2004). Democratization had a significant impact on industrial relations systems in Latin America as "it restored collective rights to workers where these were dismantled under authoritarian regimes" (Cook, 1998: 315). Similarly, democratization enabled unions to restore ties to political parties and recover their positions in the political life of the new democratic regimes (1998). "In Chile, Argentina, and especially Brazil, organized labor played an important role in resisting military rule, and its role in the transition period was also significant (Valenzuela 1989 as quoted by Cook, 1998). Democratization also brought an increase in the number of strikes in some countries, such as Brazil, and of politically motivated general strikes as in Argentina. Nevertheless, in Mexico the number of strikes declined throughout the 1980s (Middlebrook, 1989) and remained in low levels during the democratization process in the 1990s.

Grugel (2002: 103) underlines the role of labor unions in the democratization process:

> In Spain, labor opposition was the most important sign of the far-reaching rejection of the Franco regime in the 1960s and 1970s (...). In Chile, the copper workers' union, the strongest union in the country, was the initial force behind the Days of Protest in 1983, the first mass opposition to the Pinochet regime. In Argentina, the powerful national labor

> federation eventually came out against the dictatorship after 1979 (…). In Brazil the emergence of independent unions, especially in the cities, was a focal point for social protest against the military dictatorship in the 1970s. The Brazilian labor movement, in fact, consciously moved beyond narrow labor-related demands to articulate the concerns of the working and lower-class generally (…).

Labor unions, therefore, have been important actors not only in the transition to democratic societies but also during periods when authoritarian regimes endure in power. Nevertheless, unions have failed to boost their leverage within the new democratic environment. As has been stated by Smith (2005: 240): "One might have expected that as a result [of the participation in the democratic struggle], labor would receive substantial benefits from the new post-1978 democracies throughout the [Latin American] region". In contrast, observes Smith, "unions have faced a wave of neoliberal reforms that have endangered their economic welfare and compromised their political clout" in democratic regimes (2005: 240).

In the case of Mexico, a different landscape prevailed. During the period 1980–2000 Mexico remained authoritarian, when the democratization wave swept Latin America. Therefore, we cannot say that democratization opened new opportunities for the revitalization of labor unions during this period. Political liberalization opened new opportunities, albeit limited, regarding the revitalization and internal democratization of the main labor organizations in Mexico. This can be seen in actions towards more democratic procedures in the CT in the late 1980s but also in national unions, such as the SNTE (*Sindicato Nacional de Trabajadores de la Educacion*). Earlier democratization processes took place within the SUTERM (*Sindicato Único de Trabajadores Electricistas de la República Mexicana*) and STRM (*Sindicato de Telefonistas de la República Mexicana*) in the 1970s. But it was not until the late 1990s and 2000s, when real and clearer opportunities for labor unions started.

Although union membership levels declined in most of Latin American countries in the 1980s and 1990s, the restoration of political freedoms led to an initial increase in union density in some countries, such as Chile and Paraguay (Cook, 1998: 315). In the case of Argentina, despite the fact that this country saw a dramatic decline of union density over the 1980s, the union movement was capable of maintaining its political influence, given the restoration of collective-bargaining rights that accompanied the return to democracy in the late 1980s (Saavedra, 2003: 245–246). Organized labor in Argentina, mainly the CGT, supported the neoliberal reforms during the government of Carlos Saul Menem and obtained important organizational benefits in exchange for their support (Murillo, 1997, 2000, cited by Levitsky, 2003). The unions' longstanding social, political, and organizational ties to Peronism can explain organized labor's acquiescence to and support of the Argentinean government during the 1990s (Levitsky, 2003: 224).

Despite the obvious benefits of democracy, unions in many countries entered this new political period from a position of significant weakness (Cook, 1998: 315). In countries like Argentina, Brazil, and Mexico, union activity was encouraged by the state if it supported the corporatist system. In this way, union dependence on state intervention opened the door to intervention at all stages of the collective labor relations (to varying degrees by country): in the organization of unions, in the negotiation process, and in the resolution of conflicts (O'Connell, 1999: 19). Arguably then, there were in Latin America, like in Europe, strong unions in countries with elements of corporatist systems, although with different features.

According to Roxborough (1998), Brazil and Mexico, in their different ways, are the clearest cases of corporatist control of labor relations in Latin America. However, other countries operated one or other variant of corporatism in their industrial relations systems at different times, for instance in Argentina (during Peronist and military administrations) and in Peru (during the Velasco Alvarado presidency). Roxborough clarifies that corporatism has by no means been the universal rule in Latin America. For instance, "in Chile, Colombia, Bolivia and Peru, the norm has been for a more liberal system of industrial relations to prevail" and in Venezuela for a social-democratic type of industrial relations system. However, according to the author, there have been limits to the corporatist system and it has at times been seriously challenged in Brazil and Mexico (1998: 257).

On the other hand, the role of labor unions during the democratization wave has been quite mixed. For instance, in some cases labor unions have lost ground as crucial social partners of the state and privileged components of hegemonic parties; consequently, their access to policymaking and presence in the political structure have eroded. This is particularly true in those cases where labor organizations were linked to labor-based parties, which used to practically exert a kind of monopoly in political competition. In Mexico, official unionism maneuvered against the democratization process to preserve their privileges.

> The labor pillar of the PRI's corporatist power structure roundly opposed the 1977 reforms that labor leaders argued would jeopardize their access to elected posts, and their ability to recruit candidates if victories were less certain (...). There was also resistance within the official workers' unions to electoral reform and political opening (in the de la Madrid administration) as the PRI-state's corporatist union feared competition from the New Leftist parties and their genuine pro-labor positions. (Middlebrook, 1986, 1989, cited by Eisenstadt, 2004: 40–42)

Nevertheless, labor unions in other countries have played a crucial role in promoting democracy and have also benefited from the more democratic conditions in political practices. Argentina, Uruguay, and Chile can be considered in this regard. In the case of Chile, the expansion of union membership amongst the employed labor has not been sufficient to reach the levels prior to the Military regime headed by Pinochet, a time when labor unions had greater presence. This union representation diminished drastically during the 1970s and the 1980s. In the case of Argentina, it can be observed that the largest decline, in terms of unionization, occurred not during the period under the military rule (1976–1983, also known as the Dirty War), but it took place within the democratic environment which was followed by the neoliberalization process. According to Cardoso and Gindin (2009), unionization rates in this country fell by around 50% between 1985 and 2005. Nevertheless, labor unions in Argentina continued playing a crucial role in the political stability of the country during the neoliberal period, as they were linked to the Peronist party (*Partido Justicialista*, PJ) and inserted in the political game since the 1950s as Juan Domingo Peron became the most prominent political figure in the country.

Labor movements with more involvement in the democratization process and favorable outcomes can be seen in the region. However, the paradigmatic example of how labor unions affect the political process, and in this way the course of economic development, is Brazil. As mentioned before, labor unions played a significant role in the collapse of the military regime in the country during the 1980s. The Workers' Party (*Partido dos Trabalhadores*, PT), founded in 1989, may be regarded as an example of the relevant presence of organized labor in politics. It obtained political victory in the 2002 presidential elections when Luiz Inacio Lula da Silva, widely known as Lula, was elected. "For the first time in Latin America's history, a worker, a militant trade-unionist and founder of the Workers' Party, was sworn in as president of the world's ninth largest economy" (Leiva, 2008: 65).

As opposed to the case of Europe, where labor unions obtain their power from their presence in workplaces, in Latin America labor unions have tried to gain access to the state in order to achieve better employment conditions and protection for their members. Despite the low levels of union density in the region, labor unions have been immensely important in the labor movement in Latin America, mainly through shaping government policy. The trade-off was declining union influence in the sphere of collective bargaining and representation. This asymmetrical voice in bargaining and access to state intervention may explain why the region has one of the highest strike records in the world (O'Connell, 1999: 19).

Neoliberalism

The international economic crisis of the 1970s triggered an adjustment of the capitalist system, restructuring the model of economic development, hitherto characterized by a Keynesian economic system. In Latin America, these difficulties exploded with the debt crisis of 1982, which challenged the Import Substitution Industrialization (ISI) model, established after the Great Depression and the Second World War (Saad-Filho, 2005: 222–224). It was alleged that the crisis originated in the excessive participation of the state in the economy; thus, a group of policies associated with the supremacy of free markets was stimulated (Kingston, 2010: 6; O'Toole, 2007: 445). The period from the mid-1970s to the 2000s has been characterized as the neoliberal era, as neoliberal policies defined the overall direction of the crucial political and economic reforms that were implemented in many countries.

During the last quarter of the 20th century, neoliberalism advanced considerably and became the major economic doctrine in most capitalist countries. Neoliberalism implies the implementation of a widespread combination of prescriptions in governmental policies oriented towards the installation of a free-market economy. While reducing its participation in the regulation of the economy, the state promotes the liberalization of trade and financial flows. In terms of economic policies, the objectives of neoliberal policies comprise the stabilization of macroeconomic indicators, especially inflation and public deficits. They also include the deregulation of the economic activities, including the labor markets, leading to the reform of labor legislation.

Williamson (2000) listed the neoliberal principles that are essential in understanding this economic doctrine. The ten points of the Washington Consensus (named because the main financial institutions are based in Washington, D.C.) prescribed governments implement the following structural adjustments. (1) Fiscal discipline. (2) A redirection of public expenditure priorities toward fields offering both high economic returns and the potential to improve income distribution, such as primary health care, primary education, and infrastructure. (3) Tax reform (to lower marginal rates and broaden the tax base). (4) Interest rate liberalization. (5) A competitive exchange rate. (6) Trade liberalization. (7) Liberalization of inflows of foreign direct investment. (8) Privatization. (9) Deregulation (to abolish barriers to entry and exit). (10) Secure property rights. The prescriptions included in the Washington Consensus became the central part of the political economy in most capitalist countries during the 1980s and 1990s. Although Chile executed these prescriptions since the mid-1970s, the tide of *neoliberalization* extended throughout the developed world in the 1980s as a result of the failure of Keynesian policies.

Many regard neoliberalism not only as a set of economic policies and practices but also as part of a political and hegemonic project. According to Duménil, neoliberalism is the expression of the desire of a class of capitalist owners and the institutions in which their power is concentrated to restore–in the context of a general decline in popular struggles– the class's revenues and power, in long-term decline since the Great Depression and World War II. Far from being inevitable, this was a political action (2004: 1–2). Harvey (2005) has also identified neoliberalism as a "political project to re-establish the conditions for capital accumulation and to restore the power of economic elites". Indeed, neoliberalization has not been very effective in revitalizing global capital accumulation, but it has succeeded remarkably well in restoring the power of economic elites (2005: 19). Saad Filho and Yalman (2009: 1) maintain that neoliberalism is "based on the systematic use of state power to impose, under the veil of 'non-intervention', a hegemonic project of recomposition of the rule of capital in most areas of social life".

Neoliberalization does not represent a single homogenizing process but leads to variations across different places (Ibid). This is particularly applicable in the case of Latin America and Mexico, wherein "the neoliberalization of Latin American societies grew out of particular localized contexts, which then reverberated, reinforced, and interacted with political economic shifts in the global north" (Martin, 2007: 53). In this way, neoliberal policies were adjusted by the national government, which had played an important role in the economic sphere from 1940 to 1980.

Nevertheless, the use of the term 'neoliberalism' has been overstated sometimes and its meaning exaggerated. As expressed by Panizza (2009: 9), neoliberalism "should not be conceived as a closed totality of ideas diffused across nations and through time, but rather as a loosely connected set of concepts, distinctions and arguments that gained meaning as they were articulated and then stabilized in specific ways, depending on the particular discursive and political contexts in which this occurred". In this sense, it is not the intention here to use neoliberalism as the phenomenon that explains the transformation in various spheres in the economy, politics and labor in the last three decades in wide regions of the world, but rather the intention is to identify its components and analyze them separately in light of their outcomes. Discussing neoliberalism in this way serves our purpose, to identify neoliberalism's impact on labor and unions.

Neoliberalism is taken here as a group of guiding principles of political economy, not necessarily related but included in the same package, designed by international financial institutions for implementation by national governments, oriented to a free-market economy integrated into the international economy and global financial markets. The execution of these policies is supposed to result in economic prosperity and thus develop into the main engine for solving social domestic social problems especially in developing countries. However, the role of the government becomes crucial as it regulates the political and institutional framework necessary for such principles to be put into practice. In summary, the role of the government is determinant in the performance of such policies.

Neoliberal ideas were propounded since the 1940s in opposition to Keynesianism, both in Europe and the United States. The early critique of Keynesianism came from the doctrine of monetarism, developed by such scholars as Milton Friedman and Alan Walters, inspired by the earlier, wider critique of state involvement in the economy associated with the Austrian school, specifically with Friedrich Hayek (Gamble, 2001: 128).

While Keynesianism was being implemented during the second post-war period through capitalist democracies, these scholars strongly criticized state intervention of social provision and economic regulation. These critics were not considered relevant during this period as the overall economic performance was sound, but once the economic shock emerged their postulates became more significant. After the collapse of the world economy in 1973, neoliberalism's advocates emphasized their critique of Keynesianism and demanded its replacement by neoliberal policies. Even though neoliberal ideas had been supported by a group of scholars since the 1940s, it was not until the 1980s that these ideas came to be widely adopted, notably by Ronald Reagan in the United States and Margaret Thatcher in the United Kingdom, and subsequently most developed countries.

It has been claimed that while neoliberal globalization and supranational institutions have advanced and become more significant, nation states have lost ground (Khan, 1996; Ohmae, 1995). Yet, the forces leading the neoliberal process have required strong nation-states in order to foster the neoliberal agenda. Although the neoliberal ideals seek to shape a depoliticized world, paradoxically, these have been achieved by political activity. In order to succeed, the neoliberal program requires a strong state with the support of political elites at both national and supranational levels. In this sense, nation states played a crucial role: to remove restraints on free trade and the global market and integrate their nation into the global economy.

Gamble (2000: 52) argues, "Despite its disparagement of politics and its dreams of a world without politics, neoliberalism is an intensely political doctrine with a very strong sense of the different dimensions of the political and what has to be done to ensure that its priorities become political reality". Far from the nation-state withering away, neoliberalism has actually to accord it greater importance, and it does so in the name of globalization. It is the need to integrate the economy fully into the global market that creates the necessity for a state able to facilitate that integration by removing obstacles and aligning domestic institutions with international ones (2000).

Harvey (2005) identifies a neoliberal state, whose role is to create and preserve an institutional framework appropriate to the neoliberal practices. In the same way, "the neo-liberal state extols the virtues of free competition and it is opposed to, and works against, groups (e.g. unions, social movements) that operate to restrain business interests and their efforts to accumulate capital" (Ritzer, 2010: 118).

Neoliberal policies were promoted and required as a pre-condition for financial loans by international financial institutions (IFIs), such as the IMF and WB, in the developing world including the majority of countries in Latin America, Asia, and Africa (MacDonald & Ruckert, 2009). For instance, after the debt crisis of 1982, Mexican President Miguel de la Madrid adopted gradually neoliberal policies as a condition set by financial institutions to release monetary loans (Harvey, 2005: 29). Nonetheless, neoliberal policies were adjusted by domestic political actors. While Mexico initially sought to alleviate the effects of the debt crisis- through heterodox economic strategies, eventually it embraced neoliberalism since the mid-1980s. In this manner, neoliberal reforms in this country, especially the liberalization of trade as a component of the development model, became more evident by the second half of the 1980s.[2]

The conversion to neoliberalism was a diversified process, in which Latin American countries opted to adopt this economic doctrine in different years between the mid-1970s and the mid-1990s. Within a period of twenty years or so, the largest economies of the region turned to neoliberal prescriptions to overcome domestic problems. In Latin America, Chile was the first country to embrace neoliberalism in 1976 under the dictatorship of Augusto Pinochet (1973–1990), then, during the 1980s, Bolivia (1985), Mexico (1986), Argentina and Venezuela (1989) followed the neoliberal route. During the 1990s, other countries were influenced by this doctrine, such as Colombia (1990), Ecuador (1990), Paraguay (1991), Uruguay (1991), Peru (1992), and Brazil (1994).

Although the beginning of neoliberal policies varied among countries, the implementation took place in a short period. Rodrik (1996: 18) highlights the speed with which the neoliberalization process took effect in the region: "it is striking how many Latin American countries have come within reaching distance of completing the items on the Washington consensus in a period of no more than a few years". For instance, "Mexico, Bolivia, and Argentina, to cite some of the more distinguished examples, have undertaken more trade and financial liberalization and privatization within five years than the East Asian countries have managed in three decades" (1996). Nevertheless, the process of neoliberalization constituted of different kinds of policies. The first set of policies was implemented successfully, but the second stage encountered several difficulties. It could be said that neoliberalism, understood as the implementation of different policies, is neither a finished process nor a homogeneous development.

Neoliberalism and Democracy

A diverse landscape can be seen in Latin America regarding the arrival of democracy and the turn to neoliberal policies. There, however, is not a strong relation in the progression of these two processes. For instance, Chile and Mexico started the road to neoliberalism within military and authoritarian regimes, respectively; but both Argentina and Brazil became democratic countries before the adoption of neoliberal prescriptions. Certainly, these conditions affected and determined the execution and outcomes of these developments and may help explain the peculiarities observed in every country.

For others, neoliberalism helped to boost the democratization process in Latin America. In assessing the effects of neoliberalism in the region, Weyland (2004: 137–138) argues that neoliberal reforms appear to have made a significant contribution to the strengthening of democratic stability, but at the same time such reforms have weakened the quality of democracy. On the one hand neoliberalism influenced the arrival and installation of democracy, but on the other hand, it affected its quality in most of the region. Regarding the influence of neoliberalism on democracy, Weyland argues that integration of Latin America into the world economy has made the region more susceptible to international pressures to sustain democracy as the system of government. He also highlights that neoliberal policies have been implemented not only in countries with authoritarian regimes (Chile, is the best case in this category, although Mexico is also considered) but also in semi-democratic and democratic countries. Therefore, a strong relationship between the implementation of neoliberal policies and features of political regimes in Latin America is not very clear.

Nevertheless, at the political level, while the causal relationship between economic neoliberalism and political democracy is a debatable, if not polemical, claim, the fact is that Latin America is more democratic today than at any time in the region's history (Oxhorn, 2009: 218). Certainly, there is a diverse landscape in the region, but in many cases, the panorama suggests that democratically elected governments have been unable to implement a political economy that generates opportunities of decent employment as well as an institutional framework that guarantee authentic union organization. As expressed by Smith (2005: 241), "Latin America's dual transition to democracy and free-market economics simultaneously increased the voice of actors in civil society (such as labor) while giving them more reason to protest (declines in real wages, the disappearance of trade protection, and the privatization of many state-owned industries)".

In the case of Mexico, the absence of democracy had both advantages and disadvantages. On the one hand, the PRI regime, regarded as authoritarian, could achieve many of the neoliberal reforms in a relatively short period due to the control on social groups and political actors. On the other hand, the fact that the PRI regime relied on the corporatist structure to implement these policies (for example, the support of organized labor) resulted in the postponement of democratization of the labor sphere and the internal democratic life in labor organizations.

Neoliberalism and Labor

Despite the predictions made by neoliberal promoters in that more economic integration throughout the world and market supremacy was supposed to generate prosperity, since resources would be more efficiently allocated, the employment crisis grew as the process of neoliberal globalization intensified (Moody, 1997: 41). Furthermore, developed countries did not become rich through the rigorous application of neoliberal policies; the periods of economic growth in both poor and rich countries have not coincided with neoliberalism; and the policies that actually produced fast economic growth in Latin America (1930–1982), East Asia (1960–1998), and China (1978 to the present) clearly contradict the prescriptions of the Washington Consensus in various important aspects (Saad-Filho, 2005: 116).

Several studies contend that neoliberalism triggered diverse outcomes in Latin America, and, therefore, it is not possible to blame neoliberal policies for the various setbacks in the region. For instance, according to Walton (2004: 168), in terms of economic performance, the region faired significantly better in the 1990s than in the "lost decade" of the 1980s; yet with the exception of Chile's performance, this fell far short of the achievements of the East Asian Tigers and rates of growth did not fully recover to those achieved in the 1960s and 1970s. After performing an economic analysis in the countries of the region, Walton (2004: 170) contends that "market-oriented and stabilization policies are by no means the only source of higher growth". In his cross-country analysis he also finds that education and infrastructure matter, whereas more government controlling for these other factors is a drag on a growth. Effective state action is important to these areas, and East Asia has invested substantially more in both areas. Regarding the outcomes of neoliberal reforms in Latin America, "many of the reforms associated with the Washington Consensus simply could not work because they conflicted with political practices and could not be made to fit with established patterns of state behaviour." Thus, "when they were implemented, the effect was often quite different from what was expected" (Grugel & Riggirozzi, 2009: 10).

Although the poor economic performance in Latin America has been connected to neoliberal policies, it is important to distinguish different crises in the region. For instance, after the 'debt crisis' of the early 1980s, other economic shocks proliferated in the largest Latin American economies less than a decade after the implementation of neoliberal policies (Mexico 1994–1995; Brazil, 1998–1999; and Argentina 2001–2002). While the economic difficulties of the early 1980s are connected to a debt crisis generated by external factors, the economic crises of the 1990s and early 2000s are claimed to be the result of neoliberal policies and their related effects. Furthermore, neoliberal policies did improve economic performance, although to an unsatisfactory level. As stated by Cardoso and Gindin (2009), and other international bodies such as ECLAC, the economic performance, as measured by GDP growth, in Latin America was higher in the 1990s than in the 1980s.

Despite the economic reactivation in the 1990s, labor conditions worsened. Patroni and Poitras (2002) highlight the effects of neoliberal reforms on labor markets in Latin America, stating that conditions in labor markets deteriorated consistently for the region, particularly over the 1990s. According to these scholars, this negative transformation can be connected to the growth of unemployment, rising precariousness and informality in labor conditions, and stagnant or deteriorating real wages. These changes affected the capacity for collective action and political influence of labor unions. In general terms, organized labor suffered a major setback throughout the region (2002: 207). Murillo (2003: 107) concludes that market reforms created new challenges for labor in Latin America, as "open economies made labor costs important because they could not be transferred to consumers, thereby heightening productivity concerns for international competition".

On the other hand, Portes and Hoffman (2003) reveal that neoliberal reforms have generated more inequality, crime and insecurity and have expanded the informal sector and emigration in Latin America. Munck (2003: 86) points out that in the 1980s, four out of every five new jobs created were in the informal sector of the economy, and these were as likely to be in the drug trade as in the much touted micro-enterprise sector. This author states that the changing social structure of the working population has had a clear political impact, and in particular there has been a relative decline of the more traditional forms of association such as labor unions that depended on relatively stable industrial development. Certainly, the structural changes in the labor markets and employment but also the policies adopted by the government affected organized labor during the period of neoliberal reforms. As mentioned by Panniza (2009: 104): "the politicization and mobilization of class cleavages were made more difficult by the fragmentation of labor markets, deindustrialization, privatization and public sector spending cuts that affected the large concentration of workers in the most heavily unionized sectors of the economy".

Features of Neoliberalism

Several neoliberal policies were selected in order to assess the effects of neoliberalism on the labor sphere and especially on labor unions. These are the reduction and control of inflation; deregulation and *flexibilization* of labor markets; privatization, and trade liberalization or economic globalization. First, neoliberal prescriptions include the control and reduction of inflation as a condition for the stabilization of macroeconomic indicators. The reduction of inflation and the stabilization of other macroeconomic indicators were crucial and also part of the first package of neoliberal reforms in Latin America (CEPAL, 2004; Grugel & Rigarrozzi, 2009).

The reduction of inflation was a success of neoliberal policies that contributed to the improvement of macroeconomic indicators in the region. Walton (2004: 170) assures that "two of the major changes in the region between the 1980s and 1990s have been the reduction of high inflation and some improvement in the fiscal and debt positions". The overall rates of inflation in Latin America fell from more than 200%

in the 1980s to less than 10% by the second half of the 1990s (Grugel & Riggirozzi, 2009: 9). Indeed, "during the 1980s, inflation in some countries reached new heights: nearly 600 percent in Brazil on average, 800 percent in Argentina, 1,200 percent in Peru, and more than 5,000 percent in Nicaragua. In just a few years, however, hyperinflation was controlled, and inflation rates were stabilized in a lasting way. By 2000, these rates reached a level below 10 percent for the region as a whole" (Santiso, 2006: 87–88). Argentina, Bolivia, and Peru dropped rapidly from hyperinflation in the 1980s to two-digit inflation and then continued to the single-digit level; Chile did the same in the 1970s, as did Brazil in the 1990s (Stallings & Peres, 2000: 53). The policies implemented in these countries to produce stabilization varied, with some countries using exchange rate policy while others relied mainly on monetary or fiscal policy (Ibid.). Similarly, in Mexico, inflation was a major obstacle to stimulating the economy, but it was brought under control by the late 1980s, following a stabilization program included in the neoliberal strategy of the de la Madrid and Salinas administrations. Inflation rates in Mexico were in three digits in the mid-1980s but this high rate was reduced notably; between 1987 and 1991 inflation dropped from 159.2 to 18.5% (Aspe, 1993: 47) and then to 7.1% in 1994.

Nevertheless, towards the end of the 1990s, the success of neoliberal policies for addressing high inflation was tempered by low growth in per capita gross domestic product, high urban unemployment, and increasing wealth disparities (Biglaiser & DeRouen, 2004: 564).

Neoliberal economic policies privileged the reduction of inflation rates, whereas the stimulation of employment was disregarded, especially as a result of the reduction of public spending. For instance, "neoliberals argued that the way to fight inflation was to reduce growth in the money supply (monetarism) by cutting public spending and raising interest rates" (O'Toole, 2007: 443). The reduction of inflation has been accompanied by the deterioration of real wages, as in the case of Mexico. This occurred because the instruments of political economy used to control inflation included the freeze of wages and prices. The fact that the reduction of inflation has to be achieved by the compression of real wages is not clearly a specific recommendation as described by the Washington Consensus (Williamson, 2000), but rather it was a specific form of public policy followed by Mexico during the administrations of de la Madrid and Salinas (Lustig, 1998; Moreno-Brid & Ros, 2009).

Deregulation was another important component of neoliberal reforms. Most of the larger Latin American countries are among the world's most regulated market economies, at least on paper. Among the economic regulatory mechanisms are limits on firing employees (Williamson, 1990). One of the essential recommendations of neoliberalism is the *flexibilization* of labor markets, supposedly in order to increase rates of productivity and employment. This includes the deregulation of labor legislation to hire and fire workers, the decentralization of labor relations, the reduction of union's rights and duties, the suppression of collective bargaining and protective regulation, as well as the deletion of social benefits (Saad-Filho, 2005: 114).

The advent of labor *flexibilization* was the result of a singular inversion of an historical trend: while significant labor reforms were preceded by union proposals (8 hour working-days, among others), the philosophy and practice of labor market *flexibilization*, were the result of employers' initiatives, which suddenly obtained significant intellectual and institutional support and soon were received with general benevolence by the experts and sometimes the consent of labor unions. *Flexibilization* emerged as a response to the economic crisis of 1970s and has become so strongly consolidated that now it seems difficult imagine a return to the classical model of protectionism in labor relations. Although the protectionist model was definitely beneficial for workers, at the same time it came into conflict with a productive system increasingly challenged by national and international competition that exerted pressure to cut down the costs of the production factors, among them, labor. The key to implementing *flexibilization* is the easing of restrictions on the firing and hiring of workers (Montoya, 1991).

The 'flexible' worker lacks a job for life, but instead moves and retrains to meet altered market demands. To facilitate such mobility most countries have loosened laws on hiring and firing. Workers are also expected to be 'flexible' in respect of hours, wages, benefits, health and safety standards, and so forth. 'Flexible' jobs are often casual, part-time, and temporary, with few, if any benefits beyond the (often low) wages offered. The workers involved frequently lack collective bargaining arrangements and other union protections (Scholte, 2000: 223).

The *flexibilization* of labor in Latin America during the 1990s generated diverse outcomes (Cook, 2007). For instance, in Argentina and Brazil, moderate flexibility reforms were implemented; in Chile and Peru, changes in labor law were extensive; while in Mexico and Bolivia, labor law reform did not occur despite extensive economic liberalization (Cook, 2007: 3). Cook classifies these countries in state corporatist (Argentina and Brazil); radical (pro-worker) and flexible (radical-pro-employer) (Chile and Peru); and revolutionary-states (Mexico and Bolivia). In the cases of Mexico and Bolivia, Cook states that "labor organizations were relatively strong in exerting their influence to halt reform of labor laws" because "their alliance with prominent political parties and/or their mobilization potential". Furthermore, in such countries "there was less pressure to reform the laws because of the limited enforcement" (Cook, 2007: 20). On the other hand, Anner (2008) detected that most labor reforms in the 1980s and 1990s in Latin America was favorable in terms of union rights. However, the decline of unions, measured by union density, was present in most of the region. Thus, while collective labor rights have become stronger, unions have become weaker in Latin America (2008: 36).

The third aspect is privatization, an important policy tool in the neoliberal process. Privatization involves a transfer of property rights over productive assets from the public sector to private hands. It has been claimed that privatization will yield higher efficiency outcomes and better levels of service than could be obtained through public agencies (Scholte, 2005: 8–9).

In a wide study covering Latin American countries, Lora (2001) found that the privatization process has been notable although uneven in the region. Between 1986 and 1999 there were almost 400 transfers and sales from the public to the private sector which represented more than half of the value of privatization operations in developing countries. 57% of the value of the privatizations in the region during the 1990s took place in the infrastructure sectors, which were traditionally closed to private participation and where the potential for obtaining productivity and efficiency gains is greater. Another 11% came from the sale of banking and similar entities, thereby strengthening tendencies toward financial reform. The composition of privatizations by sector has differed notably between countries. In the Dominican Republic, Colombia, El Salvador, Argentina, and Bolivia, the electricity sectors have absorbed over half, whereas in Venezuela, Uruguay, and Mexico, practically no privatizations have taken place in this sector (Lora, 2001: 15).

On the other hand, the privatizations of state-owned monopolies neutralize the power of labor unions. With the dismantling of the public sector, wherein unions are particularly strong, union membership is dramatically eroded. Most jobs suppressed in the public sector were unionized. At the same time, union membership in the private sector remained at the same level, thus, there was an overall reduction of union membership. According to the neoliberal agenda, the decrease of union membership in the employed labor force brings about more profits for corporations since fewer unionized workers generate more earnings (George, 1999). Privatization has also had implications for party systems in Latin America (O'Toole, 2007). In Mexico, privatization helped to erode the centralized, single-party system under the PRI because it restrained valuable sources of patronage in state corporations for the politicians who had controlled them. In this manner, "privatization has greatly empowered the private sector at the expense of groups formerly represented within the corporatist state, such as organized labor" (O'Toole, 2007: 261).

Nevertheless, privatization has also generated varied outcomes. Tuman (2007) demonstrated that there were differences in the privatization of the telecommunications sector in Mexico and Argentina. In the case of Argentina, employment decreased, subcontracting augmented and the unions–company relations became locked in a pattern of conflict and strikes over the lack of job stability. In contrast, in Mexico the privatized company (Telmex) offered significant protection to workers. The number of jobs in Telmex remained around the same level and later expanded (2007: 173).

Moreover, the liberalization of trade and inflows of foreign direct investment (referred to here as globalization) has been identified as another determinant of unionization. Trade liberalization boost the economic performance; for instance, "East Asian countries in particular provide empirical evidence to support the contention that export performance, especially of manufactured goods within a market-oriented production system, is positively associated with economic growth" (Dussels, 2006: 125). Trade liberalization, as mentioned in Chapter 5, has been implemented in Mexico since the mid-1980s, especially with the increase of *maquiladora* plants. In this country, "a combination of effective incentives, access to the US market via the North America Free Trade Area and the decisions of TNCs appear to have ensured that large manufacturers have successfully made the shift to exporting. Automotive products, cars and parts, as well as consumer electronics and electronic machinery have been particularly significant" (Weiss, 2002: 161).

Globalization, on the other hand, is deleterious for workers and unions because a growing proportion of core workers are now in direct competition with semi-peripheral workers (Clawson & Clawson, 1999). In addition, international trade and finance capital mobility are regarded as damaging consequences of globalization for unions since the displacement of productive activities is a potential threat (Piazza, 2002). Currently, entire industrial sectors may withdraw their production activities and relocate them into regions with lower labor costs. This possibility has impacts on workers and unions because it moderates their labor demands for better working conditions and remunerations. In this way, labor unions must accept reduced wages or benefits and pass on less utility to members and potential members (Piazza, 2002: 425).

Finance capital has become highly mobile and multinational corporations can move between countries, sometimes to the detriment of the workforce (Bealey, 1999). This relative easiness to perform financial movements makes capital mobility feasible; in some developing countries this may lead to bankruptcy. For example, in Mexico this is claimed to be the main factor behind the economic crisis of 1994–1995, which triggered the international financial crisis known as *efecto tequila* (tequila effect), and contributed to increased unemployment, inflation, the erosion of average real wages (Ffrench-Davis, 2005: 179–180), and decline of union density. In this manner, it could be said that this specific characteristic of globalization has been adverse for workers and labor organizations in a group of countries, including Mexico.

Considering the aforementioned events, one of the most common beliefs is that the decline of labor union presence in the employed labor force is caused by the globalization of the economy and production. However, many have found out diverse results. For instance, Scruggs and Lange (2002) argued that rather than being a direct result of neoliberal globalization, union density decline has been determined by institutions regulating labor relations, specifically those related directly to the recruitment of members. They refute the general assumption, which states that the openness of economies (free trade, financial flows and direct investment) generates the decline of labor union density. After performing an analysis including 16 OECD countries, it was demonstrated that union density fluctuations follow different trends, even when many of these countries had already adopted public policies to encourage free trade and financial market liberalization. With respect to the argument that 'convergence' among countries is stimulated by globalization, significant empirical evidence has demonstrated a great divergence among countries inserted in the global economy (Scruggs & Lange, 2002). They conclude that "much of the economy, even in the private sector, is not directly affected by the capital mobility promoted by globalization; for instance, personal services, domestic transport, and communication are more sheltered from international competition than export manufacturing or financial services" (2002: 151).

Anner (2008) demonstrated that Latin American countries with greater degree of trade openness are not always the ones with largest decline in unionization rates. For example, in Ecuador, where imports and exports account for 55% of GDP, unionization declined by 6%; while in Peru, where trade as a share of GDP stands at 39%, unionization declined by 67% (2008: 38).

Sano and Williamson (2008) classify countries according to their levels of union density, for instance, countries with High Union Density (HUD),[3] Middle Union Density (MUD),[4] and Low Union Density (LUD)[5] countries. They confirmed that globalization is not a strong predictor in the HUD countries, but it is significant in the MUD countries. In the case of the LUD countries, again, globalization is not significant for union density. The explanation they provide consists in that while unions in HUD countries may be able to pressure corporations not to outsource jobs and investments–with the result that the impact of globalization attenuated–, the unions in MUD countries do not have this power. Regarding LUD countries, they argue that the union density in countries of this group was declining before the age of globalization began in the 1980s. The effect of globalization on the union densities of this group appears to be weaker than in those that did not experience large declines prior to 1980.

Regarding the specific case of union density decline in the United States during the period 1977–1997, Baldwin (2003: 65–66) found that "global forces, often mentioned as an important contributor, play only a modest quantitative role". He also found that "other familiar de-unionization suspects (such as the temporal shift in production toward less unionized service sectors and the less-unionized South) play at best a modest role in explaining the decline in unionization rates". Baldwin claims that the decline is ubiquitous in all sectors and regions, suggesting deep fundamental sources such as growing employer opposition, unfavorable legislative trends, and declining worker trust in union institutions.

Conclusions

This chapter has analyzed the features of neoliberalism in terms of their implications for organized labor. Neoliberal policies in general have not encouraged a significant economic expansion in the region. In the same way, they have not alleviated unemployment, which has generated more insecurity for workers. During the 1990s, Latin America saw an economic reactivation, but the informal sector in labor markets could not be reversed. However, a deeper analysis suggests a diverse landscape in the region. Therefore, we cannot establish a direct relation regarding the effects of neoliberalism on economic performance and labor markets. The outcomes of neoliberalism differ greatly in Latin America, which suggests that domestic political factors and the relations among political actors play an important role. Chile, for instance, had the highest rates of economic growth in the region in the period of neoliberal reforms. In contrast, other countries, including Mexico, did not achieve the best outcomes in the economy and employment in this period.

The relevance of domestic political frameworks and institutions as well as the specific economic and social policies are more relevant in accounting for economic performance. The outcomes of neoliberal policies depend to a certain extent on the response of organized social groups and their relations with the state and alliances with political actors. It is also relevant in this regard, to note the existence of corporatist structures and political alliances. The same argument can be used to account for the decline of union density in the employed labor force in the region. Therefore, it is necessary to analyze developments in specific countries if we are to explain the changing situation of labor unions during the neoliberal period.

One of the main conclusions is that economic performance is not a strong determinant of union density decline. It is also complicated to relate neoliberal policies to the decline of unions since the 1980s. The persistence of very strong unions in places where wide neoliberal reforms have been implemented suggests that other elements must be considered in this regard. In view of such panorama, the argument that trade liberalization and economic integration has determined union density fluctuations in developed countries, cannot be sustained.

Nonetheless, neoliberalism changed the basis of social relations between the state and social actors. This transformed the sources of power of organized labor and reduced its leverage in the political realm that it enjoyed during the period of Import Substitution Industrialization. Although there is a varied landscape, we can confirm the unionization declined in the largest economies but also in the majority of countries in Latin America. This, on the other hand, does not suggest the demise of labor unions in all the sectors and occupations. Unions continue playing an important role in some strategic sectors of the economy and in the public sector.

This chapter has provided the political and economic landscape required to analyze the factors accounting for union decline. Nevertheless, the impact of neoliberal policies on economic performance has not been very clear, as the picture is mixed in the Latin American region. The same could be argued regarding political and institutional factors, especially the institutional framework regulating labor relations. In the following chapters, the main purpose is to detect what kind of factors have been decisive for the evolution of union density and labor union power, focusing on the case of Mexico.

Notes

1. In this section, I will concentrate on Latin America as this transition took place in the countries of the region but also because similarities between the countries of the region and Mexico.
2. In the case of Mexico, see for more detail: Lustig (1998).
3. Belgium, Denmark, Finland and Sweden.
4. Austria, Australia, Canada, Germany, Italy, New Zealand, Norway, and UK.
5. France, Japan, Netherlands, Switzerland, Ireland, and US.

Bibliography

Anner, M. (2008). Meeting the challenges of industrial restructuring: Labor reform and enforcement in Latin America. *Latin American Politics and Society, 50,* 33–65.

Aspe, P. (1993). *Economic transformation: The Mexican way.* Cambridge, MA: MIT Press.

Baldwin, R. (2003). *The decline of US labor unions and the role of trade.* Washington, DC: Institute for International Economics.

Bealey, F. (1999). *The Blackwell dictionary of political science.* Oxford and Malden, MA: Blackwell Publishers.

Bensusán, G. (2007). Trade unionism in Mexico: Current situation and obstacles to renewal. In C. Phelan (Eds.), *Trade union revitalisation. Trends and prospects in 34 countries*. Oxford: Peter Lang.

Biglaiser, G., & DeRouen, K. (2004). Expansion of neoliberal economic reforms in Latin America. *International Studies Quarterly, 48*(3), 561–578.

Bruhn, K. (1996). Social spending and political support: The *lessons* of the National Solidarity Program in Mexico. *Comparative Politics, 28*, 151–177.

Cardoso, A., & Gindin, J. (2009). *Industrial relations and collective bargaining: Argentina, Brazil and Mexico compared* (Working Paper No. 5). Industrial and Employment Relations Department International Labor Office, Geneva.

CEPAL. (2004). *Anuario estadístico de América Latina y el Caribe*. Santiago de Chile.

Clawson, D., & Clawson, M. A. (1999). What has happened to the U.S. labor movement? Union decline and renewal. *Annual Review of Sociology, 25*, 95–119.

Cook, M. L. (1998). Toward flexible industrial relations? Neo-liberalism, democracy, and labor reform in Latin America. *Industrial Relations, 37*(3), 311–336.

Cook, M. L. (2007). *The politics of labor reform in Latin America: Between flexibility and rights*. University Park: Pennsylvania State University Press.

Duménil, G., & Levy, D. (2004). *Capital resurgent: Roots of the neoliberal revolution*. Cambridge: Harvard University Press.

Dussel, P. E. (2006). The Mexican economy since NAFTA. In D. Plehwe (Ed.), *Neoliberal hegemony: A global critique*. New York: Routledge.

Eisenstadt, T. A. (2004). *Courting democracy in Mexico: Party strategies and electoral institutions*. Cambridge: Cambridge University Press.

Ffrench-Davis, R. (2005). *Reforming Latin America's economies after market fundamentalism*. London: Palgrave Macmillan.

Gamble, A. (2000). *Politics and fate*. Cambridge: Polity Press.

Gamble, A. (2001). Neo-liberalism. *Capital and Class, 75*, 127–134.

George, S. (1999). *A short history of neoliberalism*. Conference on economic sovereignty in a globalising world, Bangkok.

Grugel, J. (2002). *Democratization: A critical introduction*. Basingstoke: Palgrave.

Grugel, J., & Riggirozzi, P. (2009). *Governance after neoliberalism in Latin America*. London: Palgrave Macmillan.

Harvey, D. (2005). *A brief history of neoliberalism*. Oxford: Oxford University Press.

Khan, L. (1996). *The extinction of nation-states: A world without borders*. The Hague: Kluwer Law International.

Kingstone, P. (2010). *The political economy of Latin America: Reflections on neoliberalism and development*. New York, London: Routledge.

Leiva, F. I. (2008). *Latin American neostructuralism: The contradictions of post -neoliberal development*. Minneapolis: University of Minnesota Press.
Levitsky, S., & Mainwaring, S. (2006). Organized labor and democracy in Latin America. *Comparative Politics, 39*(1), 21–42.
Levitsky, S. (2003). *Transforming labor-based parties in Latin America: Argentine Peronism in comparative perspective*. New York: Cambridge University Press.
Lora, E. (2001). *Structural reforms in Latin America: What has been reformed and how to measure it*. Washington, DC: Inter-American Development Bank.
Lustig, N. (1998). *The remaking of an economy*. Washington, DC: Brookings Institution Press.
Macdonald, L., & Ruckert, A. (2009). Post-neoliberalism in the Americas: An introduction. In L. Macdonald & A. Ruckert (Eds.), *Post-neoliberalism in the Americas* (pp. 1–18). New York, NY: Palgrave Macmillan.
Martin, P. (2007). Mexico's neoliberal transitions: Authoritarian shadows in an era of neoliberalism. In H. Leitner, J. Peck, & E. S. Sheppard (Eds.), *Contesting neoliberalism: Urban frontiers*. New York: Guilford Press.
Middlebrook, K. J. (1986). Political liberalization in an authoritarian regime: The case of Mexico. In G. O'Donnell et al. (Eds.), *Transitions from authoritarian rule: Latin America* (pp. 123–147). Baltimore: John Hopkins University Press.
Middlebrook, K. (1989). The sounds of silence: Organized labor's response to economic crisis in Mexico. *Journal of Latin American Studies, 21*(2), 195–220.
Montoya, A. (1991). El contrato de trabajo, entre la estabilidad en el empleo y la precariedad. In G. Vidal (Ed.), *El cambio laboral en la década de los 90*. Madrid: Espasa-Calpe.
Moody, K. (1997). *Workers in a lean world*. New York: Verso Publishing.
Moreno-Brid, J. C., & Ros, J. (2009). *Development and growth in the Mexican economy: A historical perspective*. London: Oxford University Press.
Munck, R. (2003). *Contemporary Latin America*. Basingstoke and New York: Palgrave Macmillan.
Murillo, M. V. (1997). Union politics, market-oriented reforms, and the reshaping of Argentine corporatism. In D. A. Chalmers, C. M. Vivas, K. Hite, S. B. Martin, K. Piester, & M. Segarra, (Eds.), *The new politics of inequality in Latin America: Rethinking representation and participation*. Oxford, UK: Oxford University Press.
Murillo, M. V. (2000). From populism to neoliberalism: Labor unions and market reforms in Latin America. *World Politics, 52*(2), 135–168.
Murillo, M. V. (2001). *Labor unions, partisan coalitions and market reforms in Latin America*. Cambridge: Cambridge University Press.

Murillo, M. V. (2003). Latin American labor. In J. I. Domínguez & M. Shifter (Eds.), *Democratic governance in Latin America and the Caribbean*. Baltimore: Johns Hopkins University Press.

O' Donnell, G. (1994). Delegative democracy. *The Journal of Democracy, 5*(1), 55–69.

O'Toole, G. (2007). *Politics: Latin America*. Harlow, UK: Pearson Longman.

O'Connell, L. D. (1999). *Collective bargaining systems in 6 Latin American countries: Degrees of autonomy and decentralization*. Inter-American Development Bank, Office of the Chief Economist, Working Paper 399. Washington, D.C.

Ohmae, K. (1995). *The end of the nation state: The rise of regional economies*. New York: Free press.

OIT. (2003). *Panorama Laboral 2002. America Latina y El Caribe*. Lima, Peru: OIT.

Oxhorn, P. (2009). Beyond neoliberalism? Latin America's new crossroads. In *Beyond Neoliberalism in Latin America?* (pp. 217–233). New York: Palgrave Macmillan.

Panizza, F. (2009). *Contemporary Latin America: Development and democracy beyond the Washington consensus*. London: Zed Books.

Patroni, V., & Poitras, M. (2002). Labour in neoliberal Latin America: An introduction. *Labour, Capital and Society, 35*(2), 207–220.

Philip, G. (2003). *Democracy in Latin America: Surviving conflict and crisis?*. Cambridge: Polity Press.

Piazza, J. (2002). *Going global: Unions and globalization in the US, Germany and Sweden*. Lanham, MD: Lexington Books.

Portes, A., & Hoffman, K. (2003). Latin American class structures: Their composition and change during the neoliberal era. *Latin American Research Review, 38*(1), 41–82.

Ritzer, G. (2010). *Globalization: A basic text*. London: Wiley Blackwell.

Rodrik, D. (1996). Understanding economic policy reform. *Journal of Economic Literature, 34*(1), 9–41.

Rodrik, D. (2001). *The global governance of trade as if development really mattered*. United Nations Development Programme (UNDP).

Roxborough, I. (1998). Urban labor movements in Latin America since 1930. In L. Bethell (Ed.), *Latin America politics and society since 1930*. Oxford: Oxford University Press.

Saad Filho, A., & Yalman, G. L. (Eds.). (2009). *Economic transitions to neoliberalism in middle-income countries: Policy dilemmas, economic crises, forms of resistance*. London: Routledge.

Saad-Filho. (2005). *Neoliberalism: A critical reader*. London: Pluto press.

Saavedra, J. (2003). Labor markets during the 1990s. In P. Kuczynski & J. Williamson (Eds.), *After the Washington consensus: Restarting growth*

and reform in Latin America. Washington, DC: Institute of International Economics.
Sano, J., & Williamson, J. B. (2008). Factors affecting union decline in 18 OECD countries. *International Journal of Comparative Sociology, 49*(6), 479–500.
Santiso, J. (2006). *Latin America's political economy of the possible: Beyond good revolutionaries and free marketers*. Cambridge, MA: MIT Press.
Scholte, J. (2000). *Globalization, a critical introduction*. Basingstoke: Palgrave Macmillan.
Scholte, J. (2005). *The sources of neoliberal globalization*. Geneva: United Nations Research Institute for Social Development.
Scruggs, L., & Lange, P. (2002). Where have all the members gone? Globalization, institutions, and union density. *The Journal of Politics, 64*(1), 126–153.
Shadlen, K. (2004). *Democratization without representation: The politics of small industry in Mexico*. University Park, PA: Pennsylvania State University Press.
Smith, P. H. (2005). *Democracy in Latin America: Political change in comparative perspective*. Oxford: Oxford University Press.
Stallings, B., & Peres, W. (2000). *Growth, employment and equity. The impact of the economic reforms in Latin American and Caribbean*. Washington, DC: Economic Commission for Latin American and Caribbean, Brookings Institution Press.
Tuman, J. P. (2007). Comparing modes of privatization: A study of the telecommunications sectors in Argentina and Mexico, 1990–2000. *Industrial Relations Journal, 38*(2), 155–177.
Visser, J. (2003). Unions and unionism around the world. In J. Addison & C. Schnabel (Eds.), *The International Handbook of Trade unions* (pp. 366–413). Cheltenham: Edward Elgar.
Walton, M. (2004). Neoliberalism in Latin America: Good, bad, or incomplete? *Latin American Research Review, 39*, 165–183.
Weiss, J. (2002). *Industrialisation and globalization: Theory and evidence from developing countries*. London: Routledge.
Weyland, K. (2004). Neoliberalism and democracy in Latin America: A mixed record. *Latin American Politics and Society, 46*(1), 136–157.
Williamson, J. (1990). What Washington means by policy reform. *Latin American Adjustment: How Much Has Happened, 1*, 90–120.
Williamson, O. (2000). What should the World Bank think about the Washington consensus? *World Bank Research Observer, 15*(2), 251–264.
Wynia, G. (1990). *The politics of Latin American development*. New York: Cambridge University Press.

CHAPTER 4

The Rise and Decline of Labor Unions in Mexico: Political and Institutional Factors

Introduction

During the last century, labor unions in Mexico played a key role in the political system that emerged from the revolution, as part of the corporatist structure of the state. They also had a privileged position within the PRI, the dominant political party from 1929 to 2000. However, the relation of labor unions both with the state and the PRI underwent major transformations as a result of the implementation of neoliberal policies and the political transition to democracy since the 1980s. While the alliance of labor with the state was modified, the position of unions in the labor and political spheres diminished. In this context, the neoliberal governments managed to weaken labor organizations. Internal divisions occurred among the official labor organizations, such as the CT and among its main labor confederations: the CTM, CROC, CROM and others. Union membership underwent a significant decline in the period of neoliberal democracy. A new kind of independent labor organization emerged, opposing the CT supremacy in the top labor leadership but also confronting the outcomes of neoliberal reforms in the working class.

Despite the outcomes of the Mexican Revolution, such as the approval of the 1917 constitution providing extensive labor rights, it was after the 1930s that labor unions would become an essential sector of the political regime and experienced their golden era. In the second half of

R. Zepeda, *The Decline of Labor Unions in Mexico during the Neoliberal Period*, Governance, Development, and Social Inclusion in Latin America, https://doi.org/10.1007/978-3-030-65710-9_4

the 1930s, the policies advanced by president Lázaro Cárdenas created a solid political regime relying on a corporatist structure with the inclusion of workers, peasants, and urban employees within the official party. This structure prevailed until the 1980s when it cracked up, but remains significantly reduced in the current political regime. In the late 1980s and early 1990s, President Carlos Salinas implemented diverse neoliberal policies that undermined the relevance of organized labor and maneuvered to weaken the official confederations such as the CTM and the CT. At the same time, Salinas supported the emergence of new unions that would become more prominent in the following years.

Labor Unions in Mexico

There are diverse categories of labor unions in Mexico. First, labor organizations subordinated and tied to the state as part of the former official party and therefore identified as "official unions".[1] Second, labor organizations with an independent position with regard to the state and the official party, therefore, identified as "independent unions". Third, labor organizations controlled by employers without any relevance in the labor and political sphere also known as "white unions". Considering these definitions, two categories of the labor organizations are prioritized: on the one hand, the official unions and, on the other, the independent unions. Finally, a large share of official and white unions has been created with labor contracts of protection, created by the companies with the acquiescence of the government in order to prevent the organization of authentic labor unions.[2]

I do not find any hint to Table 4.1... please include where appropriate in the text, and here below (if that is the convenient place for it to appear).

The Hegemonic Party and the Corporatist Framework

The Mexican political regime, which emerged from the Revolution of 1910–1920 but consolidated in the 1920s and 1930s, was based mainly on a dominant political party. This regime required for its operation and continuation a corporatist system that integrated diverse sectors, among them the labor unions, identified as the *sector obrero* (Cosío Villegas, 1972). In this political regime, the presidential institution used to have the support of the official political party (the Revolutionary National

Party, PNR, 1929–1938; the Party of the Mexican Revolution, PRM, 1938–1946, and the Institutional Revolutionary Party, PRI, 1946 to the present time),[3] which incorporated and exerted control on its three sectors: peasants, workers, and urban employees. In this way, as part of the ruling party, the labor sector paid loyalty and support to the official party and consequently to the state and its policies. Labor unions in Mexico, observed one analyst, "were an integral part of the 'revolutionary' state apparatus and did not really articulate an independent social voice" (Munck, 2003: 37).

Therefore, the operation of labor unions in Mexico and their relationship to both the state and the party can be understood more comprehensively considering two crucial aspects. First, the hegemony of a political party that became the main source of power in the country between 1929 and 2000, and the inclusion of organized labor in this party with a privileged position. The second element is a corporatist structure that sustained the political system during the PRI hegemony, which was determinant for the position of labor organizations. In this way, these two features of the political system in Mexico, the hegemony of the official party and the corporatist framework, regulated labor-state relations and determined the bargaining position of unions before employers and their access to public resources and political positions.

González (2008: 54) identified a "state corporatist system" in Mexico that operated through the hegemonic official party, conceding a "monopoly of voice and representation to the co-opted leaders of organized workers, peasants, and members of the middle class". Such a system, according to the author, generated political stability, relative inclusion, and enduring political control, factors that made the one-party regime of Mexico the envy of other Latin American countries between 1940 and the late 1960s. Indeed, "Mexico's authoritarianism differed from the rest of Latin America, particularly for its stability and durability" (Hogenboom, 2004: 93). Mexico's political system could be described as one of a flexible authoritarianism, with a hegemonic party system and a constitutional separation of powers, yet with actual decision-making concentrated in the federal executive (Hamilton & Kim, 2004: 71). "From 1929 to 1989 Mexico had a uniquely stable authoritarian regime requiring only a modest amount of repression because its legitimacy was enhanced both by its revolutionary ideology and by the regular change in its political leaders", observed Huntington (1991: 49). "Unlike single parties in most of

Africa and the former Soviet bloc, the PRI stayed in power without constitutionally banning opposition parties or employing systematic repression" (Magaloni, 2006: 121).

From 1929 and until the 1980s, the PRI succeeded in basing its dominant position on images of unity for national development and used little repression when compared to other Latin American authoritarian regimes. Through control over the presidency, the state bureaucracy, official unions, elections, and (during the years of import substitution) a large apparatus of state-owned companies, the PRI state ensemble built an enormous institutional framework for structural domination (Hogenboom, 2004: 94).

In broad terms, corporatism is a system of interests' representation between the state and diverse organized groups. The term has been employed by many academic scholars in the subject in order to define the framework in which the relations between the state and organized social sectors, among them labor unions, take place in Mexico; they refer to state corporatism (Bensusán, 2004; Cook, 1995; De la Garza, 2003). However, corporatism is a widespread concept and it is pertinent to limit its meaning in the case of Mexico. One of the most recurrent definitions is provided by Schmitter (1974: 93), who defines corporatism as:

> a system of interest representation in which the constituent units are organized into a limited number of singular, compulsory, non-competitive, hierarchically ordered and functionally differentiated categories, recognized or licensed (if not created) by the state and granted a deliberate representational monopoly within their respective categories in exchange for observing certain controls on their selection of leaders and articulation of demands and supports.

Schmitter (1974: 104) also identifies two kinds of corporatism. On the one hand, societal corporatism that is a component of democratic and liberal states (for example, Sweden, Switzerland, the Netherlands, Norway, and Denmark). In contrast, state corporatism can be "a defining element of, if not structural necessity for, the anti-liberal delayed capitalist, authoritarian, neo-mercantilist state"; for example, Portugal, Spain, Greece, Mexico and some Latin American countries such as Brazil, Chile and Peru. State corporatism, in Schmitter's words, "tends to be associated with political systems in which territorial subunits are tightly subordinated to central bureaucratic power; elections are non-existent or plebiscitary;

party systems are dominated or monopolized by a weak single party; executive authorities are ideologically exclusive and more narrowly recruited and are such that political subcultures based on class, ethnicity, language, or regionalism are repressed" (1974: 105).

This definition implies a subordination of organized social groups before the state; however, the subordination of social partners towards the state is not perceived in other sectors, such as the business sector (Patroni, 2001: 253–254); rather, labor-state relations have depended on political and economic contexts, as well as the ideological tendencies of the governments in power. Furthermore, the relations between labor unions and the state have undergone different stages and, in some cases, the official trade unions have been capable not only of influencing public policy formulation but they have also impeded the sanction of crucial reforms such as the labor code amendment. The fact that official unions had a privileged status did not mean that tensions between government and labor were absent. Consequently, labor leaders in Mexico had political influence not only because they controlled big labor organizations but also because they were involved in party politics at both national and state levels (Cook, 1995: 78)

Even though corporatism in Mexico implied several authoritarian characteristics such as vertical style in decision-making, it also facilitated the negotiation with organized groups. Bizberg (1993: 303) contends that "corporatist control over the working class has not been based solely on coercion, but also on exchange". The scholar argues that prior to 1982, "Even when salaries were falling or growing very slowly, there were mechanisms to distribute income indirectly".[4] Nevertheless, it is clear that the relation between labor organizations and the state was dominated by the latter.

Corporatism is not only a complicated part of the political history of Mexico but also the most important element required to understand its political system. Without the description of corporatism, the 70 years of PRI government could not be explained (Vazquez-Anderson, 2004: 20). Indeed, corporatism "was an essential ingredient in Mexico's one party-state" (Camp, 2007: 130).

Corporatism comprises both formal and informal provisions. That is, it includes elements of national and labor legislation but also informal arrangements between the state and organized groups. For instance, the privileged positions of official unionism as one of the PRI sectors;

the elected political positions (in the legislature, governorships, municipal presidencies) occupied by union leaders as a quota in the official party in rewards for its electoral support which enabled it to influence policy-making; diverse social benefits for workers such as medical care, pensions and housing through tripartite official institutions (Imss, Infonavit, among others); and the labor related legislation that enabled the state to control the union registration and union mobilization through labor boards (JLCA and JFCA); all of these aspects were included in the corporatist alliance between workers and the state. However, the modification of these arrangements was crucial to explain the power and influence of labor unions in the labor and political realms. Corporatism marked the fate of labor unions not only in Mexico but also in diverse countries.

The CTM creation was the outcome of previous organizational efforts by relevant labor unions that abandoned or opposed the CROM in the 1920s and became more relevant in the early 1930s. Although they were characterized by diverse ideologies and positions towards the state, these unions gathered in 1936 and organized successfully the most powerful labor organization in the twentieth century. These organizations received support from the state, whose purpose was to gather labor movement and accordingly to be able to control it more effectively (Córdova, 1976).

In the words of Collier (1992), the CTM represented the reunification of two distinct tendencies. The first, based on relatively small, weak unions that were more dependent on state support, was the "pragmatic" tendency led by Fidel Velázquez. The second consisted of the stronger, more independent, and often more combative unions, particularly several national industrial unions and unions in which the Communist Party had significant influence (1992: 27). The latter took the leadership in the foundation. Lombardo Toledano, the first secretary-general and one of the CTM founders, had more radical ideas about trade unionism that facilitated the organizing activities and the creation of one sort of leftist unionism during the Cárdenas government. Yet since the 1940s, the revolutionary regime expelled the most radical currents within the labor organizations in sectors such as the railroad, oil, and mining. In this manner, the CTM became more conservative and subordinated to the government. Therefore, the corporatist system was more broadly consolidated in Mexico since the 1940s when Fidel Velázquez[5] became the CTM secretary-general, supported by President Ávila Camacho, who had a more center-oriented ideology. During the subsequent period, 1950–1970, as the industrialization process intensified, labor unions began organizing a large share of the labor force; this period would be regarded as the golden era for labor organizations.

In the public sector, Cárdenas encouraged the creation of the federation of employees in the public sector (FSTSE), as part of his political project to bring together different sectors into single nationwide organizations affiliated to the official party. With the FSTSE creation, most workers in this sector became members of the official party (Leal, 1986: 44–45), as it belonged to the CNOP, the urban sector of the party-state. According to labor-related legislation in this area, all public sector employees with full-time positions and permanent jobs are supposed to be unionized. However, in order to reduce the capacity of mobilization of the CTM, Cárdenas maneuvered to divide the labor movement, keeping apart the public employees. Hodges and Gandy (2002: 79) put it in this way:

> As the organizing moved forward in 1937, the government worked to bring the office workers into unions outside the CTM. The labor central repeatedly attacked the official policy, and between the State and the CTM there developed a struggle for public employees. Cárdenas maintained that since public employees formed part of the state organization, their duty was to identify with its interests. He threw the weight of his office against Lombardo, and in 1938 the CTM's bureaucrat unions transferred to a new labor central, the Federation of unions of Workers at the Service of the State (FSTSE). (...) The organization of teachers also took place outside the CTM (...). Thus Cárdenas continued the policy of divide and rule. (2002: 79)

A crucial component of corporatism is clientelism. As indicated by Cornelius (2003: 492), the political system in Mexico is permeated by clientelism, in which the 'patrones' (those who have a higher political status) provide benefits to their 'clients' (individuals with a lower political status). Such benefits provided by the patrons include protection, support in political struggles with rivals, and opportunities for political ascendancy or economic prosperity. In exchange, the clients provide loyalty and useful services such as voters' mobilization, political control, and solutions to the problems of their patrons within the official party or governmental bureaucracy (Ibid.). In this way, one of the main features of the corporatist system was the patron–clientelism (Teichman, 1997).[6] This characteristic defined the cooperation of union leaders with the state and consolidated the corporatist system (Córdova, 1976).

As an example of the aforementioned, we can situate the interactions between the official labor movement (specifically the CTM) and the PRI, in which the exchange of workers' votes for spaces of political representation for the union leaders and social benefits for workers have effect. In this manner, the state promoted the creation of social institutions focused on workers (Imss, Issste, Infonavit, Fonacot, and others) that operated with the contribution of workers, employers, and government. Furthermore, the labor sector had access to the official bureaucracy in the government and tripartite labor organisms (such as the JFCA and JLCA). In addition, the CTM and other official confederations controlled political seats in the legislative branch, but they also governed several local governments. However, the pernicious aspects of this relationship comprised the subordination of the labor movement to official policies, the reduction of strikes and the cancellation of democracy within labor organizations. Such characteristics, operating to the detriment of workers' liberties, at the same time strengthened top union leaderships and made more feasible the control of the union movement by the government.

Labor-state relations are not precisely uniform, but they have been through different dynamics, even during the PRI hegemony labor mobilizations and protests took place. Furthermore, the corporatist model of unionism headed by the CTM did not encompass the totality of labor organizations. Initially, in the second half of the 1930s, the government championed the labor movement and since 1940, the CTM headed by Fidel Velázquez (except for the 1947–1950 period), subordinated to the government's interests. Velázquez "endorsed all state policies without hesitation, from the pro-labor policies of President Cárdenas to the pro-business policies of President Salinas, despite huge sacrifices for labor" (Levy & Bruhn, 2006: 75). Several national unions evaded the corporatist system controlled by the CTM. During the 1940s and 1950s, important labor unions, from sectors such as railroad, mining and oil, among others, abandoned the CTM and organized labor movements for the vindication of their labor demands; these protests were repressed in violent ways by the state.[7] These demonstrations partly pressured the government of Adolfo López Mateos[8] (1958–1964) to make a number of concessions to these labor unions to appease them. However, the support only reached some labor unions, in the sectors mentioned above, which obtained benefits in their labor collective agreements higher than average wages and benefits.[9]

In the early 1950s, the organized labor movement in Mexico became more fragmented. Although the CTM was the largest labor organization, other official organizations were competing with it for union members. In these circumstances, while preventing these conditions affected its control of labor, the government sought the unity among these organizations. In 1952, President Miguel Aleman (1946–1952) encouraged the creation of the Revolutionary Confederation of Workers and Peasants (CROC), which brought together diverse labor organizations, mainly the CNT, COCM, CPN, and the CUT. In this way, the CROM became the second largest organization in the country by the mid-1950s (See Table 4.1) .

In 1966, President Díaz Ordaz fostered the creation of the Congress of Labor (CT), an umbrella organization that facilitated the control of the organized labor movement by the government but also gathered together

Table 4.1 Selected official labor organizations in Mexico

Acronyms	*Title*		*Foundation*
CROM	Confederación Regional Obrera Mexicana	Regional Labor Confederation of Mexico	1918
CGT	Confederación General de Trabajadores	General Confederation of Workers	1921
CGOCM	Confederación General de Obreros y Campesinos de México	General Confederation of Workers and Peasants of Mexico	1933
CNT	Cámara Nacional del Trabajo	National Chamber of Labor	1934
FSTSE	Federación de Sindicatos de Trabajadores al Servicio del Estado	National Federation of State Workers	1938
CTM	Confederación de Trabajadores en México	Confederation of Mexican Workers	1936
COCM	Confederación de Obreros y Campesinos de México	Confederation of Workers and Peasants	1942
CPN	Confederación Proletaria Nacional	Proletarian and National Confederation	1942
CUT	Confederación Única de Trabajadores	Unique Confederation of Workers	1947
UGOCM	Unión General de Obreros y Campesinos de México	General Union of Workers and Peasants	1949
CROC	Confederación Revolucionaria de Obreros y Campesinos	Revolutionary Confederation of Workers and Peasants	1952

Source Elaborated by the author

the main PRI-affiliated labor organizations (that is, the CTM, CROM and CROC), consolidating the PRI hegemony over the labor movement.

> (T)he CT serves chiefly to facilitate state relations with the labor sector by giving coherence to a disparate union movement, by furnishing a formalized channel of communication with the regime, and by providing an additional mechanism for state control of workers organizations. Through orchestration of its activities with the PRI, the Congress of Labor helps to bring more than three-quarters of organized labor into the party's fold. (Grayson, 1989: 44)

Although the CT played the role of a coordinating body composed of national labor organizations, it was not a confederation of unions; in fact, it is not officially registered by the government. However, what has given it support was neither legal recognition nor the support of the rank and file of the unions derived from its labor struggles, as well as the definition of initiatives and actions, but its political and ideological identity; its PRI membership and the fact that the CT was a supporter of the political regime. Since its foundation, the CT has become the voice of corporatist unionism, with respect to the most relevant political issues, and the vehicle to face independent unionism (Escobar, 2006: 80).

Considering the details mentioned above, the corporatist framework was consolidated with the creation of the CT, as it implied the creation of a national organization that represented the majority of the labor organizations, one of the features of corporatism identified by Schmitter.

Even though the CT was the umbrella organization gathering national unions, centrals, and confederations, in practice, the CTM had determinant influence on the CT. The CTM controlled the Congress of Labor. Camacho (1980: 104) explains that the most relevant feature of the real structure of the CT would be the considerable and continuous influence of the CTM and its secretary-general Fidel Velázquez. The power of the CTM and Velázquez over the CT stem from various factors, among them: the role played by the CTM both in the political regime and the PRI, the personal ascendancy of Velázquez on the majority of the CT members, its affiliated nationwide industrial unions, the moments when it exercised the formal leadership and the autonomy offered to CT members (Camacho, 1980: 104–105).

The centerpiece of official unionism was the CT which was strongly dominated by the CTM and at the same time the leadership of the CTM relied to a great extent on its secretary-general, Fidel Velázquez. Therefore, it could be suggested that the decline of the CTM influence in terms of its relationship with the state and other CT-affiliated labor organizations, diminished drastically as a result of the death of Fidel Velázquez in 1997.

Even though economic performance during the 1950s and 1960s showed satisfactory signals, serious problems such as exclusion, poverty and inequality were still present among large shares of the population. Furthermore, discontent over the lack of democracy and the authoritarian PRI regime led to students' protests in the late 1960s and early 1970s that demanded a more democratic and egalitarian regime. However, the CTM, as the major labor organization in those years, decided to support the PRI regime and counter the attempts to democratize the country. Hathaway put it in this way (2000: 41):

> (…) before he carried out this repression, the interior minister, Luis Echeverria, secured the support of CTM leader Fidel Velázquez. Unions joined in denouncing the students and in supporting the official denial that a massacre even occurred. As a payoff fort this essential political support, in 1972 President Echeverria created the National Worker Housing Institute (INFONAVIT). Not only did workers benefit from the subsidized housing, but CTM got to allocate most of the housing units to reward workers who were behaving "properly". Again, we see that the power of the PRI and CTM was predicated on repressing challengers while rewarding and controlling collaborators.

Within this context emerged a labor movement more independent regarding official organizations and the PRI-government that opposed corporatist control and fought for more freedom and democracy. As mentioned above, independent unionism had mobilized since the 1940s, fighting against the corporatist model of unionism and the party-state regime. The government's response was to organize both the official and independent unions into the Congress of Labor (CT), the umbrella organization. However, during the 1970s, workers' protests and mobilizations were led by democratic and independent unions and dissident streams inside the official unions such as the dissident stream of electricity workers (SUTERM), the Mexican Union of Electricity Workers (SME), the Mexican Telephone Workers Union (STRM), University Workers (STUNAM), and other independent organizations such as the Authentic Labor Front (FAT) (Barba, 2004). Furthermore, independent unions assumed more radical positions. However, the government repressed these mobilizations using the army, as it had occurred by the end of the 1950s with the rail workers union.

In 1972, some of these unions created the *Unidad Obrera Independiente* (UOI), which included some of the highest-earning Mexican laborers such as those in the automobile and the air transport industries. Other workers preferred working "inside the system" and created democratic blocs inside the official union, for instance, the group *Tendencia Democrática* within the SUTERM. An explosion of industrial action accompanied labor activism. Eventually government tamed labor activism through cooption and, when this failed, through force. For example, Echeverria used the army to break a general strike in July 1976 brought on by the *Tendencia Democrática* (González, 2008: 57–58).

The independent labor movement of the 1970s was regarded as an attempt by a fraction of the unionized working class to democratize unions (De la Garza & Melgoza, 1991: 155).[10] The independent labor movements' fight against the official labor structure was not necessarily intended to break up organic relationships; rather, it sought to transform unions' internal dynamics by increasing worker representation and influence in the decision-making process. In this way, the labor insurgency was mainly a democratizing movement (Ibid.: 155). Confronted with this antagonism in the labor sphere and with other social movements, the Echeverria administration (1970–1976) responded through the expansion of the state. For instance, he increased the number of parastate enterprises. Similarly, Infonavit (National Workers Housing Institute), the national institute in Mexico to provide housing for workers that functioned through a tripartite scheme was created during this administration.

As mentioned before, the ISI model exhausted during the 1970s and impacted in the political context. Since that decade, political power was concentrated in the agencies in charge of planning and implementing the expenditures of the government. The 1970s represented a transition in the political elite which implied the redistribution of power in the top ruling elite, from the official party to official bodies in the federal government, especially the Presidency and the Department of Budget and Planning (*Secretaria de Programacion y Presupuesto, SPP*). In this decade, the ISI model faced various challenges, and the economy became the main concern of the government. Consequently, the positions related to the planning and implementation of economic policies concentrated political

Table 4.2 Political features and Labor unions in Mexico 1934–82 /1982–2006

1934–1982	*1982–2006*
• Solid corporatist framework	• Weakened corporatist framework
• Authoritarian regime	• Transition to a democratic regime
• Hegemonic party system	• Multi-party political system
• Predominance of the official unionism (CTM, CT) in the labor sphere as interlocutors with the state	• Decline of CTM and CT as privileged organizations. Emergence of independent labor union organizations
• Strong alliance between the state and unions. Rise of the corporatist pact between employers, state and workers	• Weak alliance between state and labor unions. Decline of the corporatist pact

Source Prepared by the author

power with the technocratic *camarilla*. This political group or *camarilla*[11] within the PRI would take the political power during the 1980s and 1990s with the ascent to the presidency of Miguel de la Madrid (1982–1988) and Carlos Salinas (1988–1994).

Such episodes involved changes in the political economy and the undermining of the traditional sectors of the official party, such as the official labor organizations. Since 1982, the labor union-state relations would be modified as a result of the democratic transition in the political system, from authoritarianism to a period of political liberalization and democratization, which implied the end of the hegemonic party system and the advent of a multi-party system. This political transition eroded the corporatist structure, although it remains as a weakened corporatist framework. In the labor sphere, the weakening of the corporatist framework was evident in the loss of hegemony of the CTM over the labor movement and the emergence of independent nationwide labor organizations, such as the UNT, and the deterioration of the corporatist alliance between the state and the official labor unions (Table 4.2).

The Erosion of the Corporatist Framework

Following 1982, a new era started in Mexico redefining the political sphere. This period occurred from 1982–2000, which saw three separate administrations: De la Madrid (1982–1988), Salinas (1988–1994), and Zedillo (1994–2000). It started with the debt crisis and made the government to implement changes in the economic model of development. With implications on the hegemony of the official party and its sectors on the corporatist framework that had developed since the 1930s during the Cárdenas administration. The democratization process was more evident since the 1980s and in the 1990s it undermined the political power of the PRI. In this context of political democratization, the CTM and the CT could not preserve their power in this transition, although they survived and represent part of the new democratic landscape in the twenty-first century.

The Period of Miguel de La Madrid

The inauguration of the presidency of Miguel de la Madrid (1982–1988) marked a watershed in the political orientation of the regime and the economic model advanced by the state. As summarized by La Botz (1995: 101): "between 1982 and 1994, Miguel de la Madrid, Salinas and their followers, transformed the state-party and its relations with Mexican society". According to La Botz, under their leadership the PRI abandoned its revolutionary nationalist ideology, revamped its old corporatist structure, and gave up its protectionist economic development model for the panacea of free trade (Ibid). In this respect, the origins of de la Madrid were of special relevance. As remarked by Harvey (2005: 99): "De la Madrid was reform-minded, less embedded in the traditional politics of the PRI and had close relations with capitalist class and foreign interests".

In this way, the most important transition occurred after 1982, when the technocratic elite in the government decided, for critical circumstances in the economy, to modify the economic development model, which implied the reduction of the ISI model and the progressive adoption of neoliberal policies. The most prominent transition, considering its effects on the corporatist structure of government, is not related to the democratization of the late 1990s and 2000, when the PRI was defeated in different elections, but it is related to the ascent to power of a technocratic elite, in a period marked by the deterioration of the ISI model, which represents a watershed. This event would transform the basis of the corporatist framework, but most remarkable is the adjustment of this corporatist structure even during and after the neoliberalization process of the Mexican economy.

Although Mexico's political system was dominated by a hegemonic party during most of the past century, it was ruled by diverse political currents within the party–the presidents adopted different kind of policies;

for instance, leftist, right and center oriented administrations occupied the federal government (Skidmore & Smith, 2005: 252). The solid political structure, which enabled the PRI to remain in power for decades, was designed in the presidency of Cárdenas (1934–1940), which was considered a left-wing oriented administration. The subsequent administrations fluctuated between the center and the left in the political spectrum. However, since 1982, with the election of Miguel de la Madrid (1982–1988), the political orientation of the government changed its direction and became more right-wing oriented in the political spectrum regarding the policies adopted. Such policies were reinforced during the Salinas (1988–1994) and Zedillo (1994–2000) administrations. Vicente Fox (2000–2006) and Felipe Calderón (2006–2012) of the PAN, continued this same trend regarding economic policies.

Therefore, a crucial transformation in the ruling elite started during the de la Madrid government. Diverse studies highlight a process of decline of traditional politicians and the rise of a new group of technocrats within the Mexican political elite, initiated with the election of de la Madrid (1982–88) but in essence, this *camarilla* retained the political power among the different PRI factions in the following decades. According to Demmers (2001: 163), the rise of the technocratic elite is closely linked to the growing power of the Presidential Office, the SPP (Ministry of Planning and Budget), and the PRI's institute IEPES (Institute of Political, Economic and Social Studies). From the 1970s to the 1980s, an institutional change took place in Mexico in favor of these agencies and away from the Ministry of the Interior (*Secretaria de Gobernación*) and the PRI (Ibid.).

Regarding the technocratic elite in Mexico, Centeno (1994: 40) argues, "Unlike technical experts in other authoritarian regimes, this new elite established not just behind the scenes influence, or control within limited policy areas, but commanded the helm of the state as a whole". The rise of the new elite would have been impossible without the maintenance of networks of patron-client relationships popularly known as *Camarillas*. These networks cement the political system, and they assured the integration of the new elite, facilitated its rise to power, provided the channels through which they centralized control of resources, and contributed to the development of the political mentality that characterized the process of *salinastroika* (1994: 40).

The changes in the form of doing politics, in the design and implementation of economic policies adopted by the state and the reconfiguration of its alliances with social groups; all of these were brought about by the rise of new technocratic elites in Mexican politics. As stated by Demmers (2001: 162), "technocrats clearly dominated the de la Madrid administration, and again in the Salinas cabinet comprised the largest group". Indeed, President Zedillo was regarded as the last technocratic president (1994–2000), although he distanced himself from his former *camarilla*. Fox's presidential victory in 2000 "ensured the rapid decline of technocratic control over national political institutions" (Camp, 2007: 130).

La Botz (1995: 103) explains that, as opposed to many PRI leaders, the group of technocrats did not emerge from the mass political organizations, such as unions or other organizations of the party, but rather came into the party at the top, working in the IEPES think-tank or in the shadow cabinet of the elected president. The technocratic elite, according to La Botz, was also a political vanguard that aimed to take control of the Party and the state in order to transform their own society and their relations with the world order. But most importantly, "technocrats believed in neoliberalist capitalist economic values, such as privatization of the economy and integration into the world market", and "they were committed, above all, to bureaucratic and economic efficiency as the highest goals" (Ibid.).

In this way, a transformation within the ruling elite in Mexico can be seen since the 1980s. From the 1930s to the 1970s, the nucleus of political power was the PRI, but then it transferred to the Presidential Office controlled by technocrats. As the technocrats represented a *camarilla* without a strong commitment to the official party and its sectors, they were not very responsive to organized sectors, such as organized labor. Considering these circumstances, the change of the political economy in the 1980s, which were not very favorable for organized labor, can be comprehended.

During the de la Madrid *sexenio* (six-year term), the government implemented diverse strategies to suppress the labor movement and the force of the state was used against the working class. In a major increase in levels of repression, police or military? were used against strikers at DINA (1983), URAMEX (1983), TELMEX (1984), SICARTSA (1985), Renault (1986), Luz y Fuerza (1987), Ford (1987), and AeroMexico (1988). The government also employed strategic insolvency to break labor contracts or they allowed it to be used by private companies. With this method, the company would declare itself bankrupt and close, leading to the firing of the workforce. A few weeks later it would reopen and demand a new and harsher labor contract; the strategy was used at Aeromexico (1980 and 1988), Mexicana (1982 and 1987), TELMEX (1984 and 1987), CLFC (1987), and Ford at Cuautitlan (Minns, 2006: 112).

Organized labor was not able to overcome the impact of the political and economic transformations. Since the 1980s, the labor movement in Mexico has had limited power in the political and labor landscape as its main partner and ally, the PRI-government, changed the essential elements of the corporatist alliance with it. At the same time, the official labor movement has lacked a proper strategy to overcome the limitations of the economic and political transition in recent decades and its role has been just to survive and conserve their former privileges among these conditions.

The Period of Carlos Salinas

The Salinas administration (1988–1994) deepened neoliberal policies introduced by de la Madrid but went further than his predecessor encouraging significant political and economic transformations, impacting on the corporatist structure. "The rise to power of Carlos Salinas represented a kind of counter-revolution within the Mexican government and the Institutional Revolutionary Party" (La Botz, 1995: 101).

As mentioned in previous chapters, the major transformations in the neoliberal reforms in terms of the outcomes for labor organizations occurred mostly during the government of Salinas (1988–1994). The development of the labor movement in Mexico during the last decade of the twentieth century may be attributed to the reallocation of labor organizations during the Salinas administration. Over this period, two trends occurred: on the one hand, the erosion of the main official labor organizations, since their privileged position before the state as major actors in the labor policy process became less relevant; on the other hand, the emergence of a new kind of independent unions, which grew out of the official corporatist organizations. This independent unionism was more democratic. The developments taking place over this period paved the way for the organization of new forms of unionism beyond the official corporatist spaces, represented by the CT and CTM. The Salinas's *sexenio* becomes essential in order to understand the reallocation of labor unionism in Mexico during the 1990s. This period is also crucial to understand the decline of labor unions in terms of union density and the erosion of the workers' real wages.

As noted earlier, Salinas implemented a modernizing program in various spheres, including the reorganization of the labor organizations. As part of this program, the Salinas administration not only weakened the traditional labor corporatist structure by the division between the Congress of Labor (CT) main centrals (CROC, CROM and CTM), but also encouraged the creation of independent union organizations; for instance, the Federation of Goods and Services Unions (FESEBES), which included CT unions, as the STRM, SNTSS and SME. In this context, Salinas supported new union leaderships, such as that of Francisco Hernández Juárez (STRM leader), and protected unions as the SME, whose employer, CLyFC, a state-owned corporation, was excluded from the privatization process (Burgess, 2004; Murillo, 2001).

Notwithstanding, attempts to reform the labor code (LFT) during the Salinas administration were unsuccessful, mainly because of the CTM opposition. Meyer (Interview, 2007) considers that such a situation demonstrated the influence of the official unions, as they could prevent the modification of the labor code because that possibility could transform the privileges of these labor organizations. On the other hand, the privatization program did not reach strategic sectors, including electricity and petroleum. The Salinas administration was not able to privatize PEMEX and CFE, the main energy state corporations. These companies remained under state control despite the increasing privatization process in specific internal areas, in a gradual way. Similarly, labor unions in these companies, affiliated with the CTM, played a crucial role to prevent the privatization.

Nevertheless, it is evident that the main labor organizations in Mexico lost influence during the Salinas government. As stated by Cook (1995: 284) "in general, those organizations that had for decades formed the central pillars of the PRI and the regime–the CTM, CNOP, CNC–lost status and preferential access to government in the early years of the administration of Salinas in favor of more independent organizations that had risen in the 1970s and 1980s".

During the 1980s, but more clearly during the Salinas administration, the restructuring of labor organizations was generated by significant developments. The relation between labor unions and the state was substantially modified. The official unionism ruled by the CT lost ground as the main interlocutor with the state. In this way, Salinas attacked the oil workers' union-STPRM (the most important CTM-affiliated union in terms of financial resources) and imprisoned its leader Joaquin Hernández Galicia, known as *La Quina*. The *New York Times* explained the episode:

> Mr. Hernández strongly opposed the selection of Mr. Salinas as presidential nominee of the PRI, and when Mr. Salinas became the candidate anyway, Mr. Hernández was said to have secretly urged oil workers to vote for an opposition candidate, Cuauhtémoc Cárdenas. When Mr. Salinas won a narrow and disputed victory in the popular vote but then faced problems in the Electoral College, Mr. Hernández reportedly threatened to withhold the votes of a block of congressional members he controls unless Mr. Salinas granted him political concessions. (Rother, 1989)

Salinas also removed the top leadership of the teachers' union, the SNTE. Instead, he promoted a leadership more in tune with his administration, deposing the SNTE leader Carlos Jongitud and imposing Elba Esther Gordillo as the new chief of the most relevant labor union in the country. The SNTE, grouping all teachers in primary and secondary education, is the most important union in terms of union membership not only in Mexico but also in Latin America and perhaps the most powerful in the Americas. With these actions, Salinas not only managed to control the most important labor unions in both the private and public sectors, but also set limits on the actions that eventually would be undertaken by the rest of the official labor organizations.

Considered as one of the most relevant reforms for labor organizations, the reform of the worker housing agency INFONAVIT, engineered by the Salinas administration, limited the role of the unions to monitoring the overall dynamic of the system, but without having the power to intervene specifically in its regulation, administration or direction. In this way, under the regulations approved for Infonavit in September 1992, the unions lost their control over housing construction contracts, as well as their capacity to assign housing credits to union members (Burgess, 2003: 86).

A labor union density decline occurred in the period 1989–1996, a period mostly governed by President Salinas. In such a period there was an internal restructuring of the PRI. Cornelius (2003: 497) contends that after the poor performance of the sectors and organizations of the official party to generate votes in the presidential elections of 1988, the dysfunctional nature of the corporatist system of interests' representation became an urgent issue of concern. Then, it was necessary to modify the essential terms of the relation between the PRI and its mass organizations, among them labor unions. The votes for the PRI were not in the sectorial organizations, but in the homes of workers. The Salinas administration decided to replace the traditional corporatist structure within the PRI, and created organizations and committees territorially based, led by new teams that could be separate of the party leaders who controlled the sectorial organizations. This meant that a more direct relationship between the PRI and the citizens was forged (Cornelius, 2003: 498).

In this way, Salinas's government adopted two strategies that affected labor organizations and distorted the corporatist alliance between the state and labor unions. First, it modified the structure of sectors within the PRI, changing the nature of the urban sector, from CNOP to FNOC (*Frente Nacional de Organizaciones y Ciudadanos*) and configured this sector along territorial lines and appointed new leaders. Despite the fact that these changes were reversed in a PRI assembly (Burgess, 2003) in such a way that the PRI sectors (labor, peasants and urban sectors) remained valid and the territorial movement became another section of support for the party, it was evident that the labor sector lost ground and was relegated by the government in the late 1980s and early 1990s, especially during the Salinas administration.

The Salinas government also created a parallel structure of interests' representation through the *Programa Nacional de Solidaridad* or *Pronasol*, which was territorially based and was not dependent on the PRI traditional sectors. More than 150,000 solidarity committees were established in less than five years in low income urban areas and in rural communities throughout the country. This was partly to rebuild the electoral support for the PRI by demonstrating that the system could respond more quickly and accurately to the demands of citizens for more infrastructure and services. The success of the *Pronasol* could be seen in the Congress elections of 1991 when the PRI won the vast majority in the Chamber of Deputies (Cornelius, 2003: 498). According to Morton (2003: 643), there were three objectives of *Pronasol*. First, it attempted to adapt the state's traditional role to new economic constraints and to redefine the limits of its intervention in the context of a neoliberal strategy of accumulation. Second, it attempted to diffuse potential social discontent through selected subsidies, to accommodate social mobilization through 'co-participation', and to undermine the strength of left-wing opposition movements. Third, it attempted to restructure local and regional PRI elites under centralized control. Clearly, *Pronasol* was therefore a targeted attempt to buttress both the accumulation strategy of neoliberalism and the hegemony of the PRI that was under threat from these very changes (Ibid.).

In this way, with the implementation of programs to distribute benefits and financial assistance to alleviate poverty and solve local problems, such as *Pronasol*, the relevance of the traditional corporatist and clientelist structure controlled by the official unions was reduced, undermining the position of the CTM and other labor confederations of the Congress of Labor. During the Salinas *sexenio*, the presidential office became the channel to deliver most of the social benefits, and the labor confederations saw their influence on the rank and file significantly reduced. Even though union affiliation is not always voluntary, it certainly lost significance as the workers did not perceive any benefits from being unionized or for supporting their union leaders. In this context, since the early 1990s the former powerful official unions have lost influence on their rank-and-file as their influence on wages determination, political positions and access to public resources have also declined.

As mentioned before, Salinas continued with the *Pactos* initiated in the last year of the de la Madrid administration and maintained this strategy throughout his administration. The government of Salinas became the only administration that implemented tripartite pacts (among employers, unions, and government) throughout the complete tenure. The de la Madrid government relied on this formula to reduce inflation in the last year of his tenure, whereas Zedillo's was unable to maintain this policy strategy as the peso crisis harmed labor unions and they refused to endorse these agreements.

The Term of Ernesto Zedillo

In 1994, "President Zedillo became the first Mexican chief executive to take office with a credible democratic mandate, derived from more or less honest competitive elections" considered Whitehead (2002: 208). However, the political legitimacy was not accompanied by positive signals in the economic sphere. Three weeks after taking office the national currency collapsed and capital fled. As mentioned in Chapter 6, the negative effects of the peso crisis on the economy, employment levels and real wages, limited the capacity of action of the Zedillo administration. In the initial months of his *sexenio*, the president negotiated and reached an emergency loan with the government of the United States to face the economic commitments with international financial institutions. His administration faced political turmoil and many political forces pushed for a reform of the electoral system. As a result, an institutional framework was created that guaranteed free and democratic elections sanctioned by an independent body known as the Federal Electoral Institute (IFE). Zedillo attempted to link the newly liberalized economy to a broader democratic political agenda more inclusive of various interest groups (Steger & Roy, 2010: 108).

As was the case in the economic crises of the 1950s, 1970s and 1980s, when governments faced difficult circumstances to control labor mobilizations and unrest, the Zedillo administration relied on the official labor organizations. Once more, the official labor movement, especially the CTM, gained new momentum as a crucial partner of the government in order to counter the workers' protests, which derived from their discontent about the effects of the economic crisis on wages, incomes, and living standards. The support of the official unions for the Zedillo administration in the difficult beginning of his government was evident in the cancellation of the labor parade of First of May in 1995. Similarly, despite the severe repercussions, the relatively low number of strikes in the early years of this *sexenio* is remarkable, both in the local and federal jurisdictions and in the strikes petitions to the labor bodies, registered by labor organizations in those years.

As a result of the collaboration of the CTM with the government, the position of the official organized labor was strengthened within the PRI but also in its access to political positions. For instance, the number of governorships in the country where CTM leaders were elected has been notable since the 1970s and increased slightly in the 1990s. Between 1955 and 2005, eleven CTM leaders became governors in various states of Mexico such as Sinaloa (3), Campeche (2), Querétaro (2), Nayarit (2), Durango and Zacatecas with one governor in both cases (Pastrana, 2004).[12]

However, the leadership of the CTM and of the official unionism was truncated with the death of Fidel Velázquez in 1997. Velázquez concentrated significant authority and influence not only in the official labor movement but also in the PRI regime. For instance, the CTM performed the role to announce the PRI candidate for the presidential elections. One of the most distinguishing practices of the PRI regime was the selection and appointment, by the Mexican president, of the next PRI's presidential candidate. This practice was known as *dedazo*.

However, the announcement of the decision was supposed to be taken within the party. In this way, as one of the party's sectorial organizations, the CTM, through Velázquez, used to pronounce before the mass media the decision of the labor sector to support the candidate for the presidential elections. However, it does not mean that the CTM appointed the PRI candidate and subsequent president of the country, or influenced the election process, but this organization was merely the instrument of the president to communicate such decision. Nevertheless, this kind of practice, that practically became a ritual reflecting the way of doing politics during the PRI regime, awarded to the CTM and its leader, significant influence within the hegemonic party. As mentioned earlier, the CTM leader successfully opposed many governmental proposals, among them the proposal to reform the labor code during the 1990s. One of the regional CTM leaders and former deputy in the Chamber of deputies (1994–1997) from northwest Mexico stated that the crucial problem of the CTM is that after the death of Fidel Velázquez there was not a renovation in the top leadership that could preserve the political power of the CTM. The subsequent leaders of the CTM such as Leonardo Rodríguez Alcaine (1997–2005) and Joaquín Gamboa Pascoe (2005–2016) have not had the leadership of Fidel Velázquez and the CTM influence has reduced (Meléndez, 2007, personal interview).

During the Zedillo government, the privatization process advanced in strategic sectors. One of the most striking cases for the organized labor was the railway sector, which was controlled by a state-owned company *Ferrocarriles Nacionales*. The main union in this sector (*Sindicato de Trabajadores Ferrocarrileros de la República Mexicana*, STFRM) also saw shrinking membership. During the early 1990s, the number of unionized workers of the company was approximately 84,000, but this figure reduced drastically to around 7,000 in 1998 after its privatization.

During this *sexenio*, a dialogue between unions and employers' confederations took place. In this context, the CTM and the Coparmex (*Confederación Patronal de la República Mexicana*), the most important labor organization and one of the most important employer confederations in the country, discussed the reform of the labor code and how to enhance productivity in workplaces. Granados Chapa (1995) considered such an agreement as a landmark in the history of social relations. "The agreement between the CTM and the Coparmex brings in a new kind of interlocution, especially significant because it comprises the main forces in the labor sphere and because it implies a deposition of attitudes firmly sustained for a long time" (Ibid., 1995 PAGE?). Furthermore, such a pact effectively ended the CTM's resistance to labor law reforms that it had assumed during the Salinas administration, and later the CTM endorsed the labor reform proposed by the Fox government. Indeed, the New Labor Culture has to be considered as a way of formalizing a power shift in favor of employers in the workplace through consensus built on a post-Fordist view of the global economy and relations of production (Kohout, 2008: 147). Despite the fact that this dialogue did not result in the reform of the labor code, it was important for the CTM to recover power and influence in the political arena and also to regain its position as a crucial interlocutor with the government and employers.

Nevertheless, in general, the official labor movement lost influence and membership during the period 1982–2000, which included the PRI administrations of de la Madrid, Salinas, and Zedillo, considered as the technocratic wing of the PRI. The change in the political and labor spheres was less significant during the Fox government (2000–2006) and Calderon administration (2006–2012), because of the opposition of the PRI, PRD (Party of the Democratic Revolution), and other parties to implement reforms in various sectors. Therefore, the major transformations in the last decades took place in the period from 1982 to 2000 and perhaps more clearly during the Salinas administration, which concentrated significant political power. Although the Congress of Labor, the most important umbrella organization, was weakened during this period, some of the CTM-affiliated national unions remained with leverage during the 1980s and early 1990s, which was the period of decline of the overall union density in the country. The CTM and other unions, which have survived and adapted to an environment of union density decline, are in diverse sectors, mainly in electricity and oil industries. Also, in the education sector, organized labor became more powerful and influential especially as a result of its alliance with the PAN administrations in the period 2000–2012.

Independent Labor Unions

As mentioned above, during the beginning of the Zedillo administration, several unions of the CT refused to continue with the *Pactos* initiated in the last year of the de la Madrid administration and maintained during the Salinas government. Instead, several of these unions, for instance, the SNTE, SME and others decided to organize the forums 'Unionism before the nation' to discuss the challenges and perspectives of labor unions in the country, especially as a result of the ineffective representation of the official leadership of the CT. Other national unions joined the forums and became the base for an independent nationwide labor organization in that decade.

The fragmentation and division among the labor organizations became more evident during the second half of the 1990s. One of the results of this fragmentation among the top labor confederations was the emergence of new labor organizations more independent from the PRI and the state. During such a period, several independent unions founded the National union of Workers (UNT) and the Mexican union Front (FSM). In this way, the organized labor movement turned out to be fragmented and heterogeneous and its viewpoints on relevant topics such as labor reform also differ. While official unionism promotes minor changes in labor related legislation, independent promotes more profound reforms.

Independent unionism challenged, on the one hand, the dominium of the CTM and, on the other hand, the strong control of the state facilitated by labor-related legislation. Independent labor organizations flourished during the Zedillo administration after the economic crisis generated by the peso devaluation in the mid-1990s. Since the late 1980s, but more clearly after 1995, an important number of labor unions adopted more independent positions with regard to the official CT, but they also created independent organizations. For instance, the FESEBES was founded in 1990 by the STRM and other national unions in the services sector with the support of President Salinas. As a result of the economic crisis of 1994–1995, the First May Inter-union Coordinator (CIPM) was created in 1995. The CIPM represents the most radical labor organization in Mexico. Its origins are found in the unions struggles of the 1950s and 1970s, which were repressed by the government; its name derives from the mobilizations, in May 1st 1995, after the economic crisis of 1994–1995 (Medina, 2001).

These events marked the beginning of a process that culminated in the formation of the National union of Workers (UNT) in 1997 and the Mexican Union Front (FSM) in 1998. In this restructuring process, several unions played a relevant role, such as the STRM, SME, SNTSS, STUNAM, FAT, SITUAM, SUTIN, ASPA, ASSA, ATM, and others. However, the supremacy of the UNT is evident as the most relevant organization within the independent trade unionism.[13] These independent unions were opposed to the monopoly of representation of the

CT and CTM as interlocutors with the state. However, the fragmentation among the labor movement has prevented an effective response to the neoliberal agenda. Several of these organizations, such as the SME, STRM, among others, abandoned the official CT and have maintained distance from the PRI. In contrast, they have strengthened links with the left-wing PRD. Although they are not affiliated with this party, in various social movements and protests, they have formed alliances with aims in common.

The CT foundation in 1966 contributed significantly to enhance state control of the labor sector. Functioning as an umbrella organization, the CT brought together the CTM, CROM, and CROC, unifying these PRI-affiliated organizations into a coherent and coordinated body. However, this control was contested during the period 1989–1997 as a result of the rupture within the CT, leading to the FESEBES foundation. The major transformation, however, occurred in the second half of the 1990s with the emergence of the UNT and the FSM as the major umbrella organizations gathering a significant group of independent unions, peasants, and social organizations. In this way, a diversified labor movement can be observed with multiple umbrella organizations but without a unified relationship with the state. It is revealing how the most relevant stream of independent unions emerging in the late 1990s, the UNT, was initially sponsored by the Salinas administration to divide the CT.

The forums put together both the FESEBES unions, being the CT dissidents, and more ideologically radical unions stemming from the independent unionism of the 1970s, most of them grouped in the CIPM. Also, other peasants and social organizations were included. The UNT was formally constituted in 1997, integrated by unions such as STRM, SNTSS, STUNAM, FAT, ASSA, and others. The SME and SNTE, affiliating workers from the electricity sector and teachers respectively, were two of the most important unions at these forums. They decided not to join the UNT and instead to form their own labor organizations. The SME promoted the creation of the FSM in 1998, along with other unions that participated at the forums, identified as the radical wing of unionism in Mexico. On the other hand, the SNTE decided to remain within the CT, but later it created the FEDESSP, organizing workers from the public sector, with the support of President Fox.

Conclusions

Within the institutional and political realm, the decline of labor unions in Mexico can be explained more clearly by three interrelated factors that transformed the political system and the ruling elite in the last two decades of the twentieth century. First, the political liberalization, noticeable in the late 1980s evolving into the democratization of 2000, eroded the hegemony of the official party, which was one of the main features that maintained a strong labor movement. Second, the fracture of the corporatist framework, including the alliance between the state and organized labor, diminished the influence of labor organizations in the political system. Finally, a set of governmental policies that restrained the role and perspectives of trade unions in both the public and private sectors, was designed by a technocratic elite that gained ascendancy within the PRI government, especially during the administrations of de la Madrid, Salinas and Zedillo. During the 2000s, under the administration of President Fox, labor unions generally have not seen significant modifications regarding their previous conditions including the levels of membership in the employed labor force, but also they have not seized the opportunity of a more democratic environment in the country.

The political system, which emerged from the revolution and was consolidated during the PRI hegemony, determined not only the operation and characteristics of labor unions but also the relation between the state and organized labor within a corporatist structure in Mexico during most of the twentieth century. The special characteristics of the authoritarian political system in Mexico required a corporatist structure. It is suggested here that such a corporatist framework became an important element within the political-institutional realm to induce the development and regression of trade unions, measured both in terms of union membership and political influence.

The interrelations between labor unions, employers and the state were synchronized by such a framework established immediately after the Revolution but cemented during the Cárdenas administration (1934–1940). In this context, from the late 1930s to the early 1980s, labor unions became increasingly relevant actors within the political system given its strong ties with the official party. An important characteristic of this political system was the corporatist framework designed by the state with the purpose of promoting the industrialization process in Mexico during the post-war period, which required an acquiescent and manageable labor movement in terms of its position towards capital and the state. The relationship of organized labor to the state contributed to the relative stability of Mexico during that period. This situation facilitated the creation of various institutions dedicated to the improvement of the working class, providing social benefits such as health care, pensions, and housing, among others. Nevertheless, these features were adjusted with the advent of neoliberalism and political democratization in the last two decades of the twentieth century, which undermined the position labor unions used to enjoy during the post-war period.

The corporatist framework encompassed the alliance between the state and labor confederations; it originated in the 1920s with the CROM but deepened in the 1930s with the CTM. This framework molded the labor relations system during the past century. Despite the opposition to the CTM dominance over the rest of nationwide labor unions and confederations, this corporatist system was strengthened in the late 1940s and throughout the 1950s with the purge of radical left-wing unions within this confederation. Subsequently, various labor union confederations merged in 1966 with the creation of the Congress of Labor (CT), which gathered the majority of the PRI-affiliated labor organizations. However, the advent of neoliberalism since the 1980s and the political transition in the 1990s changed the landscape for labor unions. There has been a clear decline of labor unions in terms of power and influence in the political and labor spheres, especially in the period 1989-1996, as demonstrated by the statistics of union density, but also by the reduced number of political positions occupied by union leaders in the Congress, the deterioration of real wages, and the planning and execution of policy-making without the participation or influence of labor organizations.

The erosion of union power occurred within the authoritarian regime headed by the PRI. Nonetheless, other factors must be considered. For instance, the ascent to political power of the PRI's technocratic wing during the 1980s and 1990s contributed to the relocation of power in the ruling class, from the party and its traditional sectors to the presidency and the bodies controlled by the technocrats (IEPES, SPP and others bodies in the party and government). The technocratic ruling elite changed many aspects of the old corporatist structure, most importantly the political economy based on the ISI model and the relationship of the state to organized groups. Such a reconfiguration of the political elite could explain the changing situation of trade unions along with the process of political liberalization. Indeed, there was a transition, but it occurred within the PRI. This situation could explain not only the profound economic transformation in the 1980s and early 1990s but also the postponement of political democratization to the late 1990s and early 2000s.

During the de la Madrid and Salinas administrations, dominated by technocrats, some policies were crucial for the decline of labor unions, such as the reduction of social spending and subsidies, the privatization of parastate enterprises, the *Pronasol* program, the tripartite social pacts to control inflation which affected real wages and social benefits of workers; and the restructuring of the PRI's organizations, especially the deterioration of the privileged position of the labor sector in the official party. The policies implemented by the Salinas administration, especially *Pronasol*, modified the channels of clientelism and reduced the power of labor unions as one of the main contacts between the party-state and the citizens. On the other hand, the official figures (see Chapters 6 and 7) show that the largest decline of union density rates and the most severe deterioration of real wages occurred during the period 1989–1995 (Fairris, 2005; Fairris, Popli & Zepeda, 2008). Under the governments of De la Madrid and Salinas, trade unions not only saw a regression in their representation in the employed labor force but also workers suffered a drastic erosion of their wages.

During the last two decades of the past century, the change in the PRI's ideology towards the right in the political spectrum, the implementation of macroeconomic policies driven by a technocratic ruling elite, as well as the absence of an institutional framework that guarantees the strict observance of workers' rights, created an adverse environment for the working class and impacted negatively unionization trends.

The deterioration of the corporatist structure since the 1980s explains to a great extent the decline of labor unions, not only in terms of union membership but also in terms of its political representation, which was the source of power and influence of labor unions in Mexico during most of the twentieth century. However, as can be seen in official statistics, organized labor has not increased its representation in the employed labor force since the mid-1990s when the decline of labor union density occurred. The representation of unions in the labor force has remained stagnant and its influence on policymaking has not been significant.

Notes

1. I prefer not to use the term corporatist unions since independent unions have also been identified as corporatist unions. See De la Garza (2003).
2. As will be mentioned in this chapter, most unions in the private sector have 'labor contracts of protection', that is, false contracts negotiated between corporations and union leaders, but without the consent and knowledge of unionized workers. This kind of union is located within both official and independent unions.
3. As the political party emerged from the revolution had three different names during the period 1929–1946, I will use the term "official party" to refer to the PNR, PRM and PRI.
4. For instance, social benefits were distributed through a variety of channels: the CONASUPO, a government body which used to control the prices for basic food items by buying directly from producers and selling at subsidised prices in mainly urban areas; the continuous expansion of social security services as well as the services given directly by some state firms such as PEMEX; the creation during the Echeverria administration (1970–1976) of the INFONAVIT, which oversees the construction of housing for workers; and the FONACOT, a loan system to help workers and employees purchase furniture. See Bizberg (1993: 303).
5. Fidel Velázquez headed the CTM from 1941 to 1947 and from 1950 until his death at age ninety-seven on June 21, 1997.
6. The term "patron-clientelism" is used by Judith Teichman (1997). This term is also known as "clientelism" or "clientelar system", which refers to the interchange of specific services or public resources between individuals (usually unequals) in exchange of political support, for instance, in electoral processes (see Cornelius, 2003).
7. About the union of railroad workers, (see Caulfield, 1998).
8. Adolfo López Mateos was the minister of labor in the administration of Adolfo Ruiz Cortinez (1952–1958). He was selected by Ruiz Cortinez to be the President of the Republic in 1958–1964 because of the labor protests during the 1950s.
9. Ilan Bizberg (1990) and Ilan Bizberg and Anselmo García (2004).
10. For a more detailed description of the rise of independent unionism in the 1970s, see De La Garza Toledo and Melgoza (1991).
11. A camarilla is a group of people who have political interests in common and rely on one another to improve their chances within the political leadership (Camp, 2007: 123).
12. For instance, in the period 1955–1961, Alberto Trueba Urbina in Campeche; in 1975–1980, Alfonso G. Calderón in Sinaloa; 1979–1984, Rafael Camacho Guzmán in Querétaro; in 1981–1987, Emilio González Parra in Nayarit; in 1985–1991, Abelardo Carrillo Zavala in Campeche; in

1986–1992, José Ramírez Gamero in Durango; in 1991–1997, Enrique Burgos García in Querétaro; in 1992–1998, Arturo Romo Gutiérrez in Zacatecas; in 1993–1999, Rigoberto Ochoa Zaragoza in Nayarit; in 1998–2004, Juan Millán Lizárraga in Sinaloa and in 2004–2010, Jesús Aguilar Padilla. Daniel Pastrana, "La CTM: más viva que nunca", *La Jornada*, December 12, 2004.

13. About the UNT creation, (see Xelhuantzi, 2000).

Bibliography

Barba, H. (2004). La contratación colectiva en México. In A. Bouzas (Ed.), *La reforma laboral que necesitamos* (pp. 123–150). Mexico: IIE-UNAM.

Bensusán, G. (2004). A new scenario for Mexican trade unions: Changes in the structure of political and economic opportunities. In K. Middlebrook (Ed.), *Dilemmas of political change in Mexico*. London: Institute of Latin American Studies; San Diego, CA: Center for U.S.-Mexican Studies, University of California.

Bizberg, I. (1990). *Estado y sindicalismo en México*. el Colegio de México.

Bizberg, I. (1993). Modernization and corporatism in government labor relations. In N. Harvey (Ed.), *Mexico: Dilemmas of transition*. London: ILAS and British Academic Press.

Bizberg, I., & García, A. (2004). *'El sindicalismo en Mexico'. Seminario Permanente de Estudios del Trabajo*. Mexico: STyPS.

Burgess, K. (2003). Mexican labor at a crossroads. In J. S. Tulchin & A. Selee (Eds.), *Mexico's politics and society in transition*. Rienner: Boulder.

Burgess, K. (2004). *Parties and unions in the new global economy*. Pittsburgh: University of Pittsburgh Press.

Camacho, M. (1980). *La clase obrera en la historia de México: el futuro inmediato*. México: Instituto de Investigaciones Sociales, UNAM.

Camp, R. A. (2007). *Politics in Mexico: The democratic consolidation*. Oxford: Oxford University Press.

Caulfield, N. (1998). *Mexican workers and the state: From the Porfiriato to NAFTA*. Texas Christian University Press.

Centeno, M. A. (1994). *Democracy within reason: Technocratic revolution in Mexico*. University Park, Pennsylvania: Pennsylvania State University Press.

Collier, R. B. (1992). *The contradictory alliance: State-labor relations and regime change in Mexico*. Berkeley: International and Area Studies, University of California.

Cook, M. L. (1995). Mexican state-labor relations and the political implications of free trade. *Latin American Perspectives, 22*(1), 77–94.

Córdova, A. (1976). *La política de masas del Cardenismo*. Mexico: Ediciones Era.

Cornelius, W. A. (2003). Politics in Mexico. In G. A. Almond et al. (Eds.), *Comparative politics today: A world view* (pp. 469–520). New York; London: Longman.

Cosío Villegas, D. (1972). *El sistema político mexicano*. Mexico: Mortiz.

De la Garza, E. (2003). La crisis de los modelos sindicales en Mexico y sus opciones. In E. De la Garza & C. Salas (Eds.), *La situación del trabajo en Mexico, 2003* (pp. 349–377). Mexico: Plaza y Valdez.

De la Garza, E., & Melgoza, J. (1991). Los sindicatos frente a la productividad: telefonistas y electricistas. *El Cotidiano*, (41).

Demmers, J. (2001). Neoliberal reforms and populist politics: The PRI in Mexico. In J. Demmers et al. (Eds.), *Miraculous metamorphoses: The neoliberalisation of Latin American populism*. London: Zed Books.

Escobar, S. (2006). *Los trabajadores en el siglo XX. Sindicato, Estado y sociedad en México: 1907–2004*. México: STUNAM.

Fairris, D. (2005). *What do unions do in Mexico*. Working Paper, University of California, Riverside.

Fairris, D., Popli, G., & Zepeda, E. (2008). Minimum wages and the wage structure in Mexico. *Review of Social Economy, 66*(2), 181–208.

González, F. E. (2008). *Dual transitions from authoritarian rule: institutionalized regimes in Chile and Mexico, 1970–2000*. Baltimore: Johns Hopkins University Press.

Granados Chapa, M. A. (1995, July 27). *Plaza Pública / Nueva cultura laboral. Reforma*.

Grayson, G. (1989). *The Mexican labor machine: Power, politics and patronage*. Washington, DC: The center for strategic and international studies.

Hamilton, N., & Kim, S. (2004). Democratization, economic liberalisation, and labor politics: Mexico and Korea. *Comparative Sociology, 3*(1), 67–92.

Harvey, D. (2005). *A brief history of neoliberalism*. Oxford: Oxford University Press.

Hathaway, D. (2000). *Allies across the border: Mexico's authentic labor front and global solidarity*. Cambridge: South End Press.

Hodges, D. C., & Gandy, R. (2002). *Mexico, the end of the revolution*. Westport, CO: Praeger.

Hogenboom. (2004). Governing Mexico's market democracy. In J. Demmers et al. (Eds.), *Good governance in the era of global neoliberalism: Conflict and depolitisation in Latin America, Eastern Europe, Asia and Africa*. London: Routledge.

Huntington, S. P. (1991). *The third wave: Democratization in the late twentieth century*. Norman: University of Oklahoma Press.

Kohout, M. (2008). The new labor culture and labor law reform in Mexico. *Latin American Perspectives, 35*(1), 135–150.

La Botz, D. (1995). *Democracy in Mexico: Peasant rebellion and political reform*. Boston: South End Press.
Leal, F. (1986). Las estructuras sindicales. In F. Leal (Ed.), *El obrero mexicano 3. Organización y sindicalismo*. Mexico: IIS-UNAM.
Levy, D., & Bruhn, K. (2006). *Mexico: The struggle for democratic development*. Berkeley: University of California Press.
Magaloni, B. (2006). *Voting for autocracy: Hegemonic party survival and its demise in Mexico* (Vol. 296). Cambridge: Cambridge University Press.
Medina, I. (2001). Sindicalismo Mexicano en transición. *Universidad de Guadalajara* (21).
Meléndez, M. (2007, October). *Former leader of the CTM*. Personal Interview, Mazatlán, Sinaloa.
Meyer, L. (2006, February). *Academic scholar, El Colegio de Mexico*. Mexico City.
Minns, J. (2006). *The politics of developmentalism: The midas states of Mexico, South Korea and Taiwan*. Basingstoke: Palgrave.
Morton, A. D. (2003). Structural change and neoliberalism in Mexico. *Third World Quaterly, 24*(4), 631–653.
Munck, R. (2003). *Contemporary Latin America*. Basingstoke and New York: Palgrave Macmillan.
Murillo, M. V. (2001). Partisan loyalty and union competition: Macroeconomic adjustment and industrial restructuring. In Ch. Candland & R. Sil (Eds.), *The politics of labor in a global age*. New York: Oxford University Press.
Pastrana, D. (2004, December). La CTM: ¿más viva que nunca? *La Jornada, 12*.
Patroni, V. (2001). The decline and fall of corporatism? Labor legislation reform in Mexico and Argentina during the 1990s. *Canadian Journal of Political Science XXXIV, 2*, 249–274.
Rother, L. (1989, January 12). Battleground of Mexicans; president takes aim at the unions' power. *The New York Times*.
Schmitter, P. C. (1974). Still the century of corporatism? *The Review of Politics, 36*, 85–131.
Skidmore, T. E., & Smith, P. H. (2005). *Modern Latin America*. New York and Oxford: Oxford University Press.
Steger, M. B., & Roy, R. K. (2010). *Neoliberalism: A very short introduction*. Oxford: Oxford University Press.
Teichman, J. (1997). Neoliberalism and the transformation of Mexican authoritarianism. *Mexican Studies / Estudios Mexicanos, 13*(1), 121–147.
Vazquez-Anderson, A. (2004). Democracia en Mexico: transición hacia un corporativismo social. *Espiral, X*(29), 11–44.
Whitehead, L. (2002). *Democratization: Theory and experience*. Oxford: Oxford University Press.
Xelhuantzi, M. (2000). *La democracia pendiente: la libertad de asociación sindical y los contratos de protección en México*. Sindicato de Telefonistas de la República Mexicana.

CHAPTER 5

The Restructuring of the Corporatist Pact

Reactions of Organized Labor to Neoliberal Reforms

During the 1980s, the government practically broke the corporatist alliance with the official labor organizations. In 1983, amidst the effects of the economic crisis including the peso devaluation and high inflation rates, the CTM and the CT-affiliated labor organizations threatened to carry out a general strike demanding wages increases according to the inflation levels. The government responded against the CTM petitions and only some regional unions realized the strike. In order to accomplish its objective to reduce salaries and disarticulate the CTM demands. The de la Madrid administration promoted the division of the official unionism gathered in the CT. The government supported other less relevant labor organizations within the official unionism such as the CROM and CROC and undermined the more powerful CTM (Escobar, 2006: 99; Middlebrook, 1989: 202–203). As observed by Levy and Bruhn (2006: 74), "Mexico's rulers never gave any union a monopoly over labor. Instead, they used competition among unions to limit any single union power". The CTM wanted a wage increase of 50% but, after the CTM's threats to strike, the de la Madrid administration only conceded a rise of wages between 10 and 30% (Collier, 1992: 82). The strategies of the official unionism to face the deterioration of wages and living conditions

R. Zepeda, *The Decline of Labor Unions in Mexico during the Neoliberal Period*, Governance, Development, and Social Inclusion in Latin America, https://doi.org/10.1007/978-3-030-65710-9_5

during the 1980s failed and its position of privileged interlocutor with the government also undermined its bargaining position. Paczynska (2009: 9) indicates that the willingness of the government to disregard the claims of labor union organizations after the economic crisis of 1982 was "the first sign that the PRI was prepared to abandon its long alliance with organized labor as the former shifted economic policies". Similarly, the tight control that the state maintained over the PRI controlled unions throughout the crisis determined the limited labor response during the 1980s (Haber, 2006: 66). Labor organizations were notably absent and played an insignificant role in the protest cycle of that decade; despite the 44% plummet in real manufacturing wages between 1982 and 1989, the number of strikes decreased by 83%, petitions to strike decreased by 58%, and the number of striking workers declined by 73% during that same time period (Cook, 1991, cited in Haber, 2006: 66). On the other hand, independent labor unions mobilized during the 1980s, but these actions were repressed by the government. For instance, workers from the mining, iron and steel sectors, but also public bus drivers, airline employees, university and the IMSS employees as well as teachers participated in public demonstrations against the government policies affecting the working class in that decade.

In contrast to other countries, the majority of the organized labor movement in Mexico, especially the official unionism, consented with acquiescence the implementation of a macroeconomic stabilization policy that harmed labor unions and impacted on real wages. Although the reforms were detrimental for workers, the official union leaders only showed a critical discourse, but without significant protests, mobilizations or strikes. Despite the impacts on the workers generated by the structural adjustment policies in the 1980s, the official union leaders only focused on reporting the effects of the economic restructuring on the working class; most official labor unions transited from the verbal confrontation with the state's economic policy to an acceptance without any alternative program. In general, the reactions of the official labor unions before these developments have been passive and union leaders from the official organizations (CTM and CT) have neither modified their strategies nor activities to overcome this situation. However, the independent unionism has relied on the defensive confrontation before the restructuring process of corporations (De la Garza, 1994).

The most relevant confederation of the official unionism, the CTM, adopted a strategy of negotiation with the state rather than mobilizations.

Murillo (2001a: 65) claims that the CTM responses to neoliberal reforms were influenced by its adherence to the government and the PRI. As the CTM feared the loss of resources and a subsequent drain in membership, it subordinated to the state. The CTM subordination contributed to the governance of the De la Madrid, Salinas and Zedillo administrations and to the effective implementation of the economic reforms.

In countries where unions develop institutional ties with parties, such as in Mexico, the governing coalition tends to manage potential threats to the system. Where unions do not have such ties, they tend to challenge the state from outside, using strikes and demonstrations that may threaten the economic elite (Levy and Bruhn, 2006: 73). Utilizing this logic, the official unions relied on the strategy of the relation and negotiation with the government to reach their demands, rather than using mobilization and strikes, as they were tied to the official party and the state. As mentioned before, one of the features of corporatism was that labor unions relied on its access to governmental institutions to channel their demands. This could explain the reduction of strikes in the period of economic reforms during the 1980s and 1990s. However, most of the times, the official confederations were ignored by the government to formulate and implement neoliberal policies impacting on labor unions and workers. For instance, over the 1990s labor-related institutions such as Infonavit and IMSS (Social Security Institute) underwent significant reforms designed by the government, with the acquiescence of the official labor centrals. These reforms became detrimental for workers and unions, as they removed or limited some benefits previously won by the labor movement.

The strategy of the government to appease the labor movement also included the concession of benefits to selected labor organizations which were strategic allies of the government in the period of neoliberal reforms. In the case of several national unions, such as the SNTE, SME and STRM, they negotiated significant advantages and benefits with the government (Murillo, 2001b). The SME avoided the privatization of Company of Light and Power, which threatened its survival. The STRM obtained concessions with the privatization of TELMEX, such as the 5% of the total shares of the company (Middlebrook, 1995; Murillo, 2001b).

Thus, during the neoliberal period, the government utilized diverse methods to reduce labor mobilizations; these included the division among labor confederations, the cooption of union leaders and the repression of labor union mobilizations and protests. Consequently, the total number of strikes per year in the private sector including both the federal and local jurisdictions reduced considerably in the period 1982–2006. According to official statistics, during the 1980s strikes decreased notably. For instance, in 1982 there were 2,646 strikes in the private sector in both jurisdictions, but this number reduced to no more than 650 in 1989; the most important slope was from 1987 to 1988, the last year of de la Madrid government and the first year of the tripartite pact to reduce inflation. The reduction of strikes continued in the Salinas administration and it was relatively stable in the Zedillo and Fox administrations.

The fluctuation of the total number of strikes per *sexenios* demonstrates an evident decline in the period 1976–2006 but also the effectiveness of the political regime to control or repress the protests and demands of the working class. During the López Portillo *sexenio* (1977–1982), the average number of total strikes per year was 1,272; in 1982 alone the strikes reached 2,646, the highest number in the last three decades; the total number in this 6-year period was 7,637. In contrast, in the de la Madrid administration (1983–1988) the average number of strikes in the private sector was 930, reaching the peak in 1983 with 1,208, under this government the total number was 5,579. During the Salinas administration (1989–1994), on the other hand, the average number of strikes per year declined notably to 686, with 1989 the most important in terms of labor mobilization with 875 strikes; the total number of strikes amounted to 4,118 during the Salinas period. The number of strikes continued the free fall in the Zedillo administration (1995–2000) in which the average was 356, whereas 1995 was the most important in terms of strikes with 577; during this government, the total number of strikes amounted for 2,141. Finally, the advent of the democratic regime did not result in more labor mobilizations, as the number of strikes per year averaged 253 in the Fox *sexenio* (2000–2006); in 2005 alone there were 274 strikes in the private sector, both local and federal jurisdictions (see Table 5.1). As can be seen, the number of strikes declined progressively across *sexenios* in the period 1982–2006, especially during the 1980s and early 1990s and remained relatively stable in the late 1990 and early 2000s.

It is pertinent to highlight that according to labor legislation, the strikes have to be approved by the official institutions (JFCA, JLCA and STPS). "Mexican unions must convince the government that their demands are legitimate; otherwise, they cannot legally strike" (Camp, 2007: 154). In the period 1977–2006, the percentage of strike petitions in the federal sector that was approved by the official bodies was 1.5%

Table 5.1 Number of strikes in the federal and local jurisdictions in the private sector in Mexico 1977–2006

	Year	*Federal-jurisdiction strike petitions*	*Federal-jurisdiction strikes*	*Local-jurisdiction strikes*	*Total number of strikes*	*Percentage of strikes approved in the federal jurisdiction (%)*
López Portillo	1977	5,033	128	476	604	2.5
	1978	5,572	87	758	845	1.6
	1979	6,021	141	795	936	2.3
	1980	5,757	93	1,339	1,432	1.6
	1981	6,589	108	1,066	1,174	1.6
	1982	16,095	675	1,971	2,646	4.2
De la Madrid	1983	13,536	230	978	1,208	1.7
	1984	9,052	221	548	769	2.4
	1985	8,754	125	489	614	1.4
	1986	11,579	312	903	1,215	2.7
	1987	16,141	174	949	1,123	1.1
	1988	7,730	132	518	650	1.7
Salinas	1989	6,806	118	757	875	1.7
	1990	6,395	149	670	819	2.3
	1991	7,006	136	438	574	1.9
	1992	6,814	156	477	633	2.3
	1993	7,531	155	474	629	2.1
	1994	7,490	116	472	588	1.5

(continued)

Table 5.1 (continued)

	Year	*Federal-jurisdiction strike petitions*	*Federal-jurisdiction strikes*	*Local-jurisdiction strikes*	*Total number of strikes*	*Percentage of strikes approved in the federal jurisdiction (%)*
Zedillo	1995	7,676	96	481	577	1.3
	1996	7,621	51	410	461	0.7
	1997	8,047	39	356	395	0.5
	1998	7,352	33	245	278	0.4
	1999	7,972	32	225	257	0.4
	2000	8,282	26	147	173	0.3
Fox	2001	6,821	35	219	254	0.5
	2002	6,042	45	213	258	0.7
	2003	5,909	44	202	246	0.7
	2004	6,122	38	205	243	0.6
	2005	6,646	50	224	274	0.8
	2006	7,390	55	186	241	0.7

Sources Prepared with data obtained from Middlebrook, 1995: 164–165 (period 1977–1993). STPS, 2009 and ILO, 2009 (period 1994–2006)

(3,800 out of 239,781) and the *sexenio* with more strikes approved in the period in this sector was the one of López Portillo with 2.3% and the lowest rate of strikes recognition was in the Zedillo administration with 0.6%.[1] In this sense, if the official bodies do not recognize the workers' requests to strike, then, it is not permitted to the workers to continue with the movement and they have to return to their workplaces. This situation hides the real number of strikes in the country, since not all the protests are recognized in the official statistics.

It is a paradoxical situation that an authoritarian regime emerged from a revolution advanced by wide social sectors (mainly peasants and workers) had preserved political power for such a long time with the support of these sectors, while, at the same time, their possibilities of expression and mobilization were restrained by this political regime (Middlebrook, 1995). During the 1980s the number of strikes in Mexico declined, as can be seen in Table 5.1. It is also noticeable that this slowdown of the labor struggles coincided with the implementation of economic restructuring policies during the de la Madrid administration which included the reduction of subsidies to food, transport and others social areas. These policies were aimed to harmonize macroeconomic indicators, such as the reduction of external debt and reduce the deficit in the public finances contributed to the deterioration of real wages and reduced the living conditions of the working class. Therefore, it is notable to observe that despite these impacts on workers, the number of strikes was not very high in this decade.

The Modification of the Corporatist Pact in a Democratic Environment

During the neoliberal period, the corporatist relationship between organized labor and the state was modified. The PRI governments relied on a corporatist structure with the support of social partners, among them labor unions, peasants and urban employees. During the 1980s and 1990s, neoliberal governments modified several aspects of this relationship, but they did not destroy this framework. During that period, the privileges to which the CTM had become accustomed were not so readily accommodated in an environment of greater economic and political competition. For instance, in the political arena, the party candidacies given to CTM leaders often clashed with the requirement that candidates be electable. In a more competitive political system, the CTM lost much of its capacity to deliver large number of votes on the elections and parties relied on other strategies to mobilize voters without the help of intermediary organizations such as unions (Burgess, 2004: 74).

Labor unions became stronger within an authoritarian political regime. Corporatism in Mexico was characterized by a lack of democracy within labor union organizations because their political role came first and their function of representing workers' interests was subordinated (O'Toole, 2007: 212). In this sense, the advent of a democratic regime in Mexico signified the erosion of the authoritarian corporatist structure where labor unions became strong political actors with influence in the labor and political spheres.

The collapse of the PRI as the hegemonic party in 2000 was partly the consequence of the weakening and deterioration of one of its pillars of support: the official labor unions which comprised the labor sector. With the goal of explaining the factors accounting for the debacle of the PRI in the 2000 presidential elections, Greene (2007: 104) identifies the role of labor unions within the PRI as a crucial factor. He mentions that since workers in newly created jobs were often not incorporated into formal sector unions associated with the PRI they were also outside the party's patronage network. Diminished resources also contributed to splits in the unions traditionally associated with the PRI. In the 1980s and 1990s, the CTM lost unions to alternative independent confederations such as the UNT that claimed as many members as the CTM by 1997.

The decline of labor union influence in the political arena can be demonstrated by its reduced representation in the legislative branch, both in the Chamber of Deputies and the Senate. Labor union representation, specifically that of CTM, declined during the 1990s. For example, the number of members in the Chamber of Deputies, emerging from labor unions, diminished from 70 to 42 between 1994 and 2000. Furthermore, elected representatives from CTM reduced their presence from 52 to 30 members between 1985 and 2000 in this legislative chamber. Nevertheless, in 2006 the number had almost doubled to 37 deputies from the *labor sector* (Table 5.2). On the other hand, the number of senators was also reduced. Labor unions' positions in the Senate declined during the 1990s. The number of senators reduced from 14 in 1994 to barely 2 in 2000. Moreover, the PRI senators also declined from more than 100 to 60 members in the same period (Table 5.3).

Table 5.2 Number of deputies from the PRI, labor sector and CTM

Period	*Total number of deputies*	*PRI deputies*	*Deputies from labor unions*	*CTM deputies*
1979–1982	400	294	86	49
1982–1985	400	306	77	49
1985–1988	400	296	69	52
1988–1991	500	260	54	37
1991–1994	500	320	70	41
1994–1997	500	300	70	38
1997–2000	500	211	42	30
2000–2003	500	209	14	11
2003–2006	500	222	21	10
2006–2009	500	106	37	6

Source Prepared by the author with data from García (2005), Data of 2003–2006: Aguilar and Guzmán (2006)

Table 5.3 Number and percentage of PRI and CTM senators (1976–2006)

Years	*PRI senators*	*CTM senators*	*%*
1976–1982	64	11	17.18
1982–1988	64	15	23.43
1988–1994	60	16	26.66
1994–2000	39	14	35.89
2000–2006	60	2	3.0

Source Prepared by the author with data from: Pastrana (2004)

When the PAN won the presidential elections, many predicted the dawn of a new democratic regime committed to undermining the authoritarian features set out by the PRI regime in various spheres, among them, the labor system. However, it was not the case. The Fox administration has been characterized as the lost *sexenio* (Pastor & Wise, 2005). It was a lost *sexenio* because opportunities to consolidate the democratic transition were missed and the economy did not expand; indeed, the position of the economy dropped from 9 to 14th position in the world ranking. Moreover, the boom of oil prices did not generate high rates of economic growth as was the case in other oil-exporter countries during the 2000s (e.g., Venezuela, Russia and other countries). The lack of advancements in this period was a consequence of the unfinished transition from authoritarian rule to an authentic democracy beyond the electoral realm. As explained by Rubio (2004: 27):

> Fox victory took place in an institutional and legal vacuum. While the party wielding power had changed, the old institutional structures remained the same. But instead of the traditional system of PRI rule, where the executive and legislature operated as one, Mexico now had to rely on constitutional provisions that were inadequate to bring about effective cooperation between the two branches of government. The creation of new institutional arrangements would require two-thirds majorities in congress (because most of these would involve constitutional amendments), something difficult to achieve with a relatively even split in congressional seats between the PRI and the PAN.

During his presidential campaign in 2000, Fox promised to renovate the labor system and change the labor code to democratize the labor sphere and internal life of labor unions. As a presidential candidate, Fox signed a document with independent unions, mainly with the UNT, in which he committed to achieve 20 goals to achieve democracy and freedom in the labor sphere if he won the elections. But the attempt to reform the labor code and generate new perspectives for the revitalization of labor unions was not accomplished during the Fox administration.

Fox's governmental agenda concentrated on cuts in the federal budget for social programs, the continued privatization of industry, reform and privatization of the social security systems, the passage of regressive tax legislation, and labor law reform. The Fox administration had the CT's support, while the UNT and the FSM opposed his policies. During the last years of the *sexenio*, these organizations became more critical and more militant, partly because of government attacks on their member unions. The reform of the labor code threatened independent unions, because the plan pushed by the Fox administration would give control of the shop floor and of industrial relations to the employers (La Botz, 2005).

In many regards, it is considered that Mexico did not consolidate itself as a democratic regime over the period 2000–2006, where authoritarian and non-democratic features of the old PRI regime persisted (Middlebrook, 2004). Democracy in labor unions is an unsolved agenda. In Mexico, workers can vote to elect the president, but they cannot elect their union leader (Robles, Interview, 2007). Therefore, Mexico is still in a democratization process. Furthermore, the narrow margin of difference with which President Calderón won the 2006 presidential elections was utilized by the left to argue an electoral fraud (Guarneros-Meza, 2009).

Labor organizations, especially independent organizations did not take advantage of the democratic environment in the country during the 2000–2012 period and they have not seized the opportunities to expand their presence in the employed labor force and influence the policy-making process. On the other hand, the official unions gathered in the CT conserved their privileges and positions in the labor institutions of official bureaucracy (JFCA, JLCA, and others). Meanwhile, other official unions such as the SNTE saw an expansion of their public resources and political influence.

After the defeat of the PRI in the 2000 presidential elections, official unionism became a minor player in politics but still had influence in some political spaces and official bureaucracy. Political positions of labor unions within the PRI lost relevance, as it was not any longer the party in power. Labor organizations immediately subordinated to the conservative governments, headed by Vicente Fox (2000–2006) and Felipe Calderón (2006–2012), to maintain its bureaucratic positions within the official labor institutions. For example, most of the CT-affiliated organizations endorsed government policies. In contrast to what was expected, the official labor organizations remained as instrumental actors in the political sphere, since they strengthened their links with the PAN administrations, despite their different political roots, allegedly antagonistic. In this way, official unionism has demonstrated a pragmatic ideology, as its commitment is with the government in power, but not with political parties. Many elements of the corporatist pact remain intact in labor legislation. This enables official unions to occupy spaces in the tripartite organisms and in labor boards within the federal and state spheres.

During the Fox administration, the corporatist framework prevailed but the PRI lost its former role in it. As noted by Burgess (2003: 73), "although the CTM expressed its intention to work with the Fox government, it will no longer be embedded in the network of institutionalized exchanges that characterized its alliance with the PRI-controlled state between 1936 and 2000".

Several unions with strong presence at the national level and control over their rank-and-file transferred their allegiance from the PRI-regime to the PAN government. The process towards political democratization created opportunities for some unions, such as the SNTE, to which most of the teachers in Mexico are affiliated. Thus, the arrival of democratization in Mexico has not dismantled the old corporatist structure in the labor sphere.

Nevertheless, in general, government control over the labor movement, represented by a single confederation, had been greatly weakened in the late 1990s and early 2000s; there was a broader spectrum of labor organizations from the FSM and UNT on the left to the CT and the new FEDESSP on the right (La Botz, 2005).

Another labor organization that shifted its alliances during the 2000–2012 period was the SNTMM. This union has played an important role in the Mexican labor movement featuring historical labor struggles. Founded in 1934, the SNTMM maintained an independent position regarding the CTM during the 1940s and 1950s. However, in 1965 it joined the CT and remained as one of the most important nationwide industrial unions in the country until the early 2000s. The SNTMM remained within the CT during most of the second half of the past century. The miners' union was regarded as an official union because it was tied to the government (Bensusan, 2004: 243). Napoleon Gomez Urrutia was elected secretary-general of the SNTMM in 2001 and the union began adopting more independent postures and challenging the vertical leadership of the CT. According to the categorization of the official authorities (STPS), this union was regarded as an independent[2] labor organization in 2006 (i.e., it did not have any affiliation to other confederations such as the CROC, CROM, or CTM). Its union membership was around 90,000 workers in 2003 in sectors such as coal, copper, iron and steel. This figure was almost more than double compared with 1995 when union membership accounted for 50,000 (Cardoso & Gindin, 2009: 61). According to data calculated here, the SNTMM had a membership of 60, 373 in 2006. Indeed, unionization rates in the mining sector were around 40% in the same year (see Chapter 7).

In February 2006, an explosion in the Pasta de Conchos coal mine occurred. Around 60 miners were trapped in the mine and died. Gomez Urrutia accused the company and the Labor Ministry of the government of "industrial homicide" (Bacon, 2006). The Fox government charged the union leader of corruption and at the same time recognized Elias Morales (who had been defeated by Gomez Urrutia in the union elections of 2001) as the union leader of the SNTMM. However, the workers opposed these actions and struck in the Nacozari coal mine and the Sicartsa steel plant. Furthermore, miners struck at Cananea, one hundred years after the uprising there that started the Mexican Revolution, announcing that they would not resume work until Gomez was reinstated.

The Fox administration maneuvered to depose the national committee of the SNTMM, headed by Napoleon Gomez Urrutia, and supported another committee more in tune with the government. This event was regarded as a reaction to the performance of Gomez Urrutia in the first half of the 2000s. For instance, he promoted strikes for higher salaries and better labor conditions, but he also opposed the government's proposal to reform the labor code. Moreover, Gomez Urrutia contested the process of renewing the leadership of the CT in 2003, and abandoned the organization alleging undemocratic methods for electing the new CT president. In addition, the corporations Minera Mexico and Grupo Villacero were exasperated by the labor union's claims. The government's actions were in retaliation for the independent position of the SNTMM, and at the same time, served the interests of both the mining corporations and the official unions (Alcalde, 2006). However, Gomez Urrutia was elected by mineworkers. He is currently leading the union from Canada, where he requested political asylum.

The conflict between the Fox administration and the mineworkers reflected the ineffectiveness of the old methods of state control on organized labor. It also generated high social and economic costs through the loss of production in various companies and the risk of closure. Regardless of other dimensions of the conflict, it is important to highlight that the channels of prevention and resolution of inter-union and labor-employer struggles were not functioning as in previous decades and that the repressive capacity of the state proved to be insufficient to bend the willingness of the workers as occurred in the era of strong presidentialism (Bensusán, 2006: 715–716) in the PRI regime.

The case of the mineworkers' union (SNTMM) occurring at the end of the Fox administration, suggests that the strong control of unions by the government weakened within the new democratic environment. This is opposed to other cases, when PRI governments were able to overthrow union leaders, for instance in the cases of the SNTE and STPRM in 1989 or in the 1950s. In the case of the miners' conflict in 2006, President Fox was incapable of removing the union leader of the SNTMM, Napoleón Gómez Urrutia. In summary, during the Fox administration, the official labor movement became more fragmented with the departure of the

SNTMM from the CT. This fragmentation would become even more drastic with the split of the FSTSE, as mentioned above.

The Period of Felipe Calderón

Felipe Calderón assumed the presidency in December 2006 amidst wide protests of fraudulent elections. More than half of the population believed that the presidential elections were stolen from the ballot boxes or manipulated during the computer counting. In order to distract the public opinion, Calderón launched a war on drugs to combat drug cartels in Mexico, which received significant support from the Bush administration (2001–2009). The militarization of the war on drugs also disarticulated social movements, among them, labor unions mobilizations.

The war on drugs launched by the Calderón government became a failed war, considering its deleterious outcomes; for instance, number of narco-executions, and the expansion of insecurity. Violence intensified in Mexico during the Calderón *sexenio.* Considering data on narco-executions, the number of disappeared persons, and various other indicators, the total number of drug-related deaths was approximately 100,000 from 2006 to 2012 (Zepeda & Rosen, 2014). Mexico became a more insecure, violent, and dangerous country, in which criminals and drug lords were fighting for the control of territory and drug trafficking routes. Despite the transition to democracy in 2000, various underlying problems that already existed, such as corruption and impunity, poverty, and inequality, have worsened. In this context, labor unions experienced a difficult context to pursue their interests and, consequently, reduced their mobilization; security became more important than labor rights and union membership.

The Calderón administration (2006–2012) was characterized by continued attacks against labor organizations, while the living conditions of the workers deteriorated. Calderón government confronted the independent unions but maintained corporatist alliances with some of the most important national unions, such as the SNTE and the CTM.

The living conditions of workers declined, especially after the financial crisis of 2008–2009. In the 2000–2010 period, the growth of Mexico's GDP was on average 2.1% in the period. It was the country with the lowest economic growth among the major Latin American economies in that decade. This economic context generated an adverse scenario for labor unions, as the number of jobs in the formal economy reduced but at the same time there was an expansion of the informal sector to 60% of the labor force.

In 2009, the government decided to eradicate the Mexican Light and Energy (Luz y Fuerza del Centro, LFC) Company, a public enterprise in the electricity sector, and practically eliminated its union, the Mexican Electrical Workers Union, which was also part of and led the Mexican Union Front (FSM). This labor union headed a coalition against neoliberalism and privatization of the energy sector. The federal government took over the LFC, liquidating the company and laying off around 40,000 union workers. A remaining 16,000 SME workers have continued to fight for their jobs (La Botz, 2015).

The collapse of the SME marked a major setback for the labor movement in Mexico. This labor union had been at the forefront of the independent labor movement. Even though it was one of the oldest unions in Mexico, the SME held a very active role in diverse landscapes over the 1990s and early 2000s. The SME relied on its capacity of mobilization; its ability to summon other organized groups and played a major role within the overall independent labor movement. The SME headed the FSM, an umbrella organization founded in 1998, which consists of a variety of unions identified with left wing positions in the political and social realms.

The SME participated in most of the historical union events in Mexico over the twentieth century. It was founded in 1914 at Mexico City amidst the Mexican Revolution (1910–1920), when it was occupied by the most genuine leaders (*caudillos*) of this revolution: Francisco Villa and Emiliano Zapata. From the 1930s to 1990s, the SME participated in the foundation of the main labor organizations. It was part of the labor movements that gave rise to the CTM in 1936; the CT in 1966; and the UNT in 1997. However, the SME abandoned these organizations because of significant differences in various aspects. Indeed, the SME left the CTM six months after its creation because it was subordinated to the government and because it did not accept any position in the CTM committee (Amezcua, Interview, 2007); it practically left the CT during the 1990s as the absence of alternatives proposed by this Congress in the face of the neoliberal economic crisis (Farina, Interview, 2007). Despite the fact that it had participated in the previous meetings, the SME did not join the UNT in 1997 before its founding, partly because of internal disputes with regard to leadership between the STRM, SNTE, SNTSS and STUNAM;

and because within the UNT, the SME would reduce its position as an independent union.

During the 1980s and early 1990s, the SME was able to survive because the privatization process did not reach the CLyFC, partly due to the pact accorded with President Salinas (Murillo, 2001b) to prevent these actions, which could have meant the suppression of SME's collective agreement, its membership decline and the benefits erosion. Salinas had a strategy to weaken official organizations, which comprised the promotion of independent unions. Considering these circumstances, the creation of the FESEBES in 1989 as well as the SME and the STRM protection by the Salinas administration can be understood, as they supported official policies at several key moments. Indeed, the SME was one of the first unions to offer public support to Salinas, when he was running in the 1988 presidential elections, as the PRI candidate, despite the union had previously been distant from politics (Trejo Delarbre, 1990). Towards the end of the 1990s, the Zedillo administration failed to privatize the electrical sector, as a result of the SME strategy of mobilization, including alliances with other major social and political forces, to counter this purpose not only over this period, but also in the early 2000s, during the Fox government.

In the last month of the Calderon *sexenio*, a labor reform of the LFT was approved which did not contribute to the solutions of workers problems but kept intact the corporatist structure in the legislation that regulates the labor relations between the state and workers.

The Period of Enrique Peña Nieto

The Peña Nieto government received a country with high levels of violence because of the failed war on drugs of the previous administration. In this context, Peña Nieto promoted a political and social pact with the main political parties and social organizations to achieve reforms on education, energy, and tax legislation (Rosen & Zepeda, 2016). Therefore, a new strategy to implement the recently approved labor legislation in 2012 was relegated during the Peña Nieto government. One of the main objectives of Peña Nieto was the education reform, which had staunch opposition from the largest union in Mexico, the SNTE. Elba Ether Gordillo, the union leader, had opposed this reform because she considered it as harmful to education workers, mainly teachers of primary, secondary and high schools.

In February 2013, the Peña Nieto government arrested and jailed Elba Esther Gordillo, leader of the SNTE, on well-founded charges of embezzlement (La Botz, 2015). She was accused of organized crime and money laundering since she operated with resources of illicit origin that reached the amount of 2 billion pesos (more than US$150 million at that time).

Apparently, Gordillo had not supported Peña Nieto's political campaign for the presidency in 2012, as she had supported the previous PAN candidates Vicente Fox and Felipe Calderón. It could be assumed that Gordillo's arrest and imprisonment was a settling of scores by the PRI political elite for her political support of PAN candidates in 2000 and 2006, with whom she subsequently forged strong political alliances and received wide benefits for its union (e.g., positions in the federal government cabinet, financial official support for the union and other political benefits, such as the support for the creation of a national political party [PANAL]). She was considered to be one of the most powerful women in Mexico between 2000 and 2012. In the presidential elections, the SNTE political machinery was crucial for winning the elections, as this union has members in practically all the political districts of the country.

As a result, SNTE suffered a historic political setback in the first year of the Peña Nieto government which avoided a new pact with SNTE and made education policy unilaterally; similarly, SNTE allies were not appointed to high-level positions in the Ministry of Education (SEP) (Chambers-Ju & Finger, 2016). Peña Nieto directly confronted the union to reassert the state's control over the education sector and promoted an ambitious education reform, building a multi- party coalition for thar purpose. In 2013, this coalition approved the General Law of Professional Teacher Service, which directly challenged the union's influence over the education sector. Furthermore, the approved legislative framework included the evaluation of teachers' performances (Ornelas, 2013, as quoted by Chambers-Ju & Finger, 2016), which was one of the most challenged matters by the union.

As mentioned in Chapter 4, in 1989 Salinas removed the top leadership of the SNTE and promoted a leadership more in tune with his administration, deposing the leader Carlos Jongitud and imposing Elba Esther Gordillo as the new chief of the most relevant labor union in the country. The control of Gordillo over the SNTE concluded in 2013, after more than 23 years of leadership. During the Peña Nieto *sexenio*, the union was headed by Juan Diaz de la Torre, a longtime partner of Gordillo and head of the political machine of the union (La Botz, 2015). Unlike Gordillo,

Díaz de la Torre lacked political expertise and was unable to discipline union sections in subnational states. In this way, he "was in a weak negotiating position vis à vis the federal government, and was forced to accept policies – namely, a new regime of teacher evaluations – that rank- and-file teachers firmly opposed" (Chambers-Ju & Finger, 2016). In August 2018, Gordillo was released after spending more than five years in prison. The teacher was accused of money laundering and organized crime, but a federal court cancelled the proceedings because the evidence presented at the trial did not prove her responsibility for the crimes (Nájar, 2018).

The SNTE was created in 1943, during the period of consolidation of the hegemonic party system, to control most of the teachers in primary and secondary public schools. The PRI controlled the SNTE since it served as a political machine and played a key role in elections due to its territorial dispersion. In return, union leaders were appointed positions at the legislative and executive levels (Arnaud, 1992 as cited by Murillo, 2001a). The SNTE, grouping all teachers in primary and secondary education, is the most important union in terms of union membership not only in Mexico but also in Latin America and perhaps the most powerful in Latin America.

During the Salinas administration, the SNTE participated in the design of decentralization in the education system. During the Zedillo administration this union preserved its position but was relegated by the government and during the Fox administration it became a strategic partner of the government, as can be seen in the financial resources obtained from the federal government and the fact that the union leader Elba Esther Gordillo formed a union federation and a political party in this *sexenio*.[3]

Several unions with strong presence at the national level and control over their rank-and-file were able to transfer their allegiance from the PRI-regime to the PAN governments in the period 2000–2012. The SNTE has a significant presence in the education sector, which also grants it access to state resources. Statistical data of 2007 on unionized workers confirm that this union has the highest union membership in the country (around 1.2 million). By occupation, teachers are the most highly unionized at 65% in 2000, which is down 8 percentage points from 73% in 1984 (see Chapter 7 for more details on unionization by sectors).

The democratization created opportunities for the SNTE, to which most of the teachers in Mexico are affiliated. For example, this union became more powerful as its access to public resources increased during the 2000s (Cantú, 2009). The corporatist structure did not disappear; it has survived, entrenched in the new democratic environment, but without the PRI intervention. In this sense, the SNTE benefitted from the democratic process mainly because it is no longer under the control of the PRI, but also because it strengthened its bargaining position as a labor organization regarding its relationship with the government. The SNTE created a national labor federation, the FEDESSP, but also formed a national political party, the PANAL, which has important representation in the legislative arena in both the national and regional levels.

On the other hand, democratization in Mexico has not dismantled the old corporatist structure in the labor sphere. During the 2000–2012 period, the PAN governments were not able to change or modify the corporatist system of control in the education sector in Mexico, created during the PRI regime. In contrast, they have relied on this structure to control the national union and forge political alliances on different levels. In this way, the SNTE became an important ally of the PAN governments. The Fox and Calderón administrations did not counteract the privileges of this official labor organization, but rather they ruled using the corporatist structure to control the labor movement and promote their government agenda.

Labor Legislation

Labor relations in Mexico are regulated by Article 123 of the Constitution. In this article, workers are distributed either in private sector or the public sector. The federal labor code (*Ley Federal del Trabajo, LFT*) approved in 1931, covers workers from the private sector. On the other hand, public sector workers are constrained by different legislation. From 1938 to 1960, they were regulated by an official statute decreed by President Cárdenas and approved by the Congress. In 1960, Article 123 was amended to include a special section (Apartado B) regulating federal government employees and the Department of the Federal District workers. In this year, The Federal Labor Law for State Employees (*Ley Federal de Trabajadores al Servicio del Estado, LFTSE*), which regulates the activities of workers and unions in the public sector, was enacted. Public sector workers are not allowed to strike, and they also must affiliate to a labor federation (FSTSE). The LFTSE includes provisions such as representation exclusivity and mandatory membership. Furthermore, the right to strike is too restrictive, because the LFTSE maintains that two-thirds of the affected workers must approve strikes. During the late 1990s, the Supreme Court in Mexico established that the "unique union" violated the principle of freedom of association and that the LFTSE did not bind decentralized administration agencies, thus granting this segment rights to organize collectively (Bensusán, 2000, as quoted by Cardoso & Gindin, 2009: 16).

Despite the fact that the labor code (LFT) guarantee wide labor rights, it contains elements that facilitate the control of the state over the organization and creation of labor unions and the realization of strikes (Bensusán, 2000) and has been mentioned as one of the features of the authoritarian regime (Middlebrook, 1995). With little changes, which have not modified the elements of state control, this labor code has prevailed and despite the various attempts of reform, it survived the wave of *flexibilization* that extended around Latin America in the 1980s and 1990s as a consequence of neoliberal reforms. However, as noted by Cook (2007: 152), "despite the generally protective character of labor legislation, the strong state role in labor relations allowed successive governments to modify and even violate these protections in order to adapt to changing demands of a more market-oriented economy, especially during the 1980s and 1990s".

In Mexico, labor unions require government recognition, through an official act identified as *registration* and *taking of note*, to acquire legal status and operate formally. In the federal sectors, this registration is provided by the federal boards of conciliation and arbitration (JFCyA) of the STPS (Secretary of labor and social provision), and in the local jurisdiction, it is issued by the local boards of conciliation and arbitration (JLCyA) from provincial governments. It is provided to labor unions, once they have fulfilled the requirements set by legislation. Any group of workers, at least 20 even though they represent a minority, may constitute a labor union by an official registration to obtain legal status before labor authorities and employers. Traditionally, a labor union becomes a member either of a central in the same industry or of a national federation and confederation. Once labor unions have obtained the register, they may bargain with employers and set collective contracts. If the employer refuses, then the union can call for a strike (McKennirey & Compa, 1997: 70–71).

Even though union organization is guaranteed by the labor legislation framework, in reality, it is hindered by the official labor boards during the registration process, integrated by tripartite bodies representing the employers, labor unions and official authorities of the ministry of labor (Middlebrook, 1995: 464–465). The representing body of unions is appointed by the large corporatist official organizations (CTM and CT); accordingly, the creation and registration of independent unions, not included in the main official organizations, is almost non-existent.

Even when a labor union obtains the register from the state, unions must periodically send internal documents to the administrative authorities (including their goals, structure and composition) and these documents must be approved under a system known as *toma de nota* (note-taking) as a pre-requisite for the operation of unions in the labor sphere. Furthermore, the representation monopoly is assured by the negotiation of exclusionary clauses in collective agreements, which, although not legally mandated, are widely used (Cardoso, 2009: 16–17).

The freedom and autonomy of labor unions guaranteed by the legislation framework will be insufficient if these are not accompanied by conditions which make them possible. The state guarantees labor rights, but it does not fulfil them; evidence of this situation is found in Mexico (De Buen, 2007). As previously highlighted, out of the three North American countries, Mexico includes a wide group of labor rights and fringe benefits. Notwithstanding, it also has the most adverse labor conditions and the deterioration of wages and benefits for workers has been promoted by companies with the acquiescence of the state (Guerra, 2002).

The federal labor law (LFT), according to Nestor De Buen, enforces the complete subordination of labor unions to the state. Furthermore, the state has formed an alliance with the business sector. Through multiple mechanisms included in the LFT, the state controls labor organizations, in aspects such as the registration act, the taking of notes, the regulation of strikes' actions, etc. Then, labor unions, except those with a strong spirit of struggle, are under the total dominion of the state. Thus, the state becomes a partner of the corporations for managing and controlling labor unions (De Buen, Interview, 2007).

The official labor organizations have disapproved the reform of labor code because they would lose privileges. For example, the positions in the JLCA and JFCA, IMSS, INFONAVIT, among other labor related institutions widely controlled by these unions; the possibility of forming 'ghost' unions with 'labor contracts of protection' and their position as interlocutors with the government.

The labor reform approved in November 2012 openly favors capital to the detriment of labor; as it endorses and legalizes procedures, criteria and practices that were imposed even illegally during decades of neoliberal offensive against the workers. On the other hand, several aspects such as union registration and the taking of notes were not modified; freedom of association also was absent for workers who cannot freely decide which union they join; workers do not even know if they have been included in a union organization; union bureaucracies have legal attributes and resources to control employees (Orozco & Magallón, 2013).

Labor Contracts of Protection

The organization of new unions, in which the workers from any workplace, attempt to organize by themselves in order to get a collective agreement, is relatively low, practically inexistent. In addition, it must be considered that employers' strategies to prevent the authentic union organization include simulation in labor collective contracts. In Mexico, a big share of trade unions are classified as *ghost unions* (*sindicatos fantasma*), with 'labor contracts of protection' (Bouzas, 2003). These unions are created by enterprises, in collaboration with union leaders, in order to hinder the possibility that workers organize unions by themselves to defend their labor rights more effectively. Many workers, belonging to these unions, have collective contracts set only by employers, but they are unaware of this situation. Even though the official labor institutions are aware of 'ghost unions', they have not showed any interest in solving this situation. The government agenda does not include any plan to solve this critical problematic in the short term.

As indicated by Bouzas (Interview, 2007), between 70 and 90% of the labor collective agreements in the private sector are considered as labor contracts of protection. It has been proved that diverse enterprises in the private sector (especially in departmental stores, grocery stores and gas stations) have this kind of collective agreements and unions. Gimenez-Cacho (Interview, 2007) contends that false labor contracts are a common practice in the country, with the consent of the labor authorities; indeed this situation can be noticed in the information provided by the federal and local governments, especially that of Mexico City.

However, this has also been the case of *maquiladoras* in the north of Mexico. The case of the *maquiladora* Han Young in 1997 in Tijuana, demonstrated the difficulties faced by workers to obtain the official registration for an independent union. When the Han Young workers began forming an independent union in 1996 to raise their 85-cents-an-hour wages (US$) they found that they were already represented by Government-backed labor bosses who had signed a secret contract with owners of the plant. They asked for new elections to substitute the official ghost union of the CROM. They won the election to form the new independent union affiliated with the FAT. But the government refused to recognize the independent union.

The *New York Times* (1997) reported: "When Congress debated the NAFTA, President Clinton won over some critics by including a side agreement that guarantees labor rights in Mexico, including the right of workers to choose their own unions. But the struggle for a free union at a Tijuana, Mexico, plant that makes truck chassis for Hyundai Precision America in San Diego shows that the agreement is little more than cosmetic". After pressure from the Clinton Administration, President Ernesto Zedillo's Labor Ministry intervened, and in a second election, in December 2007, the independent union gained recognition. Han Young became the first of nearly 3,000 border assembly plants in Mexico with an independent union (Dillon, 1998).

As mentioned above, labor became a central issue in the renegotiation of NAFTA, which the United States and Canada used to pressure Mexico to improve its labor standards. This involves not only labor laws, but also their enforcement, compliance and sanctioning. The U.S. and Canada claimed that wages in Mexico are significantly lower, and for that reason companies in the manufacturing sector, especially the automotive sector, are moving to Mexico. This translates into the loss of hundreds of thousands of jobs in the United States and Canada, generating a trade deficit in the United States of just over US$60 billion.

There is a wide disparity in wages in the manufacturing sector among North American countries. In the United States and Canada, the average hourly wage in the sector is around US$20, both well above Mexico, which has a wage of $3.4 in this sector. This disparity in terms of wages is mainly attributed to the existence of ghost labor unions with contracts of protection in the Mexico's manufacturing and maquiladora sectors. Workers cannot negotiate higher salaries because they cannot organize unions. In other words, low salaries of workers in this country are the result of the violation of labor rights, among them the freedom of workers to create authentic unions, with the tolerance of the state.

The labor issue is an opportunity for Mexico to become a competitive country with high wages and a skilled and productive labor force, which can become an element that helps reduce the enormous levels of inequality in Mexico.

Andres Manuel López Obrador Government

Andres Manuel Lopez Obrador (AMLO) was elected in July 2018, with the highest level of votes in the recent history of presidential elections. He obtained 53.2% of the total votes. Certainly, AMLO is not the first left-wing oriented president. As mentioned in Chapter 4, there were different political currents within the PRI. Former PRI presidents Lazaro Cardenas (1934-1940), Adolfo Lopez Mateos (1958–1964) and Luis Echeverria (1970–1976) can be considered as left-wing oriented presidents.

AMLO began his political career within the PRI in the 1970s. He earned a bachelor's degree in politics from UNAM in Mexico City. During the 1980s, there was a fragmentation within the PRI, the ideological dispute was between the nationalists and the technocrat-wings. In this dispute, AMLO left the PRI, along with other nationalist dissidents such as Cuauhtémoc Cárdenas and Porfirio Muñoz Ledo, who joined with more leftist political leaders such as Heberto Castillo of the Socialist Mexican Party. They created the Party of the Democratic Revolution (PRD), founded by a fraction emerged from the PRI but also by other social and political leaders who were stemming from leftist parties. Subsequently, in 2013, AMLO broke up with the PRD and founded his own party, the National Regeneration Movement (Morena) and run for the presidency in 2018.

As part of the requirements by the United States and Canada during the NAFTA negotiations (2017–2019), a labor reform to guarantee labor rights and their enforcement was approved in 2019 which guaranteed unionization and internal democracy in labor unions. Furthermore, the AMLO government has increased the minimum salary: 16% in 2019 and 20% in 2020. The largest increase in the last 40 years. There is a commitment to increase workers' salaries to fulfil with the new USMCA (the agreement that replaced NAFTA) in terms of labor requirements. The new free trade agreement is positive for Mexican workers as it provides guarantees to labor rights (freedom to unionize), which could help increase the levels of union density in the country.

Conclusions

In the sphere of industrial relations, certainly the creation and registration of authentic labor unions has been complex; in contrast, the organization of labor unions promoted by the official confederations has been less complicated. Furthermore, in this context, the proliferation of "ghost unions" with "labor contracts of protection" has increased significantly since the 1980s, as has been described by various scholars. In this sense, some characteristics of the labor system have not favored or facilitated union organization. On the one hand, the creation of authentic unions is obstructed and on the other hand, the formation of "ghost unions" with simulated contracts is promoted by the corporations in the majority of the private sector and this is tolerated by the labor authorities.

Diverse regulations in the labor-related legislation (for instance, the LFT) are considered by many as authoritarian, with respect to the creation of new labor unions, the recognition of strikes and the authentic representation in labor organizations. The control over labor organizations by the state obstructs the possibilities of creating independent unions. In several aspects, during the past century, the corporatist framework facilitated the official control of labor organizations in exchange for some benefits (social security, access to housing, pensions and higher real wages). Such features took place during the period of the corporatist alliance between the state and labor. However, during the neoliberal period, state control over the registration of unions and validity of strikes, for instance, has been maintained, but the benefits for the working class have been suppressed or reduced significantly. The advent of a more democratic political regime has not eliminated the corporatist structure and independent labor unions with more democratic features of operation have not expanded.

Several characteristics of the political system but also of the labor system have contributed to the decline of labor unions in Mexico. First, the freedom of workers to create authentic unions is almost inexistent. Second, the opportunities with respect to the organization of unions are not guaranteed by the labor legislation and labor boards. In this way, the creation of labor unions and the affiliation of members within the employed labor force are obstructed not only by the companies in the private sector but also by the toleration of labor authorities. These features have prevented the union affiliation and thus have influenced the relatively low levels of authentic unionization in the country. A new institutional framework is required to create the proper labor conditions and increase the number of affiliated members in the employed labor force.

Furthermore, the democratization process must progress beyond electoral democracy and extinguish the authoritarian practices in other areas such as labor organization. Mexico is a democratic country with an authoritarian corporatist structure which should be dismantled and replaced by another kind of corporatist structure more like the societal corporatism identified by Schmitter (1976). In that context, the real and authentic organization of independent unions can be guaranteed, such as in Scandinavian countries and other democratic countries where corporatist relations are common practice.

The political transition towards a more democratic regime happened in Mexico after the economic transition towards a free market economy. In this transition, the PRI, saw the reduction of its political power. This situation changed the scenario faced by labor unions, since the official unions and confederations of the CT are no longer the labor organizations representing the majority of the unionized workforce (Aguilar, 2005; Roman & Velasco Arregui, 2006: 98). However, despite the advent of political democratization and the erosion of PRI hegemony, the official unions, mainly the CTM and CT, still exert influence on the labor relations system amidst an institutional framework with limited guarantees for the organization of authentic labor unions. As opposed to the political transitions in countries like Spain, the case of Mexico has been marked by the absence of a wide political agreement or pact among the main political forces.

Regarding government partisanship, it is evident that in the case of Mexico this was not a significant factor. As mentioned before, leftist governments have brought more advantages for workers and labor unions and in contrast, conservative parties have actively resisted unions through labor legislation and in industrial relations (Wallerstein & Western, 2000). However, this has not been the case in Mexico, as most of the union density decline occurred during the era of PRI hegemony. The PRI is not exactly known as a conservative party. Other aspects were more significant in this regard, such as the orientation of the political economy.

On the other hand, since 2000, democracy has failed to generate the favorable conditions to improve the situation of workers in general and labor unions in particular. The emergence of independent labor organizations took place since the 1990s, reclaiming a new role as interlocutors with the state and as actors in the political realm. The extent of the contribution of these organizations to solve the crisis of labor unions in the country is in dispute.

Notes

1. As a result of the lack of consistent and enough official information about the strikes petitions in the local jurisdiction of the private sector, I decided not to include it in the analysis.
2. According to the STPS, the term 'independent' refers to nation-wide unions with no-affiliation to any other confederation, such as the CTM, CROM or CROC, among others.
3. The SNTE abandoned the FSTSE in 2003 and organized the FEDESSP which became the most important labor organization in the public sector. On the other hand, the SNTE organized the PANAL, a political party which occupies a reduced but significant number of deputies in the Congress.

Bibliography

Aguilar, J. (2005). *La población trabajadora y sindicalizada en México en el período de la globalización*. México: UNAM, FCE.

Aguilar, J., & Vargas, R. (2006). *La CTM en el periodo de la globalizacion. Del periodo de Carlos Salinas al gobierno de VicenteFox*. Universidad Autónoma del Estado de Mexico.

Alcalde, A. (2006). Balance sindical del gobierno de transición: promesas incumplidas. In I. González (Ed.), *Los sindicatos en la encrucijada del siglo XXI*. Mexico: Fundación Friedrich Ebert Stiftung.

Bacon, D. (2006). Hundreds of Mexican miners fired for striking. *International Union Rights, 13*(3), 4–6.

Bensusán, G. (2000). *El modelo mexicano de regulación laboral*. México: Plaza y Valdés-UAM-Flacso-FES.

Bensusán, G. (2004). A new scenario for Mexican trade unions: Changes in the structure of political and economic opportunities. In K. Middlebrook (Ed.), *Dilemmas of political change in Mexico*. London: Institute of Latin American Studies; San Diego, CA: Center for U.S.-Mexican Studies, University of California.

Bensusán, G. (2006). Le renouveau syndical au Mexique sous le premier gouvernement de transition. *Relations Industrielles, 61*(4), 708–732.

Bouzas, A. (2003). *Reforma Laboral; analisis critico del proyecto Abascal de reforma a la Ley Federal de Trabajo*. Mexico: UNAM.

Burgess, K. (2003). Mexican labor at a crossroads. In J. S. Tulchin & A. Selee (Eds.), *Mexico's politics and society in transition*. Boulder: Rienner.

Burgess, K. (2004). *Parties and unions in the new global economy*. Pittsburgh: University of Pittsburgh Press.

Camp, R. A. (2007). *Politics in Mexico: the democratic consolidation*. Oxford University Press.

Cantú, J. (2009). Los brazos del SNTE. *Revista Proceso*, 1719, October 11th.

Cardoso, A., & Gindin, J. (2009). *Industrial relations and collective bargaining: Argentina, Brazil and Mexico compared* (Working Paper No. 5). Industrial and Employment Relations Department International Labor Office, Geneva.

Chambers-Ju, C., & Finger, L. (2016). Teachers' Unions in Mexico. In D. DiSalvo (Ed.) (2017), *The comparative politics of education: Teachers unions and educations systems around the world*. New York, NY: Cambridge University Press.

Collier, R. B. (1992). *The contradictory alliance: State-labor relations and regime change in Mexico*. Berkeley: International and Area Studies, University of California.

Cook, M. L. (2007). *The politics of labor reform in Latin America: Between flexibility and rights*. University Park: Pennsylvania State University Press.

De la Garza, E. (1994). Independent trade unionism in Mexico: Past developments and future perspectives. In K. Middlebrook (Ed.) (1991), *Unions, workers, and the state in Mexico*. La Jolla: University of California; San Diego: Center for U.S.-Mexican Studies.

Dillon, S. (1998, April 30). Bias said to hurt independent Mexican Unions. *The New York Times*.

Escobar, S. (2006). *Los trabajadores en el siglo XX. Sindicato, Estado y sociedad en Mexico: 1907–2004*. Mexico: STUNAM.

Greene, K. (2007). *Why dominant parties lose: Mexico's democratization in comparative perspective*. Cambridge, UK: Cambridge University Press.

Guarneros-Meza, V. (2009). Mexico: Political parties and local participation. In S. Ludlam & G. Lievesley (Eds.), *Reclaiming Latin America: Experiments in radical social democracy*. London: Zed Books.

Guerra, T. (2002). *Derecho Laboral comparado: México-Estados Unidos*. Universidad Autónoma de Sinaloa – Facultad de Derecho.

Haber, P. L. (2006). *Power from experience: Urban popular movements in late Twentieth Century Mexico*. University Park: The Pennsylvania State University Press.

La Botz, D. (2005). Mexico's labor movement in transition. *Monthly Review, 57*(2), 62–72.

La Botz, D. (2015, September–October). The agony of Mexican labor today. *Dollars & Sense, Real World Economics*. Available at https://www.dollarsandsense.org/archives/2015/0915labotz.html, consultado en junio de 2020.

Levy, D., & Bruhn, K. (2006). *Mexico: The struggle for democratic development*. Berkeley: University of California Press.

McKennirey, J., & Compa, L. (1997). *Plant closings and labor rights: The effects of sudden plant closings on freedom of association and the right to organize in Canada, Mexico and the United States*. Dallas: Bernan Press and Commission for Labor Cooperation.

Middlebrook, K. (1989). The sounds of silence: Organized labor's response to economic crisis in Mexico. *Journal of Latin American Studies, 21*(2), 195–220.

Middlebrook, K. (1995). *The paradox of revolution*. Baltimore and London: The John Hopkins University Press.

Middlebrook, K. (2004). *Dilemmas of political change in Mexico*. London: Institute of Latin American Studies; San Diego, CA: Center for U.S.-Mexican Studies, University of California.

Murillo, M. V. (2001a). *Labor unions, partisan coalitions and market reforms in Latin America*. Cambridge: Cambridge University Press.

Murillo, M. V. (2001b). Partisan loyalty and union competition: macroeconomic adjustment and industrial restructuring. In C. Candland & R. Sil (Eds.), *The politics of labor in a global age*. New York: Oxford University Press.

Nájar, A. (2018, August 8). México: liberan a Elba Esther Gordillo, quien fuera considerada la mujer más poderosa del país. *BBC News Mundo*.

O'Toole, G. (2007). *Politics: Latin America*. Harlow, UK: Pearson Longman.

Orozco, A. A., & Magallón, R. O. (2013). Reforma laboral en México: Precarización generalizada del trabajo. *El Cotidiano, 182*, 95–104.

Paczynska, A. (2009). *State, labor, and the transition to a market economy: Egypt, Poland, Mexico, and the Czech Republic*. Pennsylvania State University.

Pastor, M., & Wise, C. (2005). The lost sexenio: Vicente Fox and the new politics of economic reform in Mexico. *Latin American Politics and Society, 47*(4), 135–160.

Pastrana, D. (2004, December 12). La CTM: ¿más viva que nunca? *La Jornada*, México.

Roman, R., & Velasco Arregui, E. (2006). The state, the bourgeoisie, and the unions: The recycling of Mexico's system of labor control. *Latin American Perspectives, 33*(2), 95–103.

Rosen, J., & Zepeda, R. (2016). Una década de narcoviolencia en México: 2006–2016. In S. Aguayo & R. Benitez Manaut (Eds.), *Atlas de la seguridad y la defensa de México*. México: CASEDE- Senado de la República.

Rubio, L. (2004). Democratic politics in Mexico: New complexities. In L. Rubio & S. K. Purcell (Eds.), *Mexico under Fox*. Boulder, CO: Lynne Rienner Publishers.

Schmitter, P. C. (1974). Still the century of corporatism? *The Review of Politics, 36*, 85–131.

Trejo Delarbre, R. (1990). *Crónica del Sindicalismo en México (1976–1988)*. Mexico: Siglo XXI.
Wallerstein, M., & Western, B. (2000). Unions In decline? What has changed and why. *Annual Review of Political Science, 3*, 355–377.
Zepeda, R., & Rosen, J. D. (Eds.). (2014). *Cooperation and drug policies in the Americas: Trends in the twenty-first centuries*. Lexington Books.

Interviews

Amezcua, F. (2007, November). *Secretary of external affairs*. SME, Mexico City.
Bouzas, A. (2007, September). *Labor lawyer and academic scholar*. UNAM, Mexico City.
De Buen, N. (2007, September). *Labor lawyer and union advisor (SNTMM and others)*. Mexico City.
Farina, F. (2007, October). *Union advisor (SME and INEGI union)*. Mexico City.
Gimenez-Cacho, L. (2007, November). *Academic scholar and director of NEXOS magazine*. Mexico City.
Guerra, T. (2007, October). *Academic scholar and labor lawyer*. Universidad Autónoma de Sinaloa.
Robles, J. (2007, September). *Union leader (FAT and UNT)*. Mexico City.

CHAPTER 6

The Economic Performance and Labor Markets

Transformation of the Economic Model

From the 1940s to the 1970s, like in other Latin American countries, Mexico successfully adopted an economic model of development known as Import Substitution Industrialization (ISI) and followed an inward-looking development path over these decades. The rapid industrialization of the country took place within an economic environment protected by trade barriers (Lustig, 1998: 14). The ISI model was characterized by an economy relatively closed to the international markets as well as heavy participation of the state in the economic sphere, as owner of parastatalparastatal enterprises[1] (state owned enterprises) in sectors such as highway, telephony, banking, and mass media, among others. The major economies of the region saw an economic expansion. For instance, average annual growth rates in Brazil and Mexico between 1950 and 1980 were 7.0 and 6.5%, respectively, while their industrial sectors became powerful engines of growth and employment. Their export baskets came to include a substantial role for industrial products. Smaller economies also experienced successful growth under the ISI model. Colombia and Costa Rica, for example, grew more than 5% per year during the 1950–1980 period (Stallings & Peres, 2000: 37).

However, various limitations resulted in the collapse of this economic model in Latin America, for instance: (1) the inability of the ISI model to

R. Zepeda, *The Decline of Labor Unions in Mexico during the Neoliberal Period*, Governance, Development, and Social Inclusion in Latin America, https://doi.org/10.1007/978-3-030-65710-9_6

overcome the *scarcity of foreign exchange*, which led to persistent balance-of-payments difficulties. (2) The *fragility and inefficiency of the domestic financial system*, which failed to provide long-term finance for industrial development. (3) *Fiscal fragility* due to the wide gap between the budgetary demands and the tax revenues available. (4) High *inflation*, which was a product of distributional conflicts: social groups fought for shares of the national income through higher prices, taxes, and wage demands. And (5) *lack of policy coordination*: Latin American states could rarely exercise the degree of co-ordination of economic activity required by their developmental objectives (Saad-Filho, 2005: 223).

When the ISI model showed signs of exhaustion in the 1970s and early 1980s, it was gradually substituted by the neoliberal model, whose main feature was a trans-national productive system focused on external markets. In this context, a major economic transformation began in Mexico through the implementation of a structural adjustment program to deal with public finance problems. Mexico opened its economy and became a member of the GATT in 1986, NAFTA in 1994 and has integrated successfully into the international markets through various free trade agreements. However, the recovery has been slow; consequently, workers have seen the erosion of their wages and living standards in the process.

The Debt Crisis

During the 1970s, for the first time since the post-war period, the Mexican economy faced an adverse international context.[2] Furthermore, the ISI model showed signs of exhaustion as its core policies were not able to generate economic growth. Like other Latin American countries, Mexico's economic growth during the 1970s often relied on external borrowing (Skidmore & Smith, 2005: 58). Attempting to overcome structural weaknesses in the economy generated by the ISI model within a context of an international economic crisis, the Mexican government decided to expand its activities, including the number of parastatal enterprises. The administrations of Echeverria (1970–1976) and López Portillo (1976–1982) deepened the role of the state in the economy and continued the ISI model with an expansive fiscal policy, including high public spending. As a result of this expansive strategy, the public sector deficit increased significantly, passing from around 2% of the GDP in 1971 to 10.9% in 1982. In this period, the current account deficit raised from

US$928.9 million in 1971 to US$6,220 million in 1982, which represented 3.2 and 3.5% of the GDP, respectively (Chavez & Huerta, 2003: 64).

Although the economy spun out of control in 1982 with the debt crisis, there had been signals of weakening since the 1970s. As underlined by Aspe (1993: 13), "Mexico was already on the road to higher inflation as early as 1972. Between 1971 and 1976, the public sector deficit rose from slightly more than 2 percent to 9.1 percent of GDP, financed by a combination of inflation and external borrowing". During the 1970s, specifically in 1976, the national currency underwent a heavy devaluation, in contrast to the stability observed in the rate of exchange in the three previous decades. Since 1954 the parity between the US dollar and the Mexican peso was 12.50 pesos per dollar, but this parity rose to 20: 1 in 1976 and to 70: 1 in 1982.

In these circumstances, during the 1970s the government faced a predicament: either open the economy and stimulate an exporting economy or to reinforce the nationalist model which had been in practice since the 1940s. The government opted for the second option and the political economy included the expansion of the parastatal enterprises while it relied on oil exports as one of the main sources of income for the country. The economic policies of Echeverria and López Portillo have been regarded as populist or neo-populist because they boosted public spending and were not very concerned with the budget deficits. Nevertheless, the governments in these two administrations failed to successfully administer a basic condition for the adequate performance of the economy: a proper balance between public incomes and expenditures. During the 1970s Mexico was not *en route* toward a transition from the ISI model to an export-oriented economy as had been the case in other developing countries (especially South Korea and other Asian countries). An obese state became a burden upon Mexican enterprises inhibiting their ability to adapt to the international crisis of the early 1970s characterized by high inflation rates and economic stagnation (stagflation) that spread in many countries.

Toward the end of the 1970s, during the López Portillo administration, oil wells were discovered, and the economy found new momentum. The exports of oil were greater than before, climbing from $500 million in 1976 to $13 billion in 1981, and the Mexican economy grew 8% annually in this period. When the oil prices were high, the main source of revenues of the government stemmed from the oil exports; for instance, in

1982 Mexico depended on oil for 75% of total export incomes (Edmonds-Poli & Shrink, 2009: 251). However, Mexico suddenly became dependent on financial loans from international institutions to sustain its economy. Such financial loans were covered with income from high oil prices, helped by relatively low interest rates of foreign banks and international financial institutions (Aspe, 1993). In this manner, the correct operation of the economy depended on external factors: the high oil prices and low interest rates charged by international financial institutions and banks. Mexico's foreign debt increased from $4.2 billion in 1970 to nearly $20 billion by 1976 and to almost $59 billion by the end of 1982. A large percentage of this debt was contracted on a short-term basis, at high interest rates (Levy & Bruhn, 2007: 161–162). Mexico's external debt, which accounted for 31% of GDP in 1980, increased to 39% of GDP in 1981 (Schlefer, 2008: 169).

Therefore, domestic problems were alleviated in the short term, although the public finances became weaker: external debt increased, and the economy became vulnerable to international conditions. Nonetheless, the policies of Echeverria and López Portillo proved to be an erroneous strategy in 1982. It was not a surprise that the debt crisis emerged in Mexico, considering the fragile conditions that were sustaining the economy. Rising interest rates combined with falling oil prices to make Mexico the first among the debtor nations to experience a financial crisis (Collier, 1992: 80). The debt crisis of 1982, initiated in Mexico and expanded through all Latin America, was so severe that this country had to modify the main parameters of the economy during the 1980s and 1990s. Mexico changed direction; opening its economy to international markets became the main strategy for economic stimulation. The debt crisis became a turning point as it called into question the viability of the ISI in Mexico and Latin America, which had become dependent on a continuous infusion of capital, and it strengthened the perspective of neoliberals (O'Toole, 2007: 442) (see Table 6.1).

As in previous chapters, please insert call-outs to the tables, and make a hint in the text proper ("see Table 6.1").

The Neoliberal Era

The transition taking place in Mexico since 1982 in the economic sphere consisted mainly of a change in the development model from an Import-Substitution-Industrialization (ISI) to a neoliberal model. Whereas the

Table 6.1 Labor unions and the economic model, 1934–1982/1982–2010

1934–1982	*1982–2010*
• Import-Substitution-Industrialization	• Neoliberalism
• National productive model focused on domestic markets	• Trans-national productive model focused on external markets
• Closed economy with high level of tariffs to protect national economy from international trade	• Open economy ruled by globalization and regionalization
• Significant state participation in economy. High number of *parastate* enterprises	• Reduced state participation in economy. Low number of *parastate* enterprises
• Labor unions as relevant factors in productive system	• Labor unions as deleterious factors in the productive system

Source Elaborated by the author

ISI encouraged a national productive system focused largely on domestic markets, the neoliberal model promoted a transnational productive model directed to external markets. The ISI model was protected by high tariffs to international trade and was complemented by the heavy participation of the state in the economy with a significant number of parastatal enterprises. Labor unions found a propitious environment to flourish in such a model. However, labor organizations faced difficulties in the neoliberal period, as corporations looked for the *flexibilization* of labor agreements before international competition brought by the economic liberalization. In this economic model, according to Leiva (2008: 55), the sale or realization of production of the most dynamic sectors of the economy is executed in external markets. The result is that workers in the export sector are not the consumers of what they produce. Consequently, wages and working conditions can be depressed without significantly affecting profits. More importantly, the shared interest between capitalists and labor unions in expanding the internal market, which for decades served as the basis for the multiclass support for the national-developmentalist project, has vanished (Leiva, 2008).

The transition toward a model of export-oriented industrialization had a deep impact on the industrial relations model that had developed for decades in close cooperation with the state. In these new circumstances, the availability of cheap labor became crucial to the struggle to conquer international markets; the oppression and control of labor organization formed an important part of the new industrialization strategy. Suddenly the labor union movement in Mexico and Latin America found itself on the defensive (Thomas, 1995).

The changes experienced in the Mexican system of labor relations have been characterized as a process of transition from a system of *selective inclusion*—linked to the ISI model and the internal market—to a system of *generalized exclusion* in the context of the outward oriented model of development. The emergent system promotes competitive strategies based upon labor cost reduction, employment precariousness, and weakening of labor unions; in sum, external flexibility (Bensusán, 1999 as quoted by Bayon, 2003: 103).

The economic transition also had an impact on the political system. In Mexico, the authoritarian system experienced a process of political liberalization since the 1980s which undermined the hegemony of the ruling party. The collapse of the ISI model and the rise of neoliberalism were accompanied by the exhaustion of the PRI hegemony (Morton, 2003: 648), and affected the party's sectors. Greene (2007: 104) contends that "the move from the relatively closed ISI development model to a more open economy reduced the reach and organizational capacity of the PRI's sectorial organizations (CTM, CNC and CNOP) that previously distributed massive quantities of patronage to voters". In this manner, economic transition contributed to exacerbating a context (along with other processes) that undermined the hegemony of the PRI. Since the labor organizations were linked to the official party as one of its key sectors, they also faced unexpected circumstances during the economic transition towards neoliberalism.

In 1982, President de la Madrid took over the Mexican presidency amid a major economic debacle. It was Mexico's worst economic shock since the 1930s (González, 2008: 114). The economic activity stagnated, and inflation soared to almost 100% in 1982. Local and foreign capital fled, and the government opted for the nationalization of the banking sector in September 1982. In this context, the relation of the government with the business and financial sector deteriorated, making the government's goal of reactivating the economy more difficult.

In order to overcome the negative effects of the economic crisis, the de la Madrid government launched in 1983 the Immediate Program for Economic Readjustment (*Programa Inmediato de Recuperacion Economica*, PIRE), whose main purpose was directed to restore the public finances and set the conditions for the rapid economic recovery. In this context, the government reduced public spending and, at the same time, increased public sector prices and tariffs. The PIRE initiatives brought about an unprecedented reduction in the primary and operational deficits. However, total financing as a share of GDP continued at a high level due to the persistence of inflation (Aspe, 1993: 14).

The de la Madrid government (1982–1988) promoted a new economic model, which was significantly different from that of his predecessors, relying on a group of neoliberal policies to alleviate the precarious economic conditions in the country. Initially, the de la Madrid administration concentrated on policies to stabilize macroeconomic indicators, such as the reduction of inflation, the public deficit and debt servicing, which had soared in recent years. The government's social budget decreased, including public expenditures and subsidies to food and groceries. Subsequently, the main policy tools also came to include privatization of parastatal enterprises and free trade-oriented policies, which became more evident following Mexico's adherence to the General Agreement on Tariffs and Trade (GATT) in 1986. At the end of the de la Madrid government, tripartite pacts with the participation of employers, unions and government were implemented to reduce inflation rates through the restrain of national minimum wages and prices.

Nevertheless, the recovery of the Mexican economy after the debt crisis was slow, especially for economic reasons. The adverse economic conditions that had brought the debt crisis to a boil continued through the 1980s: in particular, high real-world interest rates, low availability of credit and low oil prices (Lustig, 2001: 87). In 1985, the drop in the international price of oil affected the incomes of the government. Inflation soared between 1985 and 1987: from 60% to more than 160% and capital fled. Furthermore, an earthquake in 1985 devastated Mexico City but also undermined the credibility of the government among citizens as it reacted slowly to alleviate the negative effects.

Since 1982 the government adopted various economic policies that affected workers and contributed to the loss of real wages and other social benefits. The core of these policies was the reduction of inflation. As mentioned by (Cornelius, 1989: 94), "the principal weapon in the battle against inflation was the de la Madrid government's own belt-tightening". Similarly, subsidies on basic food items, collective transport, electricity, natural gas, and gasoline were significantly reduced or eliminated in the early years of the de la Madrid administration (Middlebrook, 1989: 195). Under de la Madrid, central government expenditures were cut from 27.1% of GDP in 1982 to 17.1% in 1988; in the same way, education and health funding were badly hit, falling by a cumulative 29.6 and 23.3%, respectively during this *sexenio* (Minns, 2006: 112). Other policies more in tune with the neoliberal prescriptions were also implemented such as the privatization and the cutback of public spending reducing the number of employees in the public sector, which impacted union membership in this sector. The de la Madrid administration fired more than 20% of all government employees by July 1985 (Levy & Bruhn, 2007: 166).

Despite the adoption of an export-oriented strategy of industrialization in Mexico, an integral strategy to foster economic development has been absent, at least since the late 1980s, to consolidate the exporting model. Dussel (2003: 248) notes that "since 1988, Mexico's liberalization strategy has given secondary importance to industrial and trade policy; indeed, for many government economic officials, the best industrial policy was none at all". In this sense, Mexico has relied on a limited strategy to advance economic development, especially one based on the attraction of foreign investment and the expansion of *maquiladoras* and free export zones. This strategy has not triggered high rates of economic growth and formal employment has not absorbed the emerging labor force.

As mentioned in Chapter 3, one of the aims of neoliberal prescriptions consists of the reduction and control of inflation. In doing so, the government relied on the corporatist structure. In 1987 a sequence of social pacts, accorded among the government, business chambers and labor unions, were put into practice. The *Pacto de Solidaridad Economica* was valid from December 1987 to December 1988. Later, the *Pacto para la Estabilidad y Crecimiento Economico* (PECE) was promoted by the Salinas administration and was renewed every year between 1989 and 1995. These pacts comprised reductions in the fiscal deficit, a further tightening of monetary policy in the form of higher interest rates to tame inflation and stabilize the exchange rate, further trade liberalization, and a commitment by industry not to raise prices and by trade unions not to press for wage increases above inflation (Lustig, 1998 as quoted by Gallagher & Zarsky, 2007: 49).

The social pacts were successful in reducing and containing inflation rates since 1987. During the early 1980s inflation rates expanded but at the end of this decade they reduced considerably. According to official figures, inflation increased from 29.8 to 131.8% between 1982 and 1987, but then it declined to 20% in 1989, and fell further to 9.8% in 1993. It is important to highlight the utilization of the corporatist structure created in the 1930s to successfully implement some neoliberal prescriptions.

According to many scholars, these social pacts greatly contributed to the deterioration of real wages. In the manufacturing sector, despite the rise in productivity levels throughout the 1990s, average wages in this sector declined in real terms (Polaski, 2004). On the other hand, if we analyze the decline of union density rates in the last decades, we can see that the largest decline occurred in the period in which the social pacts mentioned above were implemented. In this manner, unions lost influence on wage determination. As explained by Fairris (2005): "in 1984, unions bid up wages by 21%, whereas in 1996 the union relative wage effect had fallen to 15%. Unions appear to have lost some bargaining power over wages during this period, arguably related to the rather significant decline in union density". Finally, a group of political practices that were directed to stabilize macroeconomic indicators, such as the control of inflation rates and other goals, reduced the influence of labor unions and affected the overall real wages of workers.

Although NAFTA marked the expansion of trade liberalization, it had advanced notably during the de la Madrid and Salinas administration. From 1984 to 1993, import license coverage fell from 83.5% (1984) to 21.5%, the production-weighted average tariff declined from 23.5% (1985) to 12.5%, and the maximum tariff fell from 100% (1985) to 25% (Moreno-Brid & Ros, 2009). Furthermore, in the last years of its administration, de la Madrid lowered the impregnable tariff wall around the economy to less than 15% protection (Hodges & Gandy, 2002: 128).

The government of de la Madrid initiated the road towards a neoliberal economy, but the major transformation in terms of neoliberal reforms occurred during the Salinas administration (1988–1994). The Salinas reforms comprised trade liberalization, an opening up to foreign investment, the deregulation and privatization of several major industries, the re-privatization of commercial banks, and a constitutional reform permitting the sale of communal lands; the process culminated in Mexico's entry into the North American Free Trade Agreement (NAFTA) in 1994 (Levitsky, 2003: 242). During this administration, for the first time since 1982, the year of the neoliberal turn, the economy showed steady positive rates of economic growth. The economic growth during this period was higher than during the previous administration: the economy grew almost 3.9% on average, as opposed to 0.2% in the de la Madrid government. Finally, Mexico had recovered the path towards a reactivation of the economy, a low inflation and a stable foreign exchange rate between the peso and the US dollar. However, ancestor problems like inequality persisted. As mentioned by Levy and Bruhn (2007: 12): "Standard economic indicators (like growth and inflation) were positive", but "the benefits of this growth were distributed unequally", in this way, "a few Mexicans got very rich, but most people failed to improve their lot substantially".

On the other hand, the Salinas government maintained an exchange rate policy in which the peso was pegged with the dollar. This was hazardous for the economy because the currency was overvalued and delayed currency devaluation during all the Salinas administration. Delaying devaluation certainly made the problem worse. Mexico maintained a pegged exchange rate from 1987 through 1991 as part of a program that included a substantial reduction in government expenditure. As a result, inflation fell from 160% in 1987 to less than 20% in 1991, although, in 1994 a speculative attack on the peso led to a sharp currency devaluation and a financial crisis (Gil-Alana & Barros, 2009).

During the final year of the tenure of President Salinas (1988–1994), some events exacerbated a context of political instability that affected the financial markets. The emergence in January 1994 of the EZLN (Zapatista Army of National Liberation) in Chiapas, one of the poorest states in the South and the assassination of the PRI presidential candidate during the campaign for the 1994 presidential election, created nervousness in the financial markets and triggered the mass departure of foreign financial capital during that year.

Ernesto Zedillo (1994–2000) took over the presidential office within these fragile conditions and a major economic debacle emerged. One of the first decisions that the new president had to make was to cut the peso-dollar peg, causing the currency's value to drop by more than 50% in only a few days (Steger & Roy, 2010). The peso devalued with respect to the dollar rapidly between 1994 and 1995, from 5.3:1 to 7.6:1 (Banco de Mexico); there was an economic contraction of 6.2% in 1995. Amidst these circumstances, the IMF and the United States contributed to the rescue of the Mexican economy, liberating credit for $50 billion of US dollars (Cameron & Aggarwal, 1996). This financial rescue stopped the peso from collapsing and prevented the crisis from spreading to other countries. Its success can be seen in the quick recovery of the Mexican economy and in the fact that the government repaid the loan years ahead of schedule (Lustig, 2001: 92).

During the period 1996–2000 the economy showed a significant recovery, its overall rate of growth was around 5.5% per year. On average, over the Zedillo's *sexenio*, economic growth was 3.6% annually (INEGI, 2007). The peso crisis of 1994–1995 had repercussions throughout the world and showed the disadvantages brought by a globalized economy. Similarly, it suggested that economic policies adopted by Mexico should be re-examined. As mentioned above, the Salinas administration relied greatly on foreign investment as a strategy to foster economic development. But the kind of investment was short-term and was not regulated. When financial capital departed in 1994, Mexico faced huge difficulties.

Before 1994, around 80% of capital flows into Mexico were in the form of portfolio investment; the acquisition of existing assets on the stock market. In 1994, as mutual fund managers and other institutional investors began to detect signs of an impending crisis, that share declined to 50%. Nevertheless, the amount of portfolio investment in Mexico was a far greater share of total capital inflows than in any other country in Latin America. Meanwhile, domestic savings declined from 22 to 16% of the gross domestic product (GDP) between 1988 and 1994 (Cameron & Aggarwal, 1996: 4).

The economic collapse of the mid-1990s spread its deleterious outcomes on various social sectors. The effects of the crisis on the employment conditions were remarkable. Informal employment rose rapidly because of the scarcity of jobs. In 1995 alone, one million jobs were lost, which could not be recovered in the formal economy. By the end of 1996, there were 8 million unemployed and 5 million working within the informal economy, out of a total labor force composed by 35.7 million (Becerril, 1996; Fox, 2006).[3] After the crisis of 1994–1995, average wages deteriorated even more than previous years. Between 1987 and 1997, real wages declined around 50% (González Amador, 1998). Mexican manufacturing wages fell over 20% in real terms from 1994 to 1997 and in 2003 average real wages in the manufacturing sector were still 5% below 1994 levels (Hufbauer & Schott, 2005: 99). Moreover, despite rising productivity levels throughout the 1990s, workers remunerations remained stagnated in the manufacturing sector (Polaski, 2004). Nevertheless, during the period 1996–2019, Mexico did not experience another major economic crisis of the magnitude of the crises of 1982 and

1994–1995, reflected by an accentuated negative trend in the GDP rates, high inflation, and currency devaluation.

Privatization

Since 1982 the government of de la Madrid implemented a gradual privatization program as one of the actions, among others, to overcome the negative effects of the debt crisis. Privatization in Mexico had at least three key objectives (Weiss, 1996: 67): (1) To improve the operating efficiency of enterprises by a transfer to the private sector. (2) To contribute to a reduction in the government budget deficit either from the sale proceeds, or from the disposal of loss-making enterprises whose losses no longer must be covered by the government. (3) To foster confidence in the private sector and thus encourage new investment. Privatization proceeded in three phases. In the first phase (1983–1985) non-viable and non-priority State enterprises, mostly small in size, were either liquidated or merged within the public sector. In the second phase (1986–1988) experience was built up through the sale of medium and small companies, generally in non-sensitive areas. In the third phase (1988–1994), during the Salinas administration, the larger, more strategic, public enterprises were sold, such as the telecommunications company (Telmex), the two airlines, the large steel, fertilizer and sugar companies and the commercial banks, nationalized in 1982 (Weiss, 1996: 67).

Labor unions flourished in the companies controlled by the state. As mentioned in Chapter 2, unions became stronger in the public sector, which comprised the majority of unionized workers and a significant number of labor unions. In general, unions were considered by the state as relevant factors in the productive system in the kind of economy dominated by big national industries and parastatal enterprises. During the ISI model period, the number of parastatal corporations increased in Mexico, but during the neoliberal era, these enterprises have decreased. As a result of the privatization process, the number of parastatal enterprises considerably reduced during the period 1983–1994: from 1156 enterprises in 1982 to only 252 in 1994. Previously, the figures had increased from 259 in 1960 to 905 parastatal firms in 1980 (Fig. 6.1).

The privatization in the early 1990s of the two state airlines also involved major downsizing before privatization. Most of the staff belonged to a union. In the case of AEROMEXICO a massive strike led the government to declare the company bankrupt. The company went

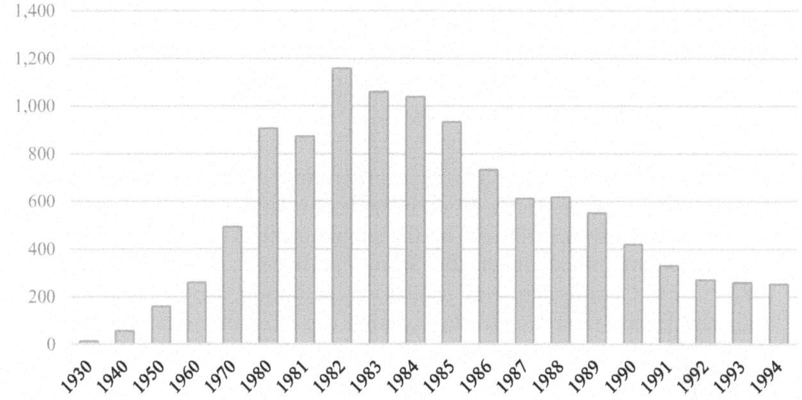

Fig. 6.1 Number of parastate enterprises in Mexico: 1930–1994 (*Source* Adapted from MacLeod, 2005)

into liquidation and its assets were sold; only a fraction of the workforce was rehired by the new owner. In the case of the second airline, Mexicana, the prospective buyers insisted the labor force be cut before privatization, and the government reduced it by more than 40% (Kikeri, 1995).

Labor unions were affected by the privatization of major sectors during the Salinas administration (1988–1994). Employment in four steel plants was cut from 35,578 in 1985 to 17,485 in 1994, with the largest declines occurring just before privatization in 1991 (Kikeri, 1995). The mining workers from Cananea had rejected the plans of the company to change the collective contract; after they went out on strike, the company went bankrupt and more than 300 workers were dismissed. A similar experience happened to unions in the steel and iron sector. Around 5.4 thousand workers from the steel plant *Lazaro Cárdenas-Las truchas* (Sicartsa) were thrown out of the company during the privatization process. In contrast, the telephone workers union faced different conditions during the privatization of TELMEX, the state-owned company in telecommunications (Clifton, 1999). The STRM, the union of telephone workers, received special conditions from the government when the firm was privatized. In this case, the political context must be considered since President Salinas promoted this union as the representative of modern unionism more in tune with neoliberal policies. During the Zedillo government, the privatization of main sectors advanced. One of the most striking cases was the railway sector. The main union also diminished its membership in the sector. During the early 1990s, unionized workers were around 100,000 but this fell to 7,000 in 1998 after the privatization of the company. Harvey (2005: 100–101) maintains:

> Privatization entailed the wholesale restructuring of labor contracts and this provoked conflict. Fierce labor struggles broke out in the late 1980s only to be put down ruthlessly by the government. The attack on organized labor intensified under the Salinas presidency that took over in 1988. Several labor leaders were gaoled for corruption, and new and more compliant leaders were installed in key labor organizations under the PRI's control. Troops were called out more than once to break strikes, and the independent power of organized labor, such as it was, was diminished at every turn.

While public enterprises were privatized, collective agreements underwent modifications, removing some benefits for workers and creating more flexible work rules at the workplaces. Moreover, privatization process harmed trade unions since most workers in the privatized enterprises were fired and replaced by sub-contracted workers, supplied by outsourcing firms. These workers were not allowed to become union members. Labor unions in the privatized enterprises were weakened by the reduction of their membership or deleted from the collective contract. Furthermore, the privatization of public enterprises, fostered by neo-liberal governments, has benefited a small group who are among the world's richest people. One example could be the area of telecommunications. As a result of the privatization process, "Mexico's stock of billionaires rose from 2 to 24 during the presidency of Carlos Salinas (1988 - 94)" observed O'Toole (2007: 448).

The *Flexibilization* of Labor

Employers in Mexico have pressed for more flexible labor markets to reduce labor costs and face more effectively the challenges imposed by international markets. The latter has impacted labor unions; for instance, the deregulation of collective labor agreements has made labor conditions more flexible in the last years. In the case of Mexico, collective agreements with labor unions in various sectors such as mining, steel, telecommunications, and airlines were dismantled during the 1990s (Williams, 2001), especially during the de la Madrid and Salinas *sexenios*. In practice, the labor relations have become more flexible in a majority of labor sectors; this process has been stimulated by employers and consented by the state and even though independent unions have denounced it, they have not overcome this situation (Bouzas, Interview, 2007).

Heckman (2000: 115–116) calculated the expected discounted cost of dismissing a worker in Latin America. An index was designed by the authors to compare the marginal costs of dismissing full-time permanent workers. The measure quantifies the impact of job security on different measures of employment and unemployment in a group of Latin American countries. As displayed, the average cost of dismissing a worker is still higher in Latin America than in the sample of OECD countries included in the study. As can be seen, the study shows that Mexico presented 3.1 monthly wages in terms of cost of dismissal, which was higher than average (2.3 monthly wages). The most flexible countries, in terms of dismissing a worker, were the United States, New Zealand, Australia, and Canada (Table 6.2). Traditionally Mexico has been considered to have a more flexible labor market, but this indicator suggests that it has rigid labor legislation regarding labor costs. After a decade of substantial deregulation, Latin American countries, including Mexico, remain with levels of regulation higher than those of the highly regulated countries of southern Europe.

Nevertheless, the theoretical rigidity of Mexico's labor legislation in many cases is incompatible with the reality, as it is not respected by employers. According to some firms, Mexico is one of the countries with the most onerous labor regulation. However, a crucial question is to what extent this extremely protective legislation is actually enforced (Kaplan, 2008). In this way, union organization has been affected by two major related processes which have taken place on labor markets in Mexico. On the one hand, the increasing labor force in the informal sector mostly located in the low-paid services sector, and on the other hand, the *flexibilization* of labor markets.

Mexico in the NAFTA Region

The NAFTA region, located in North America and integrated by the United States, Mexico, and Canada, is one of the largest free trade regions in the world. In 2006, the region accounted for a total population of more than 440 million, with a GDP of $US 14.5 trillion. It is the second

Table 6.2 Job security index across Latin America, the Caribbean and OECD countries, late 1990s

	Cost of dismissal. Monthly wages		*Cost of dismissal. Monthly wages*
United States	0.000	Trinidad and Tobago	2.548
New Zealand	0.221	Panama	2.718
Australia	0.443	Dominican Republic	2.814
Canada	0.553	Venezuela	2.955
Norway	0.912	Argentina	2.977
Germany	1.140	Costa Rica	3.121
France	1.143	Mexico	3.126
Poland	1.219	El Salvador	3.134
Switzerland	1.247	Spain	3.156
United Kingdom	1.457	Chile	3.380
Belgium	1.729	Colombia	3.493
Austria	1.784	Honduras	3.530
Brazil	1.785	Peru	3.796
Greece	1.804	Turkey	3.973
Guyana	1.890	Ecuador	4.035
Jamaica	1.920	Portugal	4.166
Paraguay	2.168	Bolivia	4.756
Uruguay	2.232		

Source Calculated from Heckman, 2000

Table 6.3 NAFTA, European Union and China, 2013

	European union	*NAFTA*	*China*
Countries	28	3	1
Population (million)	511	460	1,355
GDP (US$ Trillion)	16.9	19.8	8.8
Labor Force	228	209	797

Source Calculated from CIA, 2014

greatest free trade zone, after the European Union (EU) in terms of population. Yet, in terms of GDP, the NAFTA region is the biggest worldwide (Table 6.3). Nevertheless, with respect to the features and scope of the integration process, the EU is deeper than the North American. Unlike the EU, the NAFTA only concerns issues on free trade and its institutions are far from being considered as supranational. Each NAFTA member decides on its own labor and trade policies. The common frontiers among the three members, rather than having free transit, have become increasingly closed to workers, mainly between Mexico and the United States. The common currency appears a distant project; indeed, it is not considered in the short term.

Free mobility of workers among countries, such as in the European Union, is not the case in the NAFTA region. It only includes minimal dispositions for the mobility of workers in certain areas. Moreover, democratic and political supranational institutions have not been created as a result of NAFTA integration. In contrast to the EU, NAFTA represents a less ambitious effort to establish a common market for the trade of goods and services, with little interest toward the development of a continental policy with an institutional framework (Stanford, 2003). Curzio (2004) emphasizes that integration processes in Europe and North America are very different and encouraged by diverse ideals, with contrasting social supports and different institutional levels. While Europe traces long term objectives, North America, in contrast, does not go beyond a free trade zone, from the institutional approach. The agreement is merely a trading zone with some other elements attached, such as security issues, combating drug trafficking and ensuring security at the border to fight terrorism.

NAFTA region is dominated both economically and politically by the United States, which accounts for 68% of the total population and around 84% of economic production in the region (Table 6.4). Furthermore, the negotiation and implementation of NAFTA was more relevant in Canada and Mexico than in the US. To the US, the creation of a free trade

Table 6.4 Main features of NAFTA members, 2013

	Canada	*Mexico*	*United States*	*US as % NAFTA*
Population (million)	34	112	314	68
GDP (US$ billions)	1,826	1,260	16,800	84
GDP per capita (US$)	51,958	10,307	53,143	
Labor Force (million)	19,000	51,400	155,400	69

Sources Calculated from Statistics Canada, 2014; Conapo, 2014; US Census Bureau, 2014 CIA, 2014. World Bank (2013): http://databank.worldbank.org/data/download/GDP.pdf US Bureau of Labor Statistics, various years zone was a significant event, but it was not considered as the beginning of a new era. Indeed, NAFTA reinforced the US strategic and economic dominance in the continent (Stanford, 2003). Despite their increasing economic links, major political and economic differences still prevail among NAFTA members. In terms of per capita income, the US economy is the richest one in the region and its economic policy reflects an extreme level of deregulation and market orientation which is unique in the industrialized world. The Canadian economy is less developed than that of the US and has traditionally showed a more mixed development pattern with a more relevant economic role of the state and a wide range of social programs and protections similar to the social democratic traditions of Europe. Mexico is an industrialized economy with mid-level incomes; its per capita income is about one quarter that of the United States.

Income Inequality (measured by the percentage of incomes obtained by the highest deciles of population compared with the lowest) is more severe in Mexico than in the US, which is double that of Canada. Both Mexico and Canada depend on the production and exportation of primary resources to the United States (specifically, energy) as an important economic activity; moreover, they have encouraged manufacturing industry. Mexico relies on its low labor costs, whereas Canada depends upon innovative activities based on high technology.

Economic integration has impacted mainly exporting sectors strongly related with international trade such as the manufacturing sector and agriculture. It is claimed that a significant number of jobs have been displaced from US to Mexico during the period 1994–2004. By September 2003, "slightly more than 525,000 workers in the US had been certified as having lost jobs under the US government-sponsored NAFTA Trade Adjustment Assistance program" (Caulfield, 2004: 454). In the United States "NAFTA has contributed to the reduction of employment in high-wage, traded-goods industries, the growing inequality in wages, and the steadily declining demand for workers without a college education" (Scott, 2006: 3). While NAFTA has benefited and protected investors, it has worsened labor standards, such as employment, wages, and social security: "NAFTA tilted the economic playing field in favor of investors, and against workers and the environment, resulting in a hemispheric 'race to the bottom' in wages and environmental quality in the United States, Canada, and Mexico" (Scott, 2006: 4).

According to Salas (2006: 33), since the beginning of NAFTA, Mexico has undergone a steady increase in precarious employment. Real wages and salaries have followed a negative trend and, in most sectors, have never returned to levels achieved at the beginning of the 1990s. The development project in Mexico must be transformed to provide the most benefits for the working population and guarantee a persistent growth in production, earnings, and living standards. As mentioned above, one of the developments that has attenuated the benefits of NAFTA in the last years has been the decline of employment in *maquiladora* industry, which had been one of the most dynamic economic sectors. Many these plants closed and moved to China during the period 2000–2004. In 2001, around 500 *maquiladoras* with more than 300,000 workers closed and moved to Asia or Central America in response to the combination of the strong peso, cheap Chinese labor, and the US economic slowdown (Ramirez de la O, 2002: 9). Furthermore, from 2002 to 2003 around 400 *maquiladoras* closed and moved out of the country; however, between 2003 and 2006 the decline halted, and a slight recovery took place (INEGI, 2008).

It is argued that the union density decline in North America was generated by the process of economic integration, started in 1980s and accelerated in 1990s with the NAFTA agreement. One argument is that this economic integration has transformed working conditions and labor markets features. According to diverse sources, the gap between rich and poor people as well as the informal sector has enlarged in the last decades. Labor benefits, such as social security, decent wages, pensions, and so forth, have been cut down. This situation has not only led to precarious jobs but also has engendered insecurity for workers.

The NAFTA contribution to the creation of formal jobs has been disputed. It has been argued that NAFTA facilitated Mexico's recovery more quickly from the peso crisis of 1994–1995, since both exports and foreign direct investment increased in 1994–2004. On the other hand, it has been claimed that NAFTA contributed to the reduction of formal jobs and has not encouraged endogenous development in the national industry.

Salinas (2004) the former Mexican president, highlights some benefits brought about by NAFTA. First, while in 1993, international trade in Mexico accounted for 22% of GDP, it become to 53% in 2003. This is because during the period 1994–2004, trade between Mexico and US almost tripled and with Canada it almost doubled. Second, NAFTA prompted investment flows towards Mexico: the annual flow of foreign investment almost tripled, passing from an average of 4,000 million dollars annually until 1993, to 11,000 million by year since 1994, accumulating 72,0000 million dollars by 2004. Third, NAFTA strengthened unionization: manufacturing industry, focused on exports, registers the highest levels of unionization in Mexico: 90% of the working population in this sector is unionized (however, the author disregards that a big share of these labor unions has false or contracts of protection). On average, the jobs in exporting industries have higher salaries than non-exporting sectors.

Despite the success obtained by NAFTA regarding foreign investment attraction and the rise of exports, Mexico has lagged in jobs creation and in development of its productive capacities and has experienced low economic growth during the period 1994–2004. Zarsky and Gallagher (2004) argue that Mexico's economic strategy cannot be evaluated exclusively on data about FDI and exports. They consider that "the central goal of a development strategy is–or should be–the improvement of current living standards while also improving the prospects for broad and sustainable development in the future". In general, they highlight, among many others, the following repercussions on economy and labor markets. (1) Most of Mexico's new jobs since 1994 are in the informal sector and are generally of poor quality–55% do not provide benefits. Moreover, the average minimum wage fell by more than 7 and by 13% in manufacturing since 1994. (2) In total, some 6.5 million Mexicans entered the work force between 1994 and 2002. Only 4.4 million new jobs were created, leaving over two million people without employment. Many migrated to cities where there are manufacturing enclaves. Others sought work across the border. In the 1990s, approximately 380,000 Mexicans migrated to the United States each year compared to less than 200,000 per year in the 1980s. The neoliberal model of economic integration has not been the panacea for economic development. Even if it has succeeded in attracting FDI and expanding exports, the model can fail to stimulate domestic growth and employment (Zarsky & Gallagher, 2004: 4).

Both the liberalization strategy and NAFTA have been significant in creating a small and highly dynamic export-oriented private manufacturing sector, which is mainly integrated to the US economy, but has failed to generate a sustainable growth and development model for Mexico as a whole (Dussels, 2006).

On the other hand, Polaski (2004) concludes that NAFTA produced small net gains in employment in the countries of North America. For example, in Mexico, employment reduction in domestic manufacturing and agriculture has gone beyond the job creation in export manufacturing. The decline in domestic manufacturing employment has been the result of import competition and perhaps also to the substitution of foreign inputs in assembly operations. About 30% of the jobs that were created in *maquiladoras* (export assembly plants) in the 1990s have since disappeared. Many of these operations were relocated to lower-wage countries in Asia, particularly China.

Therefore, NAFTA has not been the *panacea* to generate employment in Mexico since outcomes have been limited. The 'window of opportunity' brought by NAFTA has been closed. The advantages offered by Mexico, such as cheap and productive labor force, have reduced, given the better advantages international capital can find in China, where labor costs are lower. In North America, Mexico displays the most adverse outcomes on job creation during the post-NAFTA period. The loss of jobs and the absence of employment growth in the formal sector of the economy have discouraged union membership expansion in Mexico. Furthermore, it has been detected that most labor unions in the maquiladora sector are 'ghost unions', with artificial labor contracts, controlled by corporatist unions, mainly from CTM and CROC (Bouzas, 2003; Quintero, 1997).

The North American Agreement on Labor Cooperation (NAALC) was created as an annex of the NAFTA to guarantee the rights of workers within each member state. The NAALC is one of the few international agreements linking labor standards and trade. It was requested by President Clinton of his counterparts in Canada and Mexico, to guarantee the ratification of the treaty in the United States. The specific objectives of this agreement are: "monitor implementation of *national* laws and regulations pertaining to labor, provide resources for joint initiatives to promote better labor practices, and establish a forum for consultations and dispute resolution in cases where domestic enforcement proves inadequate" (Hufbauer & Schott, 2005: 55). "Each country is committed to sustain these principles through enforcement of its own domestic labor laws. Notably, NAALC does not create specific regional labor provisions. Rather, it brings enforcement of domestic labor standards to regional scrutiny" (Graubart, 2009: 179). A similar agreement with the same origins and objectives on environmental issues was annexed to NAFTA.

However, the limitations of the NAALC to sanction those companies which have infringed essential labor rights have been highlighted. As pointed out by Watts: "In Canada, Mexico and the United States, fundamental workers' rights continue to be abused with impunity". Although NAALC cases have generated reports on labor issues, virtually no concrete changes have been made to countries' laws or practices to improve workers' rights (Watts, 2003: 24).

NAFTA Renegotiation 2017–2019

In general terms, NAFTA has not been successful in solving Mexico's problems with respect to issues such as economic growth, poverty, inequality, employment and working conditions. The results of neoliberal policies and NAFTA in Mexico have been low economic growth and recurrent crises that have created an environment characterized by precarious employment, informality, unemployment, and high levels of social and economic inequality. More than half of the labor force works in the informal sector, and about half of the population lives in poverty. Economic growth in the NAFTA decades has averaged no more than 2%, a level of growth far below that of the 1940s and 1980s. In summary, NAFTA has not been a panacea for Mexico's domestic problems.

Nevertheless, it is pertinent to note that NAFTA has favored specific industrial and manufacturing sectors, facilitated the attraction of foreign investment, and has increased Mexico's exports to the United States and Canada. Mexico went from having a deficit in trade relations with the United States to having a surplus. In 1993, before NAFTA, trade between the two countries was about $88 billion, with a surplus in favor of the United States economy of $2.4 billion; in 2018, NAFTA reversed the balance in favor of Mexico.

The NAFTA region produce around 30% of the world's goods and services. Trade in the region has nearly tripled during the NAFTA era, while investment has increased six-fold. The United States trade relationship with Canada and Mexico represents twice as much as United States trade with China, and 10 times as much as trade with the United Kingdom.

The Mexican economy relies on the United States in terms of exports, imports, foreign investment, and integrated supply chains which in turn generate millions of jobs in Mexico. For example, about 80% of Mexico's exports are directed to the United States, and about half of its imports come from that country, while the United States is the main investor in Mexico. Total trade between the United States and Mexico has increased more than 6 times because of NAFTA. Integrated supply chains have been created in some sectors that depend on components in the countries of the region, that is, North America is a productive zone that depends on the free flow of trade, especially in intermediate goods. The automotive sector, one of the most active in recent years in Mexico, depends on productive supply chains, which has meant greater competitiveness and have made North America one of the world's most dynamic manufacturing platforms in the automotive and auto parts sector.

Economic Performance

The analysis of GDP fluctuations permits detecting to what extent the overall economy is functioning properly. As showed in Table 6.5, Latin America experienced a notable slowdown in the economy during the 1980s in contrast to previous decades. During this decade it grew, on average, only 1.6% per annum, as opposed to the period 1965–1980, in which it showed a steady growth of 6.1% every year. However, despite the poor performance of the 1980s, it partially recovered over the 1990s with 3.3% of annual growth (Robinson, 2004: 138). Hence, it is not anomalous that labor markets in Latin America are increasingly characterized by the majority of jobs in the informal sector, lacking social security provision, with lower salaries and low-qualified occupations. These are

Table 6.5 Comparison of growth by regions (percent average annual growth rate)

	1965–1980	*1980–1989*	*1990–2000*
World	4.1	3.1	2.6
Latin America	6.1	1.6	3.3
Sub-Sahara Africa	4.2	2.1	2.4
East Asia	7.3	7.9	7.2
South Asia	3.7	5.1	5.6
OECD members	3.8	3.0	2.4

Source Calculated from Robinson (2004)

jobs not very likely to be unionized since they are in sectors and occupations difficult to organize, creating an adverse scenario for trade unions (Table 6.5).

As shown in Table 6.6, economic growth in Latin America slowed in the last two decades of the twentieth century. This period of economic slowdown coincides with the implementation of structural adjustment policies, but the outcomes have been divergent. Although Mexico has presented rates of economic growth very similar to the region as a whole in the last decades, it can be highlighted that in recent years, in the 2000–2010 period, the economic expansion of Mexico has been lower than in most Latin American countries. Nonetheless, it cannot be affirmed that neoliberal policies have propelled the low economic performance in the region, as shown in the statistical data, during the period 1980–2010, countries such as Chile have growth more than the average in the region. Therefore, it is necessary to analyze the national context in which the economic policies were implemented.

Mexico experienced recurrent economic crises throughout the final decades of the past century. Similar to the rest of Latin America, Mexico's economy also experienced poor performance in recent decades. During the 1980s, overall GDP growth registered a low of 1.9%, while in the period 1990–2000, it reached about 3.5%, on average. In contrast, in former periods, for example, between 1940 and 1980, GDP growth

Table 6.6 GDP growth rates in Latin American selected countries, 1980–2010

	1981–1990	*1991–2000*	*2000–2010*	*1980–2010*
Chile	3.0	6.6	4	4.5
Colombia	3.7	2.6	4.5	3.6
Bolivia	0.2	3.8	4.1	2.7
Ecuador	1.7	1.7	4.6	2.7
México	1.9	3.5	2.1	2.5
Paraguay	3.0	2.2	3.8	3.0
Brasil	1.6	2.6	3.7	2.6
Uruguay	0.0	3.0	3.9	2.3
Argentina	−0.7	4.2	5.6	3.0
Perú	−1.2	4.2	6.1	3.0
Venezuela	−0.7	2.0	4.6	2.0

Sources Data of 1981–1990 and 1991–2000, obtained from CEPAL, 2000. Data of 2000–2005, UNCTAD, 2008. Data of 2000–2010 (UNCTAD, 2012: 413–416)

was, on average, around 6% per decade. During the 1940s and 1950s it grew more than 5% and between 1950 and 1970 it steadily climbed around 6% per annum. However, economic activity underwent significant recessions throughout the 1980s; in this decade the overall growth was less than 2%; furthermore, despite the fact that in the period 1980–2010, it saw a higher rate, the economic growth was not more than 3%. Thus, the economic performance during the neoliberal period has been less than the half of that from 1940 to 1980 (Fig. 6.2). Therefore, a diverse landscape can be seen. In the 1980s, neoliberal policies could not trigger a significant economic growth, but in the early 1990s the economic policy tools generated higher rates of economic growth, especially during the Salinas government. Yet again at the end of 1994 and 1995 the economy faced difficulties. In this way, the constant slumps in Mexico's economy are evident and clear in the period 1980–2010, which suggest that the economic policies have proved to be ineffective in reactivating the economic cycle. Neoliberal reforms, implemented since the 1980s, have encouraged a modest performance in the economy and triggered informal employment in labor markets.

Even though the economy in Mexico experienced periods of growth between 1980 and 2010, it is clear that the general performance was poor. Furthermore, economic growth did not increase, on average, beyond 3% in the period 1980–2000. Mexico's economy not only suffered two

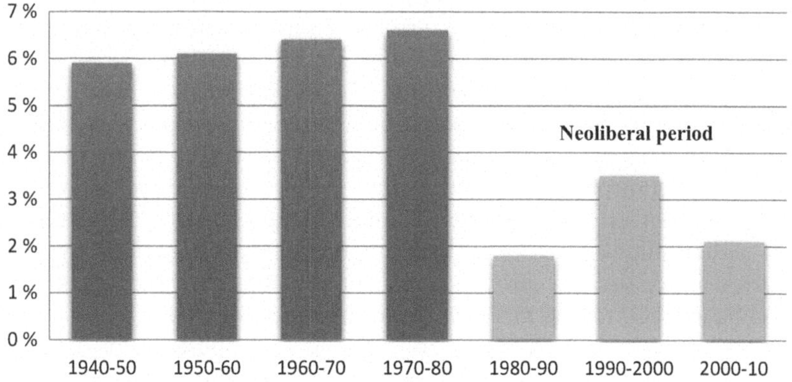

Fig. 6.2 GDP growth by decades in Mexico during period 1940–2005 (*Source* Calculated from INEGI, 1999; UNCD, 2012)

striking shocks in the 1980s (1982 and 1986), but also it had another collapse in the mid-1990s, producing negative effects for the working class. However, it quickly recovered during period 1996–2000 displaying constant rates of growth ranging between 3.7 and 6.8%. Notwithstanding, this path halted as Mexico's economy entered a recession in the early 2000s; GDP growth rate registered a −0.3% in 2001 due mainly to the heavy dependence on the United States economy. Indeed, during the Fox administration (2000–2006), the overall economic growth was only 2.3%. In comparison with its trade partners, the United States and Canada, economic performance in Mexico over the period 1980–2000 showed a lower pattern.

The poor conditions of the working class in Mexico are evident in the relative low level of incomes, measured by the GDP per capita. In contrast to the features of most countries in the developed world, Mexico shows poor indicators in terms of economic development and well-being for workers by the mid-2000s. For instance, Mexico's GDP per capita is one of the lowest not only in North America but also within OECD countries. In 2006, it was around $11,000 per year, which is very low in contrast to Norway ($52,000), United States ($43,000) and Ireland ($41,000), which registered the highest international levels of GDP per capita in that year (U.S. DOL, 2008). During the period 1980–2003 in the North American region, this indicator improved considerably in the United States (+57%) and Canada (+45%), but it barley increased in the case of Mexico during the period (+12%). Furthermore, despite the widespread economic reforms, Mexico's per capita output grew by only 0.45% per year between 1980 and 1999 (Lustig, 2001: 86).

The economic policies implemented by the government have greatly relied on a set of prescriptions to encourage economic growth, including foreign investment, export-oriented industry, as well as public policies directed to control inflation and restrain public expenditures. However, they have not created the jobs required by an emerging labor force, but rather stimulated a precarious labor market characterized by low salaries, scarce social security, wherein trade unions have no possibilities to enhance their role as major actors in the sphere of labor.

One of the main factors triggering the adverse landscape for workers in the last decades has been the economic situation of the country. Since the 1970s, Mexico has experienced not only a constant fall of real wages but also a strong state control over workers and the organization of new labor unions. Economic conditions constitute one of the factors behind the labor union decline, by reducing its leeway. Similarly, another factor in this regard is the modification of the economic policy; since 1982, Mexico has been dominated by one kind of authoritarian neoliberalism, replacing the former tutelage of the state, in which the role of the state in the economy was directed to guarantee diverse social benefits for the working class. In this context, the decline of labor unions has taken place.

On the other hand, one of the most devastating effects of the poor economic performance has been the increase of international migration, in this case, from Mexico towards the United States. Over the last decades, the exodus of Mexican workers has been accentuated by the lack of work opportunities. According to the CONAPO, in the period 1960–2000 the number of migrants augmented approximately 13 times. For instance, in the decade of 1960 the number of migrants leaving the country annually towards the United States was approximately between 26,000 and 29,000; this figure rose to 300,000 in the 1990s and to 400,000 in the early 2000s (CONAPO, 2014). Moreover, by 2007, the annual average number of Mexicans leaving their country looking for a job was around 500,000 (Farina, Interview, 2007; Ibarra, Interview, 2007). In other words, during the period 2000–2010, around 1,700 individuals leaving the country every day for better opportunities because of the lack of job opportunities and poor labor conditions. Nevertheless, recently the Mexican migration to the United States has reduced drastically, more clearly since 2009. Mexico has become a transit country for migrants coming from Central America heading to the United States.

The boom of Mexico's migration has been so remarkable that currently the remittances sent by migrants in the United States are among Mexico's main sources of income, only exceeded by oil revenues. According to the World Bank (2007), Mexico ranked third (after India and China) in a list of top remittance—recipient countries, with high revenues in this regard. In 2007 alone, these represented US$ 25 billion in total. Indeed, this figure has been steadily climbing in recent years. For instance, in 2002 the remittances sent from Mexican workers in the United States to their families in Mexico accounted for US$ 9.8 billion; however, by 2004 it had risen to 16.6 billion and to 20 billion US dollars in 2005 (Banco de Mexico, 2007).

Unemployment

Unemployment in Mexico during the period 1986–2001 remained relatively low. However, between 1995 and 1996 it expanded because of the peso crisis. In 1987, unemployment was 4%, and during 1988–1993 around 3%. In 1996, it went up over 6%. It then began to descend over the further 4 years period; it stood at 4% in 1997, and around 2% in 2000. Throughout the 2000s it saw a slight rise; in 2007 it was 3.4%. According to the cyclical approach, as unemployment increases, unionization tends to decrease and vice versa.

The analysis of data suggests that unemployment has been relatively low, although there have been some fluctuations, during the period 1980–2010. This may be attributable to various factors. First, a crucial aspect to consider is that Mexico does not have any program of unemployment compensation, which is another obvious reason for its low unemployment rate. Few people can afford the time it might take to look for the most desirable job (Martin, 2000: 8). Workers cannot be unemployed, because of the lack of unemployment insurance schemes. Second, the methodology used to measure unemployment rates needs to provide a more exact assessment of the labor situation. For instance, household surveys performed by INEGI take into account the term *occupation*, instead of *employment*. In this sense, every person who is *occupied* is not regarded as unemployed. Many people do not have wage-earning jobs, but they are occupied performing any activities, even those which are not necessarily receiving remunerations. Then, in the outcomes of the survey and accordingly in official statistics, these people are not registered or considered as unemployed. This significantly reduces the unemployment rates.

The characteristics of employment in Mexico have been shaped by economic activity. All over the last two decades, the economy has not generated as many jobs as required for the emerging labor force, which annually increases around 1.2 million. In the period 2000–2006 the number of formal jobs created represented around 500,000; in other words: there was a deficit of more than 5 million jobs in this period. This has triggered informal employment, crime (mainly drug trafficking) and migration, which have increased in the last years. In addition, Mexico's domestic industrial sector has reduced and recently the economy depends, to a great extent, on incomes from two main sectors: first, natural resources, especially, petroleum, and second, the remittances sent by Mexican migrants in the United States. In this manner, government strategy to create jobs has proved to be unsuccessful. Employment decline has led to the *flexibilization* of labor markets. In this regard, it has been claimed that a rigid framework on labor legislation (wide welfare state, social security, fringe benefits, and so forth) has prevented jobs generation in Mexico, and that this has stimulated the emergence of jobs in the informal sector. Indeed, some scholars point out the nature of these jobs, defined as 'contingent' jobs, considering the precarious conditions and benefits they comprise (Mishel & Allegreto, 2005).

The Structural Factors

This section analyzes the structural factors in Mexico. These factors comprise the main characteristics of the economically active population in Mexico and the distribution of employment by industry, services, and agriculture. The number of jobs in the informal sector is also included in this category. As already mentioned, the composition of the employed labor force is crucial for labor union organization. It has been claimed that while workers are more likely to be unionized in the industrial sector, apparently it is more difficult in the services sector. Accordingly, one of the most frequent arguments used to explain union density decline is the reduction of the industrial sector within the overall employment. However, this was not exactly the case in Mexico, as data shown here suggest.

Employment Composition

The analysis of other labor indicators, provided by INEGI, reflects the magnitude of the precarious situation of workers in Mexico. Rather than focusing on unemployment rates, it becomes necessary to identify the formal waged workers and the informal employment. For instance, in 2006 around 40% of the working population lacked formal jobs.

In Mexico, a large share of the labor force (Economically Active Population, EAP) are informal workers; that is, people who lack social security and fringe benefits; many of them are street vendors, without regular earnings, and as a consequence without any possibility to join labor unions. With respect to the workforce covered by social security benefits, the statistics also show an adverse landscape. Around 62% of the Occupied Population or 63% of the Economically Active Population in Mexico lacks various benefits and provisions derived from the social security system,

Table 6.7 Labor market statistics in Mexico, 2006 Numbers in 000s

Concept	*Reference*	*Percentage*	*Total*
Population		100	104,748
Economically Active Population (EAP)	% of population	41.6	43,584
OP (Occupied Population)	% of EAP	96.8	42,197
Unemployed/unoccupied	% of EAP	3.1	1,377
Formal waged workers	% of EAP	58.2	25,377
Informal workers	% of EAP	38.6	16, 819
Workers earning less than 1 minimum wage ($ 4.5 US dollars) per day	% of OP	13.0	5,648
Workers earning between 1 and 3 minimum wages per day		41.8	18,234
Primary sector workers (agriculture, cattle farming)	% of OP	14.3	6,033
Secondary sector workers (industry)	% of OP	25.6	10,803
Third sector workers (services)	% of OP	59.4	25,051
Workers under social security system (IMSS and ISSSTE)	% of EAP	37.1	16,175
IMSS (Permanent workers) (a)	% of EAP	31.6	13,751
ISSSTE (b)	% of EAP	5.6	2,424
Unionized workers (c) Scheme B1	% EAP	11.4	4,950
Unionized workers (d) Scheme B2	% of waged workers	19.5	4,950

Sources Calculated from ENOE 2006/II, INEGI – STPS; (a) Calderón, 2007. (b) ISSSTE, 2007. (c) STPS, 2006b. (d) STPS, 2006a; ISSSTE, 2007

such as health care and retirement pensions. Similarly, the analysis of data about permanent and temporary members in both IMSS and ISSSTE confirms the stagnation in the creation of formal jobs, although more clearly in the public sector. This pattern in the creation of jobs suggests a critical situation for union organization since the majority of union membership in Mexico is located within the public sector (Table 6.7).

Informal Employment

As mentioned above, the creation of formal jobs (measured by the number of jobs affiliated to the IMSS and ISSTE) has stagnated in the last few decades. The difficulties faced by workers in Mexico have seriously worsened since they cannot find a job within the formal economy. This situation has led many individuals to alternative options such as self-employment (workers who are in the streets offering services such as plumbing, brickwork, gardening, among others), informal employment (street vendors in small-scale commerce) or, as extreme options, other illegal activities (from stealing to drug trafficking). The situation just mentioned has taken place, on a greater extent, in Mexico, wherein the number of workers in the informal economy has significantly increased in recent years. Informal employment in the country has climbed in the neoliberal period; although there is not reliable data from past decades, around 60% of the labor force (EAP) is in the informal sector.

The proliferation of informal employment is one of the most significant repercussions of neoliberalism in Latin America, and Mexico is not the exception. Neoliberalism has encouraged an increasingly informal sector over the last decades. This has been one of the most striking effects of neoliberalism on labor in Mexico and Latin America: the creation of labor markets mainly characterized by precarious employment. Similarly, neoliberal reforms have accelerated the emergence of low paid jobs in the services sector. In the case of Mexico, between 1990 and 2010, informal jobs climbed from 40 to 60% of the employed labor force (OIT, 2008, 2010). Within the services and industrial sectors, unionization is hindered by employers using 'ghost unions' with 'labor contracts of protection' (see Chapter 4). Thus, workers in the private sector, especially in services, have false labor contracts. As mentioned in Chapter 5, these labor contracts are directly negotiated between the firms and official labor unions (advised by labor lawyers), but without the consent and approval of workers, whom in most cases ignore their union affiliation.

It is claimed that the process of *informalization* of labor markets has been crucial for the reduction of labor union membership. The latter may explain the fact that while there has been a rapid increase of the employed labor force in the last two or three decades, the union membership has not showed the same pattern of growth, which has resulted in the decline of union density rates. As the employed labor force has expanded, union affiliation has lagged behind. This is because potential union members are not found in the informal sector. Data provided by official institutions confirms the latter argument; for instance, in 1984, the labor force or EAP was around 22.3 million and union membership approximately 3.7 million; however by 2006 labor force had doubled to 44.7 million, but union membership had slightly advanced to 4.3 million.

Conclusions

This chapter has examined some economic and employment indicators to identify the landscape faced by workers in the last decades. Between the mid-1980s and 2010, the economic policies encouraged by the state in Mexico have failed to generate economic development. A variety of economic and labor indicators reveals the lack of opportunities for the revitalization of organized labor. The collapse of the ISI model in the 1970s and early 1980s led the state to modify its main strategies of political economy. This change comprised a group of neoliberal policies focused on stabilization programs, such as the containment of inflation and the reduction of foreign debt, as well as the correction of imbalances in the public current account. The conversion from a closed economy to an open economy oriented on foreign markets has two sides in Mexico. On the one hand, Mexico inserted itself very quickly into the international markets as an important exporter, mainly to the United States. The bulk of exports became more diversified and relied less on the oil industry and more on the expansion of the manufacturing sector. On the other hand, economic crises were recurrent in the period 1982–2000. For instance, Mexico experienced economic difficulties in 1982, 1985, and 1994–1995, mainly due to external factors but also to the fragility of the Mexican economy (large deficit in the current count, an increasing foreign debt and a low collection of taxes, among others).

Certainly, these underlying failures affected workers. The panorama just described has generated the corrosion of labor conditions and the weakening of labor union organizations. Since the early 1980s, the creation of formal employment has decelerated, considering official statistics such as the number of workers affiliated to the social security institutions in both the private and public sectors (IMSS and ISSSTE) but also the number of waged or salaried workers in the EAP.

These conditions have triggered diverse deleterious outcomes. First, an increase of informal employment which accounts for 60% of the economically active population, making it more difficult for unions to attract new members, as potential union membership is located within the formal sector. Second, a migration of Mexican workers towards the United States accelerated since the 1990s but this trend has reduced since 2009. Furthermore, the majority of the unemployed have invaded the streets to work in the small-scale informal commerce as 'street vendors', but some others go into criminal activities. In sum, in the last decades, workers have not only lacked decent jobs in labor markets, but also their possibilities to have access to reasonable housing, social security and pensions are limited. Mexico has some of the richest people in the world, whereas the levels of inequality of income distribution has increased over the last decades. It is essential to consider the political system featured by authoritarian practices in Mexico. In this way, not only the outcomes generated by neoliberal policies on labor markets must be analyzed, but also the form in which these policies were implemented; and the overall political context with certain features that rendered pernicious the effects of neoliberalism in Mexico.

Notes

1. In Mexican government, the executive branch of government oversees and manages a number of semi-autonomous agencies known as "parastatal" agencies. Parastatal agencies, which are often created to manage national resources or services considered either a part of the national patrimony (i.e., subsoil mineral or energy resources) or essential to the collective well-being of the nation (i.e., transportation services, utilities provision, telecommunications services, food distribution services, farming inputs provision, banking services, airports and seaports management, etc.) are the product of revolutionary nationalism and central planning ideas that jealously sought to keep control of critical elements of Mexico's economy and essential social services in the hands of Mexican authorities and away from foreign investors and corporations (Huck Jr., 2017: 78).
2. United States policies under President Richard Nixon drastically affected Mexico; they included a 10% surcharge on all imports and the elimination of the gold standard for the dollar. Because the peso had always been pegged to the dollar, the peso became unstable. Inflation did more damage. By 1973 the economy was in severe straits (Foster, 2004: 208).
3. Many workers not only lost their houses and jobs but also their financial debts increased more than double as a result of the peso devaluation. Social movements emerged, such as *el Barzon* to defend the bank debtors. This popular organization was created after the financial collapse of 1995; its main purpose was to defend the working class and families before their increasing debts with the banks; eventually it became a regional political party and obtained some local political positions in the legislative branch.

Bibliography

Aspe, P. (1993). *Economic transformation: The Mexican way*. Cambridge, MA: MIT Press.

Bayon, M. C. (2003). Trabajando en la frontera: mujeres, mercado de trabajo y globalización. In *Las expresiones locales de la globalización: México y España* (pp. 49–66). Mexico: Grupo Editorial Miguel Angel Porrúa.

de Mexico, Banco. (2007). *Las remesas familiares en Mexico*. Mexico: Banco de Mexico.

Becerril, A. (1996, December 31). Cayó 70% el poder adquisitivo durante 1996. *La Jornada*.

Bouzas, A. (2003). *Reforma Laboral; analisis critico del proyecto Abascal de reforma a la Ley Federal de Trabajo*. Mexico: UNAM.

Calderón, F. (2007). *Primer informe de gobierno*. Mexico: Presidencia de la Republica. Available on line www.presidencia.gob.mx, consulted in November 2008.

Cameron, M., & Aggarwal, V. (1996). Mexican meltdown: States, markets and post-NAFTA financial turmoil. *Third World Quaterly, 17*(5), 975–987.

Caulfield, N. (2004). Labor relations in Mexico: Historical legacies and some recent trends. *Labor History, 45*(4), 445–467.

Chavez, M. F., & Huerta, M. (2003). Tres modelos de política económica en Mexico durante los últimos sesenta años. *Análisis Económico, XVIII, 37,* 55–80.

CIA. (2014). *The world fact book*. Available on line https://www.cia.gov/, consulted in November 2014.

Clifton, J. (1999). Sindicatos y politica en Mexico: el caso de la privatizacion de Telmex. *Politica y Gobierno, VI, 2,* 407–440.

Collier, R. B. (1992). *The contradictory alliance: State-labor relations and regime change in Mexico*. Berkeley: International and Area Studies, University of California.

CONAPO. (2014). *Consejo Nacional de Poblacion*. http://www.conapo.gob.mx/, consulted in May 2014.

Cornelius, W. A. (1989). The political economy of Mexico under De la Madrid: Austerity, routinized crisis, and nascent recovery. *Mexican Studies/Estudios Mexicanos, 1*(1), 83–124.

Curzio, L. (2004). La integración en Norteamérica y la experiencia de Europa. In J. Roy & A. Chanona (Eds.), *La Unión Europea y el TLCAN*. México: UNAM.

Dussel, P. E. (2003). Industrial policy, regional trends, and structural change in Mexico's manufacturing sector. In K. Middlebrook & E. Zepeda (Eds.), *Confronting development: assessing Mexico's economic and social policy challenges* (pp. 241–274). Stanford University Press.

Dussel, P. E. (2006). The Mexican economy since NAFTA. In D. Plehwe (Ed.), *Neoliberal hegemony: A global critique*. New York: Routledge.

Edmonds-Poli, E., & Shirk, D. A. (2009). *Contemporary Mexican politics*. Lanham: Rowman and Littlefield.

Fairris, D. (2005). *What do unions do in Mexico* (Working Paper). Riverside: University of California.

Foster, L. V. (2004). *A brief history of Mexico*. New York: Checkmark.

Fox, V. (2006). *Sexto informe de gobierno*. Mexico: Presidencia de la republica. Available on line www.presidencia.gob.mx, consulted in February, 2007.

Gallagher, K. P., & Zarsky, L. (2007). *The enclave economy: Foreign investment and sustainable development in Mexico's Silicon Valley*. Mit Press.

Gil-Alana, L., & Barros, C. (2009). A historical perspective of inflation in Latin America. A new approach based on fractional integration with a structural break. *International Economic Journal, Korean International Economic Association, 23*(2), 259–279.

González, A. (1998, November 22). Los salarios, en el menor nivel de 38 anos, revelan cifras oficiales. *La Jornada*.

González, F. E. (2008). *Dual transitions from authoritarian rule: institutionalized regimes in Chile and Mexico, 1970–2000*. Baltimore: Johns Hopkins University Press.

Graubart, J. (2009). The legalization of transnational political opportunity structures: Mobilization of NAFTA's labor citizen petitions for domestic political gain. In *Contentious politics in North America* (pp. 177–194). London: Palgrave Macmillan.

Greene, K. (2007). *Why dominant parties lose: Mexico's democratization in comparative perspective*. Cambridge, UK: Cambridge University Press.

Harvey, D. (2005). *A brief history of neoliberalism*. Oxford: Oxford University Press.

Heckman, J. (2000). *Job security index: Expected discounted cost of dismissing a worker* (Working Paper 430). Inter-American Development Bank.

Hodges, D. C., & Gandy, R. (2002). *Mexico, the end of the Revolution*. Westport, CT: Praeger.

Hufbauer, G. C., & Schott, J. J. (2005). *NAFTA revisited: Achievements and challenges*. Washington, DC: Institute for International Economics.

INEGI. (2007). *Instituto Nacional de Estadistica, Geografia e Informatica.*: Available on line http://www.inegi.gob.mx, consulted in May 2007.

INEGI. (2008). *Instituto Nacional de Estadistica, Geografia e Informatica*. Available on line http://dgcnesyp.inegi.gob.mx/cgi-win/bdieintsi.exe/NIV J150008#ARBOL, consulted in March 2008.

ISSSTE. (2007). *Anuario Estadístico*. Instituto de Seguridad y Servicios Sociales de los Trabajadores del Estado. Available on line http://www.issste.gob.mx/, consulted in May 2007.

Kaplan, D. (2008). *Enforceability of labor law: Evidence from a labor court in Mexico* (Policy Research Working Paper 4483). Washington, DC: The World Bank.

Kikeri, S. (1995). *Privatization and labor: What happens to workers when governments divest. The World Bank* (Technical Paper no. 396).

Leiva, F. I. (2008). *Latin American neostructuralism: The contradictions of post -neoliberal development*. Minneapolis: University of Minnesota Press.

Levitsky, S. (2003). *Transforming labor-based parties in Latin America: Argentine Peronism in comparative perspective*. New York: Cambridge University Press.

Levy, D., & Bruhn, K. (2007). *Mexico: The struggle for democratic development*. Berkeley: University of California Press.

Lustig, N. (1998). *The remaking of an economy*. Washington, DC: Brookings Institution Press.

Lustig, N. (2001). Life is not easy: Mexico's quest for stability and growth. *Journal of Economic Perspectives, 15*(1), 85–106.

MacLeod, D. (2005). Privatization and the limits of state autonomy in Mexico. Rethinking the orthodox paradox. *Latin American Perspectives, 32*(4), 36–64.

Martín, R. (2000). Local labor markets: Their nature, performance and regulation. In G. Clark (Ed.), *The Oxford Handbook of economic geography*. Oxford University Press.

Middlebrook, K. (1989). The sounds of silence: Organized labor's response to economic crisis in Mexico. *Journal of Latin American Studies, 21*(2), 195–220.

Minns, J. (2006). *The politics of developmentalism: The midas states of Mexico, South Korea and Taiwan*. Basingstoke: Palgrave.

Mishel, L., & Allegreto, J. (2005). *The state of working America 2004-05*. Washington, DC: Economic Policy Institute, Cornell University Press.

Moreno-Brid, J. C., & Ros, J. (2009). *Development and growth in the Mexican economy: A historical perspective*. London: Oxford University Press.

Morton, A. D. (2003). Structural change and neoliberalism in Mexico. *Third World Quaterly, 24*(4), 631–653.

O'Toole, G. (2007). *Politics: Latin America*. Harlow, UK: Pearson Longman.

OIT. (2008). *Panorama Laboral 2007. America Latina y El Caribe*. Lima, Peru: OIT.

OIT. (2010). *Panorama Laboral 2009. America Latina y El Caribe*. Lima, Peru: OIT.

Polaski, S. (2004). NAFTA's promise and reality: Lessons from Mexico for the hemishphere. In Audley (Ed.), J. *NAFTA's promise and reality: Lessons from Mexico for the Hemishphere* (pp. 11–37). Washington, DC: Carnegie Endowment for International Peace.

Quintero, C. (1997). *Reestructuración sindical en las maquiladoras mexicanas*. Mexico: COLEF.

Ramirez de la O, R. (2002). Mexico: NAFTA and the Prospects for North American Integration. *C.D. Howe Institute Commentary* (172): 1–25.

Robinson, W. I. (2004). Global crisis and Latin America. *Bulletin of Latin American Research, 23*(2), 135–153.

Saad-Filho, A. (2005). *Neoliberalism: A critical reader.* London: Pluto press.

Salas, C. (2006). Between unemployment and insecurity in Mexico. Nafta enters its second decade. *Revisiting Nafta. Still not working for North America's workers (173)* (Briefing paper) (pp. 33–52). Washington, DC: Economic Policy Institute.

Salinas, C. (2004). Diez años de TLCAN y el fracaso de Cancún. *Foreign Affairs en Español, 1,* 2–16.

Schlefer, J. (2008). *Palace politics: How the ruling party brought crisis to Mexico.* University of Texas Press.

Scott, R. (2006). Rising trade deficits lead to significant job displacement and declining job quality for the United States. *Revisiting Nafta. Still not working for North America's workers* (Briefing paper 173) (pp. 3–32). Washington, DC: Economic Policy Institute.

Skidmore, T. E., & Smith, P. H. (2005). *Modern Latin America.* New York and Oxford: Oxford University Press.

Stallings, B., & Peres, W. (2000). *Growth, employment and equity. The impact of the economic reforms in Latin American and Caribbean.* Economic Commission for Latin American and Caribbean. Washington, DC: Brookings Institution Press.

Stanford, J. (2003). The North American free trade agreement: Context, structure and performance. In J. Michie (Ed.), *The handbook of globalization* (pp. 261–282). Cheltenham: Edward Elgar Publishing.

Statistics Canada. (2014). *Fact sheet on unionisation.* Perspectives on labor and incomes.

Steger, M. B., & Roy, R. K. (2010). *Neoliberalism: A very short introduction.* Oxford University Press.

STPS. (2006a). *Direccion General de Registro de Asociaciones (DGRA).* Secretaria del Trabajo y Prevision Social. Available on line www.stps.gob.mx, consulted in May 2006.

STPS. (2006b). *Trabajadores Involucrados en las Revisiones Salariales y Contractuales en la Jurisdicción Local por Entidad Federativa, 2006*, table IV.8.11. Secretaria del Trabajo y Prevision Social. Available on line www.stps.gob.mx, consulted in June 2006.

Thomas, K. (1995). *Globalization and third world trade unions: The challenge of rapid economic change.* London: Zed Books.

United Nations Conference on Trade and Development (UNCTAD). (2012). *Handbook of statistics, 2012*. United Nations.

U.S. Census Bureau. (2014). Available on line https://www.census.gov/, consulted in June 2014.

U.S. DOL. (2008). *A chartbook of international labor comparisons: The Americas, Asia-Pacific, Europe*. Washington, DC: U.S. Department of Labor.

Watts, J. (2003). *Mexico-US migration and labor unions: Obstacles to building cross border solidarity* (Working Paper 79). University of California - San Diego.

Weiss, J. (1996). Economic policy reform in Mexico: The liberalism experiment. In R. Aitken, et al. (Eds.), *Dismantling the Mexican state*. Macmillan: Basingstoke.

Williams, M. (2001). Learning the limits of power: Privatization and state-labor interactions in Mexico. *Latin American Politics and Society, 43*(4), 91–126.

World Bank. (2007). *Migration and development brief 3*. Washington, DC: Development Prospects Group, Migration and Remittances Team, World Bank.

Zarsky, L., & Gallagher, K. P. (2004). *NAFTA, foreign direct investment, and sustainable industrial development in Mexico*. Washington, DC: Americas Program Policy Brief.

Interviews

Bouzas, A. (2007, September). *Labor lawyer and academic scholar*. UNAM, Mexico City.

Farina, F. (2007, October). *Union advisor (SME and INEGI union)*. Mexico City.

Ibarra, G. (2007, October). *Academic scholar*. Universidad Autonoma de Sinaloa.

CHAPTER 7

Union Density Trends in Mexico

Union Density in Mexico: A General Assessment

Studies focused on union density in Mexico present notable differences, depending on the sources and schemes applied for their estimation. For instance, Scheme A relies exclusively on the ENIGH survey and Scheme B uses a combination of different official sources (STPS, INEGI, and ISSSTE). Despite the diversity of sources, the overall union membership is very similar, although with some differences. Even though most of the studies calculate union density from union membership and EAP, some of the scholars using Schemes A and B take only the formal waged workers for that purpose. Therefore, two sub-categories in both schemes are identified. On the one hand, while scheme A1 utilizes union membership and the Economically Active Population (EAP) to estimate union density, scheme A2 considers unionized workers and the waged workers in the formal sector. Similarly, scheme B1 considers overall union membership and EAP to estimate union density, but scheme B2 takes for this purpose unionized workers and the formal waged workers (Tables 7.1, 7.2, 7.3 and 7.4).

Aguilar (2005), using scheme B1, claims that according to official information provided by the Department of Labor (STPS), there were 4.7 million unionized workers in Mexico in 2000. This figure represented 10.8% out of the labor force (EAP); union members were affiliated with

R. Zepeda, *The Decline of Labor Unions in Mexico during the Neoliberal Period*, Governance, Development, and Social Inclusion in Latin America, https://doi.org/10.1007/978-3-030-65710-9_7

Table 7.1 Scheme A1 to calculate union density in Mexico

Union membership (a) Economically Active Population, EAP (b)	=	Union density (c)

(a) Expanded data from ENIGH, INEGI
(b) Expanded data from ENIGH, INEGI
(c) It is the percentage obtained from union membership and EAP: a/b = c

Table 7.2 Scheme B1 to calculate union density in Mexico

Union membership (a) Economically Active Population, EAP (b)	=	Union density (c)

(a) Data from STPS (unionized workers in the federal private sector and workers covered by collective agreements in the local private sector). Data from ISSSTE (workers in the public sector covered by social security provision)
(b) Data from INEGI (ENOE)
(c) It is the percentage obtained from union membership and EAP: a/b = c

Table 7.3 Scheme A2 to calculate union density in Mexico

Total union membership (a) Formal waged workers (b)	=	Union density (c)

(a) Expanded data from ENIGH, INEGI
(b) Expanded data from ENIGH, INEGI
(c) It is the percentage obtained from union membership and formal waged workers: a/b = c

Table 7.4 Scheme B2 to calculate union density in Mexico

Union membership (a) Formal waged workers (b)	=	Union density (c)

(a) Data from STPS (unionized workers in the federal private sector and workers covered by collective agreements in the local private sector). Data from ISSSTE (workers in the public sector covered by social security provision)
(b) Data from INEGI (ENOE)
(c) It is the percentage obtained from union membership and formal waged workers: a/b = c

2,155 organizations, which are 500 more labor organizations than those registered in 1986. Fairris and Levine (2004) sustain that union density was reduced by one third in Mexico during the period 1984–2000.

Regarding the waged labor force in the formal sector, these scholars noted that union density declined from 30% in 1984 to 20% in 2000 (Scheme A2). They affirm that the deepest decline occurred during 1984–1994, with a decrease of 9 percentage points, remaining at 21%. Thereafter, this rate would keep stable with a fluctuation between 22 and 20%. Furthermore, union density in the country, in relation to the formal waged labor force, has declined in the extensive spectrum of industries and occupations (Fairris & Levine, 2004: 11–13).

Relying on the ENIGH survey, Panagides and Patrinos (1994) found that the total union density in Mexico was around 30% in 1989 (using Scheme A2), an estimation that coincides with other studies based on the same scheme (for instance, Fairris & Levine, 2004). According to this study, the probability of unionization in that year increases until secondary schooling is completed, whereupon further education has no additional impact on the probabilities of union membership. In terms of unionization by region, labor in the north is 4.6% less likely to organize than labor elsewhere in the country (1994: 9). Similarly, the study reports that the probability of union membership is lower for men than for women, as opposed to many studies in developed nations, where women are found to be significantly less likely to be union members than are men.

Herrera and Melgoza (2003), using Scheme A1, indicate that union membership in Mexico was almost 10% of the total labor force (EAP) in 2000. An analysis comparing union density trends during the period 1992–2000 performed by these researchers indicates that the percentage of unionized workers diminished from 13.6% in 1992 to 9.8% in 2000. With respect to union membership in Mexico, these authors highlight the fact that over the 1990s, labor unions weakened significantly; they observe that both in absolute and relative terms (union density), the space occupied by unions in 2000 was less relevant than in 1992.

Zapata (2005) calculated union representation in the labor force, using Scheme B2, but including additional sources and statistics. He affirms that union membership in Mexico was about 5.4 million, which consisted of a combination of unionized workers in local private sectors (1.03 million), in federal private sectors (2.24 million) and in the public sectors (2.20 million). However, the union density rate he obtained was as high as 56.3%; which differed from the findings of Aguilar (2005) and those of Herrera and Melgoza (2003), who depend on the Economically Active Population (43.8 million) for their estimations, which produced union density rates ranging from 9 to 11%.

In contrast, data prepared by the Commission for Labor Cooperation (2003), reveal that union representation in Mexico passed from 23% in 1985 to 15.6% in 2001. As indicated by the *OECD Employment Outlook* (2004b: 145), Mexico's unionization rate was as high as 43% in 1990 but declining to 18% by 2000. These figures include union density rates in 30 OECD countries, during the period 1970–2000. However, the sources that allowed such estimations of union density in Mexico are not sufficiently detailed, thus it cannot be identified whether it is scheme A or B, according to the categorization used here. The OECD (2009) published more recent statistics on unionization, in which Mexico's union density declined from 43 to 18% in 2000 but has remained stable in the 2000s.

According to *The World Labor Report* (ILO, 1998), unionization rate in Mexico was at 42.8% in 1991. This report presented union density figures in a vast majority of countries throughout the world. However, in the case of Mexico, it only provides data for one year, which does not allow for making estimations of union density variations through different years in the country. As this rate of union representation is very similar to the one provided by the OECD, it is considered here that the scheme is practically the same.

Cardoso and Gindin (2009) compared the fluctuations of union density in Latin America in recent decades. Unionization rates in Mexico, Brazil and Argentina were measured. In the case of Mexico, a decline of union density during the period 1992–2002 (from 13.6 to 10%) but a slight increase of union membership was detected (from 4.1 to 4.2 million). Furthermore, they generated estimations of union density, drawing on the ENIGH survey 2006 (Scheme A2) to calculate unionization rates but considering the waged workers (a share of the EAP) to obtain the unionization rate. In this manner, union density was 16.5% in 2006. In this year, in terms of disaggregated union density, the most unionized sectors were in the mining sector (48%), in electricity, water and gas (51.1%) and in the education sector (66.6%). The less unionized sectors were: wholesale trade (5.6%), construction (4.3%), professional, scientific and technical services (3.2%), retail trade (2.8%), real estate market services (2.5%) and agriculture and fishing with 1.4% (see Cardoso & Gindin, 2009: 82, Table 7).

The Factors Accounting for Union Density Decline

As mentioned in Chapter 2, the factors accounting for union density decline may be classified as cyclical, structural and political-institutional factors. According to various scholars, labor lawyers and official bodies, there are a variety of factors determining the trajectory of union density in Mexico over the last few decades. The relative loss of labor union membership has been related to economic, structural, and political factors, taking place more clearly since the 1980s.

De la Garza (2003) identifies neoliberal policies as one of the factors linked to union density decline. For instance, he mentions that since 1982 the country has undergone crucial transformations that have affected workers and their organizations. For instance, he argues that labor-related policies executed over the neoliberal period have had damaging effects on labor unions and workers in Mexico because these policies have focused on controlling inflation rates; for this purpose a considerable number of collective labor agreements have become more flexible. On the other hand, De la Garza considers that structural factors also explain the decline of unionization in Mexico. He contends that the nucleus of labor unionism of social bases in the twentieth century (that is, the old working class of heavy industries over the stabilizing development period) has diminished substantially and has almost been substituted by a new working class, which is extremely mobile in terms of employment among firms and without identity with unions. He also notes that productive restructuring has affected labor unions, specifically the nucleus of the working class in the services, trade and exporting industrial sectors (De la Garza, 2003: 350).

Regarding the factors accounting for union density decline in Mexico, Herrera and Melgoza (2003) identify a group of varied factors explaining the decline of union density. They argue that a peculiar combination of outdated structure organizations, precariousness of labor, political transition, reorientation of the productive system and a lack of alternatives, are key factors in explaining union density variations, as opposed to post-modern hypothesis (end of work, leisure preference, and lack of interest on unions). They emphasize the relevance of structural and cyclical factors. They observe that the most significant challenge for the Mexican unions is the process of precariousness of labor, with an increasing share of unprotected and unorganized workers, which is increasingly omnipresent in the country. They note that the strong economic crisis happened in the mid-nineties had negative impacts on employment. While employment had recovered by the second half of the nineties, the union affiliation did not recover to the same level (2003). As can be noted, they identify political-institutional and structural factors, as well as democratization and neoliberal policies.

On the other hand, Fairris and Levine (2004: 10) contend that union density decline in Mexico is attributable to a greater extent to the changing structural—institutional context, within which labor unions organize new workers and retain existing members. These changes include, for instance, the modification of governmental policies and the growing employer opposition to labor unions. They argue, as opposed to De la Garza (2003), that only a small proportion of the decline is explained by changes in industry, occupations, and demographic characteristics. In sum, these authors consider that both structural and political-institutional factors are more relevant in the deterioration of labor unionism; however, there is more emphasis in the political-institutional factors.

Regarding the political-institutional factors mentioned in previous chapters in the case of Mexico, one of the factors mentioned was the exclusion clauses in collective contracts. Through this mechanism, workers were forced to affiliate to the union to obtain employment, otherwise they could be fired. Marshall (2006) identified a decline of union density in Mexico in the period 1984–2000, despite the existence of the exclusion clauses, one of the instruments that permit labor unions to organize workers in a compulsory way. She questions: "why the existence of a form of closed shop in Mexico was not effective in countering the impact of those factors that fostered the decline in union membership?"

> Closed-shop clauses often led analysts of Mexican unionization to stress the compulsory or forced nature of union affiliation in this country, and to rightly inquire about the nature or meaning of the legally established "voluntary" union membership under these circumstances. One possible explanation of the apparent ineffectiveness of closed shop clauses could be that their inclusion in collective agreements might be less widespread than in the past; another, that even if they were incorporated, they might actually be implemented less often than in the past. (Marshall, 2006: 18)

Miron Lince (Interview, 2007) identifies two main factors accounting for union density decline in Mexico, especially neoliberal policies and the performance of labor organizations. First, it can be attributed to one external factor: the neoliberal economic policies promoting a free market-oriented model. Second, related to internal factors; the lack of effective responses of labor unions before the neoliberal agenda. Evidently, the prevailing labor unions structures are not useful to the neoliberal state; on the contrary, within a free market economy, the large business sector and transnational corporations are supported by the state. Indeed, within a neoliberal economy the goal is to reduce the power of labor unionism because this doctrine pursues the *flexibilization* of labor relations.

Comparing the variations of union density in Argentina, Brazil and Mexico, Cardoso and Gindin (2009: 34) observes that "the picture, then, is one of falling density in Mexico, and increasing density in Argentina and Brazil, with union membership among women mounting in all three countries, due mostly (but not exclusively) to structural changes in the labor market, including reduced employment in manufacturing, and increased employment in social services and commerce".

Some labor analysts in Mexico affirm that rather, certain political and institutional factors that regulate labor relations in the country have been more relevant than neoliberal policies (such as economic globalization) for the decline of union membership and the erosion of labor union influence in politics and labor realms. Many claim that the labor boards, such as the JFCA and JLCA, as well as the department of labor (STPS), obstruct the organization of independent unions and contribute to the control exerted by companies on workers; indeed, they suggest that these boards are manipulated by official unionism (Alcalde, Interview 2007; Bouzas, Interview 2007; De Buen, Interview 2007). This statement can be confirmed with the observation of official statistics, especially in terms of exports and imports since the 1980s.

Furthermore, De Buen dismisses that not only the decline of union density but also the decline of labor union influence in Mexico is not exclusively a development taking place during the last two decades of the twentieth century, but it has been a process that has been a reality since the 1930s, when corporatism was established. He affirms that workers have not had freedom to organize unions in the country since the 1930s, as the labor system emerged in this decade was designed by the state to control workers and labor unions.

Dan La Botz (2005) highlights that union density rate does not afford a good measure of real union power in Mexico since so many unions are controlled by the government or by employers. Some believe that 80% of all collective agreements in the private sector may be protection contracts. La Botz points out that the decline of real union power during the period 1984–2000 was therefore even more dramatic than the figures on labor union density would indicate.

Therefore, considering the previous considerations, it is possible to identify a variety of factors accounting for the decline of labor unions in Mexico. Although there are some disagreements, these observations coincide in the fact that the decline occurred since the 1980s and is related to structural changes in the labor markets, the political transition, features in labor-related legislation and institutions, among others. The aim of the following sections is to identify more precisely the years of union density decline in Mexico, relying on official sources and subsequently to offer my own perspectives regarding the decline of union density in Mexico.

Analysis of Union Membership in 2006

After the analysis of recent literature about the variations of union membership in Mexico and the main factors accounting for such variations, an examination of various statistics was conducted to construct original figures. Firstly, Scheme A1 was used to calculate total union density, and also by gender (men and women) in the years 1984, 1989, 1992, 1994, 1996, 1998, 2000, 2002, 2004 and 2006 with the purpose of detecting the fluctuations of union membership and union density during that period. Secondly, using the same scheme, aggregated and disaggregated union density was calculated in 2006, especially by state, industry, occupation, education, and age. Thirdly, the results of 2006 were compared with previous years to detect the fluctuations of union density by specific categories; the years are 1984, 1998 and 2006. Finally, Scheme B1 is utilized to estimate union membership by labor confederations and by sector (public and private) in 2006. The purpose here is to make use of the two schemes to generate valuable findings, although in some cases the results in every scheme may differ notably.

Union Membership (Scheme A1)

The following sections present original estimates of union membership in Mexico. An analysis of data from INEGI surveys was performed to estimate the figures in the period 1984–2006. In this case, the ENIGH survey was analyzed, which is conducted by INEGI every two years since 1992. It is important to mention that the figures on union membership and union density presented and analyzed in the following sections are estimations of the author, but they are not generated or published by the government, in this case, by the INEGI. Data presented here is not a summary of data published by INEGI, but it is the result of a statistical process, as explained in the following section.

Union Membership, Total, Male and Female, 1984–2006

Relying on the ENIGH household surveys of 1984, 1989 and every two years from 1992 to 2006, a statistical analysis was conducted to obtain statistics related to total union membership in Mexico. The outcomes reveal that, by 2006, total labor force (EAP) in the country, including the unemployed and informal sector, was of 44,709,819 whereas union membership accounted for 4,343,920. Accordingly, considering these figures, total union density in Mexico, with regard to the EAP, was at 9.7%, significantly lower than 1989, when it was 17.8% (the peak in the period), although slightly lower than 1998 when it registered 9.8%. Between 1984 and 2006, EAP increased by 100% but union membership increased by just 17%, which generated a net loss of 7 percentage points in terms of union density during this period.

According to the ENIGH surveys expanded micro-data, during the period 1984–2006, the overall union density rate in Mexico declined from 16.7 to 9.7%; then the rate has remained relatively stable. It reached the peak in 1989 (17.8%) and the lowest rate in 2006 with 9.7%. Total union membership increased over this period; for example, in 1984 union members accounted for 3.7 million; this figure rose to slightly over 4 million in 2000 and continued this trend to 4.3 million in 2006 (Table 7.5).

The largest increase of union membership occurred between 1984 and 1989. During this period, the number of union members increased from 3.7 million to 4.4 million. In the same way, union density climbed from

Table 7.5 Union membership and union density in Mexico: total, men and women. 1984, 1989, 1992, 2000, 2002, 2006 (Scheme A1) Numbers in 000s

	1984	*1989*	*1992*	*1994*	*1996*	*1998*	*2000*	*2002*	*2004*	*2006*
Total										
EAP	22,312	25,222	29,583	32,827	35,261	37,891	39,299	41,505	41,045	44,709
Union members	3,725	4,480	4,123	3,752	3,559	3,732	4,011	4,124	4,705	4,343
Union density (%)	16.7	17.8	13.9	11.4	10.1	9.8	10.2	9.9	11.5	9.7
Men										
EAP	16,353	18,136	20,825	22,193	22,891	24,427	25,557	26,116	25,996	27,033
Union members	2,566	3,187	2,766	2,253	2,100	2,268	2,328	2,426	2,794	2,494
Union density (%)	15.7	17.6	13.3	10.2	9.2	9.3	9.1	9.3	10.7	9.2
Women										
EAP	5,958	7,086	8,758	10,634	12,370	13,463	13,742	15,388	15,049	17,676
Union members	1,158	1,293	1,357	1,498	1,459	1,464	1,682	1,698	1,910	1,849
Union density (%)	19.4	18.2	15.5	14.1	11.8	10.9	12.2	11.0	12.7	10.5

EAP = Economically active population

Sources Author and Raúl Perusquia with expanded estimations of ENIGH micro-data

16.7 to 17.8% in this period. Therefore, there was not a decline of union density in most of the 1980s, at least between 1984 and 1989, when compatible data can be compared, according to data obtained from the same survey. In contrast, the most significant decline occurred between 1989 and 1996, from 4.4 million to 3.5 million of union membership in the country. This period was of constant decline, as can be noted in the figures (From 4.4 million in 1989 to 4.1 million in 1992 then to 3.7 million in 1992 and to 3.7 million in 1994). Union density also experienced the most drastic decline between 1989 and 1996, from 17.8 to 10.1%. As mentioned before, the fluctuations of union density between 1996 and 2006 have remained around 10% in the period, in 1996 it was 10.1% and in 2006 9.7%, which, if rounded, is 10% (Table 7.5).

Union density was higher in women than in men by 2006. The unionization rate among female workers was 10.5%, whereas that of men was 9.2%. Indeed, these figures confirm the levels of previous years, in which union density among women was higher than among men in all the years of the survey. However, in terms of union membership, it has been higher in male than female workers, but this difference has been shortened in the period analyzed here. For instance, in 1984, union membership in women was 1.1 million but it spiked to 1.8 million by 2006. In contrast, the number of male union members declined from 2.5 million in 1984 to 2.4 million in 2006. Similarly, regarding the employed labor force, more men were employed than women. In 1984, the difference was more significant, with male workers accounting for 16.3 million, whereas female workers accounted for 5.9 million. In 2006, however, the number of employed male workers was 27 million compared to 17.6 union members among female workers (Table 7.5).

In terms of unionization by gender, even though union membership is higher in male workers, women became unionized more rapidly than men over the period. In 1984 female union members were 1.1 million, but the number picked up to 1.7 in 2000 and reached almost 2 million in 2006. Conversely, male workers registered lower increase in unionization: in 1984 male union members were 2.2 million; this figure enlarged to 2.7 in 1992 but eroded to 2.3 in 2000; then it recovered in 2006 with almost 2.5 million members. In sum, while union membership levels among female workers have increased significantly over the period 1992–2006, they have declined in the case of male workers. In total, union membership among women increased by 57% during the period 1992–2006, while the union representation among men fell by approximately 9% in that period (Table 7.5).

Union Membership by Industry, Occupation, State, Age, and Education, 2006

The highest rates of union density by industries and sectors in 2006 according to ENIGH classifications and to the original estimations were in the following categories: services in education (56%), electricity, water and gas transmission (47%), mining (40%), health services and social work (37%), government and international bodies-related activities (25%) and information in mass media (24%). On the other hand, with lower unionization rates the next sectors were: manufacturing (14%), transportation, mail and warehousing (10%), financial services and insurance (9%), services in recreation, cultural, sports and other services (6.2%), services of business support and waste materials management and related services (4.5%), services of temporary accommodation and beverage and food preparation (4%), whole and retail commerce (2.3%) and construction (1.8%). Unionization rates have declined in most industrial sectors since 1984; the most striking decline can be observed in transportation, communication, mail, and warehousing sector (Table 7.6).

In terms of union membership by industry in 2006, the sectors with more union members were: services in education (1,264,584), manufacturing (1,108,702), governmental and international bodies related activities (480,139), health services and social work (475,466) which together represented around 75% of total union membership in the sector (Table 7.6).

Among occupational groups, according to the ENIGH categories, the highest rates of union density in 2006 were in the following categories: workers in education (59%), operators of fixed machinery and equipment in the process of industrial production (32%), department managers, coordinators and supervisors in administrative and service activities (20%). On the other hand, categories between 20 and 10% of union density were: technicians (19%), managers and supervisors in handcrafted and industrial production and in repair and maintenance activities (19%), assistant workers in administrative activities (19%), professionals (14%), government officials and directors of private, public and social sectors (11%), conductors and assistants in machinery and means of transport (11%).

Table 7.6 Union membership and density in Mexico by industry, 2006 (Scheme A1)

Industry	*Economic Active Population (EAP)*	*Union membership*	*Union density (%)*
Services in education	2,246,525	1,264,584	56.30
Manufacturing	7,692,879	1,108,702	14.41
Governmental and international bodies related activities	1,910,218	480,139	25.10
Health services and social work	1,300,317	475,466	36.60
Transportation, mail and warehousing	1,929,081	194,941	10.11
Whole and retail commerce	8,617,080	194,471	2.26
Services of temporary accommodation and beverage and food preparation	3,058,530	113,014	3.70
Electricity, water and gas transmission	234,782	111,815	47.60
Information in mass media	334,290	80,090	24.00
Construction	3,935,421	70,054	1.80
Mining	150,989	60,373	40.00
Services of business support and waste materials management and related services	1,105,626	50,282	4.50
Other services, except government activities	4,009,414	40,925	1.00
Financial services and insurance	402,363	37,453	9.30
Services in recreation, cultural, sports and other services	411,662	25,324	6.20
Scientific and technical professional services	969,650	15,902	1.60
Agriculture, cattle, forest, hunting and fishing activities	6,120,027	14,648	0.20

(continued)

Table 7.6 (continued)

Industry	*Economic Active Population (EAP)*	*Union membership*	*Union density (%)*
Real estate and property services	258,646	2,056	0.80
Management of corporations	9,095	0	0.00
Others	13,224	3,681	27.84
Total	44,723,043	4,347,601	9.72

Source Calculated from ENIGH (2006)

On the other hand, the occupations with the lowest union density rates were as follows: workers in protection and surveillance services and the armed forces (8%), workers in arts, performance and sports (7%), assistants, laborers and others in craftwork/industrial production process and in repair and maintenance activities (5%), artisans and fabric workers in the transformation industry and workers in repair and maintenance activities (5%), merchants, commercial employees and sales agents with 3% (Table 7.7).

In terms of union membership by occupation in 2006, the categories with more union members were: workers in education (911,367), operators of fixed machinery and equipment in the process of industrial production (547,863), assistant workers in administrative activities (521,964), and workers in personal services in fixed establishments (374,259), which together represent more than 50% of all the unionized workers in this category (Table 7.7).

As can be seen, the industries and sectors more unionized are those related to education and manufacturing working activities. These outcomes may be explained in light of two factors: on the one hand, the largest labor union not only in Mexico but also in Latin America, is the National union of Education Workers (or SNTE), controlled by Elba Esther Gordillo since 1989, the most prominent union leader in the country who has built alliances with political leaders from diverse parties. On the other hand, the relative significant number of unionized workers in the manufacturing sector may be attributable to the fact that employment in this sector has increased considerably during the last decades. As shown in Table 7.6, a large share of union membership is found in the manufacturing sector; however, most of the union members are affiliated

Table 7.7 Union membership in Mexico by occupation, 2006 (Scheme A1)

Occupations	*Economic Active Population (EAP)*	*Union membership*	*Union density (%)*
Workers in education	1,539,120	911,367	59.2
Operators of fixed machinery and equipment in the process of industrial production	1,725,276	547,863	31.8
Assistant workers in administrative activities	2,794,815	521,964	18.7
Workers in personal services in fixed establishments	3,701,463	374,259	10.1
Technicians	1,619,475	315,376	19.5
Artisans and fabric workers in the transformation industry and workers in repair and maintenance activities	6,189,574	291,241	4.7
Conductors and assistants in machinery and means of transport	2,228,070	241,684	10.8
Department managers, coordinators and supervisors in administrative and service activities	1,158,649	232,889	20.1
Professionals	1,369,082	185,746	13.6
Assistants, laborers and others in the craftwork and industrial production process and in repair and maintenance activities	3,578,389	180,919	5.1
Merchants, commercial employees and sales agents	5,924,415	152,982	2.6

(continued)

Table 7.7 (continued)

Occupations	*Economic Active Population (EAP)*	*Union membership*	*Union density (%)*
Managers and supervisors in handcrafted and industrial production and in repair and maintenance activities	749,799	144,383	19.3
Government officials and directors of private, public and social sectors	1,136,961	125,634	11.0
Workers in protection and surveillance services and the armed forces	935,388	75,099	8.0
Workers of the arts, performance and sports	384,976	25,411	6.6%
Workers in agriculture, cattle, forestry, hunting and fishing related activities	5,929,440	11,460	0.2
Street vendors and street workers in services	1,871,644	4,844	0.3
Workers in housework services	1,865,915	582	0.0
Others	7,368	217	2.9
Total	44,709,819	4,343,920	9.72

to 'ghost unions' with 'labor contracts of protection', ruled by the official labor organizations (Quintero, 1997). As mentioned in previous chapters, 'ghost unions' are created by enterprises, in collaboration with union leaders, to hinder the possibility that workers organize unions by themselves to defend their labor rights more effectively. Furthermore, 'ghost unions' have 'labor contracts of protection', to prevent the authentic labor contract.

The highest concentration of union membership in Mexico was in a small group of states in which most of the national economic activity is concentrated. For instance, by 2006 only 5 states, among others, Federal District (D.F. or Mexico City) (21%), Mexico (9.7%),

Nuevo León (7.5%), Jalisco (6.2%), and Chihuahua (4.6%), accounted for around half of the total GDP in the country. All these states (except Chihuahua) also registered the highest levels of union membership. Moreover, these states also concentrate most of the economically active population; for instance, Mexico, Federal District and Veracruz, which represented around 30% of the EAP in 2006. In 2006, the state of Mexico was on top of the list with 640,357 unionized workers. Then, the Federal District with 366,699 union members; thereafter, Nuevo León with 333,376 unionized workers; the state of Veracruz concentrates a membership of 286,678, Tamaulipas has 242,518, Jalisco 240,858 and Coahuila 177,452. Within these six states there is around 40% of the overall union membership in the country. The rest of the states had no more than 150,000 unionized workers in each one. In addition, states with union membership between 50,000 and 150,000 included: Chiapas, Michoacán, Guerrero, Morelos, Oaxaca, Chihuahua, Sonora, Sinaloa, Durango, Nayarit, Guanajuato, Querétaro, Hidalgo, among others. Indeed, some states registered a union membership lower than 50,000, i.e. Baja California Sur, Zacatecas, Colima, and Campeche. In sum, the regions in the center and the north-east of the country concentrate the majority of the overall union membership (Table 7.8).

In terms of union density, the states with highest rates were: Tamaulipas (19%), Nuevo León (17%), Coahuila (16%), Quintana Roo (15%), Baja California Sur (14%), Tlaxcala (14%), and Querétaro (13%). In contrast, the states with the lowest union density rates were: Guanajuato (6%), Yucatán (6%), Baja California (6%), and Oaxaca (5%). These figures suggest that the highest rates of unionization are not located in the states which concentrate most of the employed labor force, leading to a low union density at the national level. In this case, a different landscape is observed: the states from the north-east, north and center display the highest rates of unionization in the country (Table 7.8).

Regarding labor union density by age in Mexico, by 2006 it was higher among the workers, whose ages fluctuated between 36 and 45 (14%) and 46–55 (13.9%). Likewise, the group of 56–65 registered 10% of unionization. On the other hand, with lower rates were the group of 16–25 (6%) and of 26–35 (10%). Accordingly, the union density tends to increase between workers whose ages are between 18 and 45 but then it falls until the age of 65 (Fig. 7.1). These figures resemble those displayed by the US, Canada, the UK, and other developed countries, where unionization rates appear higher in workers whose age is between 30 and 50 years;

Table 7.8 Union membership in Mexico by state 2006 (Scheme A1)

State	*Economic Active Population (EAP)*	*Union membership*	*Union density (%)*
Mexico	5,849,798	640,357	10.95
DF	3,988,398	366,699	9.19
Nuevo León	1,913,061	333,376	17.43
Veracruz	3,203,461	286,678	8.95
Tamaulipas	1,246,716	242,518	19.45
Jalisco	2,923,048	240,858	8.24
Coahuila	1,083,751	177,452	16.37
Puebla	2,530,798	176,121	6.96
Guerrero	1,326,918	129,399	9.75
Chiapas	1,841,552	123,122	6.69
S. Luis Potosí	1,027,817	123,070	11.97
Guanajuato	1,940,947	121,923	6.28
Chihuahua	1,365,555	120,805	8.85
Michoacán	1,638,731	108,148	6.60
Sonora	1,021,002	101,494	9.94
Querétaro	704,640	93,685	13.30
Sinaloa	1,125,572	86,450	7.68
Quintana Roo	550,758	85,317	15.49
Hidalgo	945,975	83,517	8.83
Oaxaca	1,489,305	80,015	5.37
B. California	1,235,173	72,947	5.91
Durango	555,402	69,836	12.57
Tabasco	913,240	67,713	7.41
Tlaxcala	450,608	61,248	13.59
Morelos	654,391	53,760	8.22
Aguascalientes	469,392	53,107	11.31
Nayarit	433,696	52,598	12.13
Yucatán	835,663	50,483	6.04
Zacatecas	567,477	49,804	8.78
Campeche	394,619	28,798	7.30
B. California Sur	226,286	31,350	13.85
Colima	256,069	31,272	12.21
Total	44,709,819	4,343,920	9.72

Source Calculated from ENIGH (2006)

similarly, lower density rates are found in younger workers, mainly those aged between 18 and 30 and in those workers older than 50.

The distribution of union membership by age was more located in the group of workers aged between 36 and 45, which accounted for

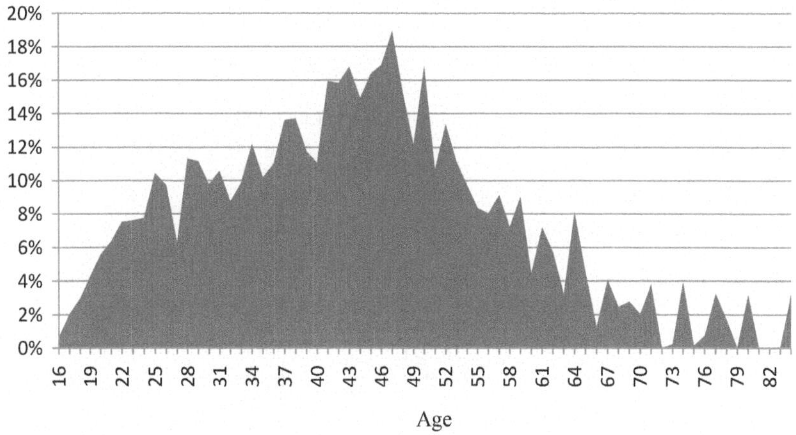

Fig. 7.1 Union density in Mexico by age 2006 (*Source* Calculated from ENIGH, 2006)

1,413,274 unionized workers, thereafter the group of workers of 26–35 with 1,151,651 and the group of 46–55 with 923,496 union members. The lower levels of unionization were in the group between 16 and 25 (580,032), 56 and 65 (233,557), more than 66 (40,501), and those between 0 and 15 (1,409) (Fig. 7.1). Data also suggest, on the one hand, the lack of interest showed by young workers to unionize, and on the other hand, the failure of union leaders to organize new members, mainly younger workers. Similarly, it may be suggested that new jobs are created in sectors unlikely to be unionized, such as in the service sectors. These figures reveal the existence of child labor in the country: around 1,400,000 workers under the age of 16 were unionized in 2006.

With regard to the different levels and type of education attained by unionized workers, unionization rates were greater in those workers with the education level of a bachelor degree in teaching and education (72%), doctorate (40.8%), Master's Degree (26.2%), technical and commercial career (18.6%), university (17.6%). On the other hand, with the lowest levels of union density, the categories are as follows: high school (10.8%), secondary (9.0%), pre-primary (4.2%), and primary (3.3%). Finally, the category of workers without education registered 1.0% (Table 7.9).

However, in terms of union membership distribution the groups with more union members in 2006 were: university (1,065,329), secondary

Table 7.9 Union membership by education, 2006 (Scheme A1)

Education level	*EAP*	*Union membership*	*Union density (%)*
University	6,066,630	1,065,329	17.60
Secondary	11,840,475	1,062,873	9.00
High school	6,281,077	678,915	10.80
Primary	13,997,799	465,752	3.30
Technical and commercial career	2,483,089	462,535	18.60
Bachelor degree in teaching and education	540,662	389,012	72.00
Master degree	609,694	159,467	26.20
Doctorate	78,591	32,039	40.80
Without education	2,775,929	26,495	1.00
Pre-primary	35,873	1,503	4.20
Total	44,709,819	4,343,920	9.70

Source Calculated from ENIGH (2006)

(1,062,873), high school (678,915), primary (465,752), technical and commercial career (462,535), bachelor degree in teaching and education (389,012). The lowest levels of union membership were located in the following categories: doctorate (32,039), without education (26,495) and finally the group of pre-primary (1,503) (Table 7.9). Therefore, the most unionized groups were in those workers with university and secondary levels of education. It is precisely the education levels attained by most of the union members in the country: the majority of workers in the education sector are graduated from universities and workers in the *maquiladoras* or manufacturing industry have completed the secondary as the highest level of education.

A Comparison of Union Density Rates: 1984, 1998, 2006 (Scheme A1)

As stated previously, research on union density in Mexico shows different rates of both aggregated and disaggregated union density; for instance, the most recent overall rates vary between 20 and 10%, but the rates by industry and sectors appear to be more similar among the various studies. In this sense, it becomes possible to perform comparative analysis in long periods with data available.

On the other hand, union density rates declined between 1984 and 2006 in Mexico in most sectors and industries. The most striking decline occurred in transportation, communications, post and warehousing which passed from 50.3% in 1984 to 18.2% in 1998 and to 12% in 2006; then, in mining, electricity, and water and gas transmission, in 1984 it comprised 63.9% but it decayed to 47.4% in 1998 and to 45% in 2006. Similarly, the decline happened in manufacturing, from 29% in 1984 to 20% in 1998 and to 14% in 2006; also, the services underwent a fall from 37% in 1984 to 28% in 1998 and to 15% in 2006. These figures were calculated relying on the ENIGH 2006 and a comparison was made with data from years 1984 and 1998 considering statistics from other sources (Fig. 7.2).

Among occupational groups, the trends illustrate a reduction of union density levels in the majority of categories. For instance: unionization in education workers was at 73% in 1984, but it fell to 64% in 1998, the trend persisted, and it fell to 59% in 2006. Another category was technicians: 47% of these workers were unionized in 1984, but it diminished to 37% in 1998 and to 19% in 2006. In the same way, the workers from arts performance and sports suffered a reduction of unionization: from 73% in 1984 to 13% in 1998 and finally to 7% in 2006. Union density among functionaries and directors went from 21% in 1984 to 13% in 1998 and to

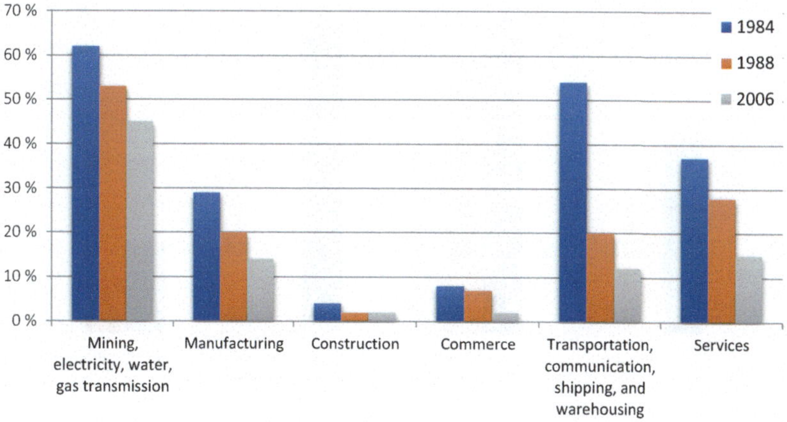

Fig. 7.2 Union density in Mexico by industry; 1984, 1998, 2006 scheme A1 (*Source* Data from 1984 and 1998, Fairris & Levin, 2004; data from 2006, calculated from ENIGH, 2006)

11% in 2006. The only category in which there was an increase of union density rate was in direct workers and industrial, oscillating between 30 and 20% in 1984–1998, but climbing to 32% in 2006. Assistants, artisanal and industrial workers saw a slump in union density from 19 to 9% in 1984–1998 and to 5% in 2006. In fact, all the other categories underwent a reduction of labor union representation. Workers in protection, security and armed forces witnessed a steady decline: in 1984 unionization was 27%, in 1998 16%, and in 2006 8%. On the other hand, unionization rate in professionals had an increase from 13 to 21% in 1984–1998, but then it decreased to 14% (figs. 7.3, 7.4 and 7.5).

Union density by age groups also reduced over the period 1984–2006. Unionization among workers aged 36–45 passed from 21 to 16% in 1984–2000 and to 14% in 2006. Similarly, union density fell among workers aged 26–35 from 16 to 10% in 1984–2006. The slump also took place in the group of 16–25, from 12 to 6% in 1984–1998, but it remained at that level to 2006. The category of workers in 46–55 reduced from 18 to 16% in 1984–1998 and to 14% in 2006 (Fig. 7.6).

Another aspect to highlight in this sector is the existence of child labor in Mexico; young workers aged below 15, accounted for 1,133,203 in

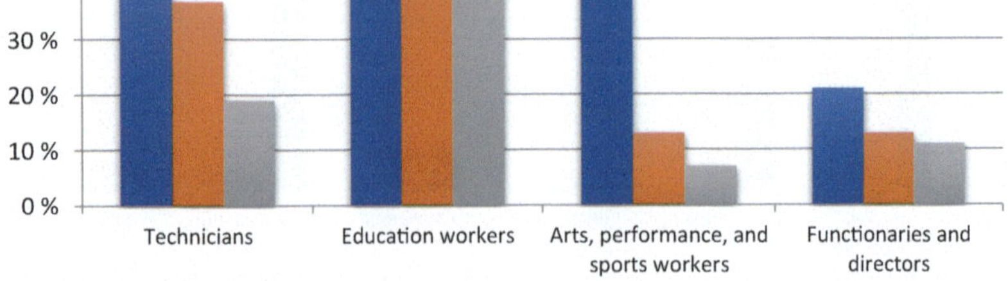

Fig. 7.3 Union density by occupations in Mexico; 1984, 1998, 2006 (I) scheme A1 (*Source* Data from 1984 and 1998, Fairris & Levin, 2004; data from 2006, calculated from ENIGH, 2006)

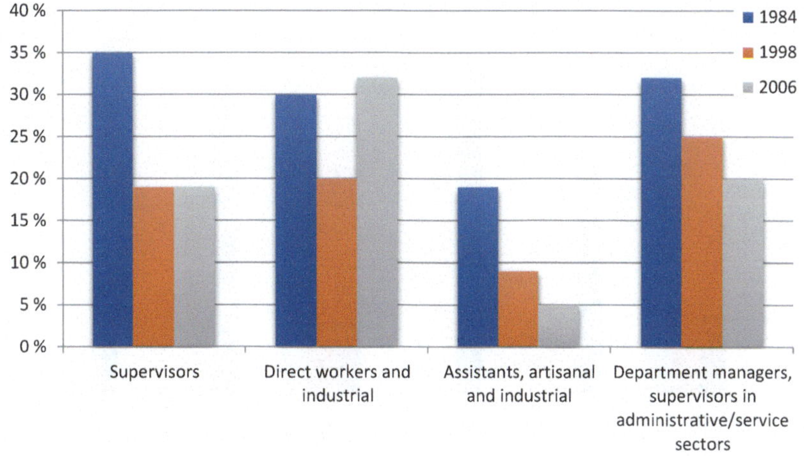

Fig. 7.4 Union density by occupations in Mexico; 1984, 1998, 2006 (II) scheme A1 (*Source* Data from 1984 and 1998, Fairris & Levin, 2004; data from 2006, calculated from ENIGH, 2006)

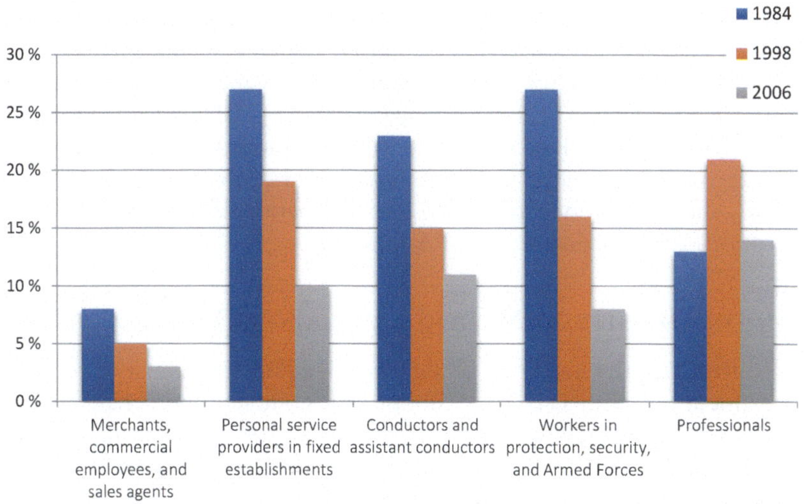

Fig. 7.5 Union density by occupations in Mexico; 1984, 1998, 2006 (III) scheme A1 (*Source* Data from 1984 and 1998, Fairris & Levin, 2004; data from 2006, calculated from ENIGH, 2006)

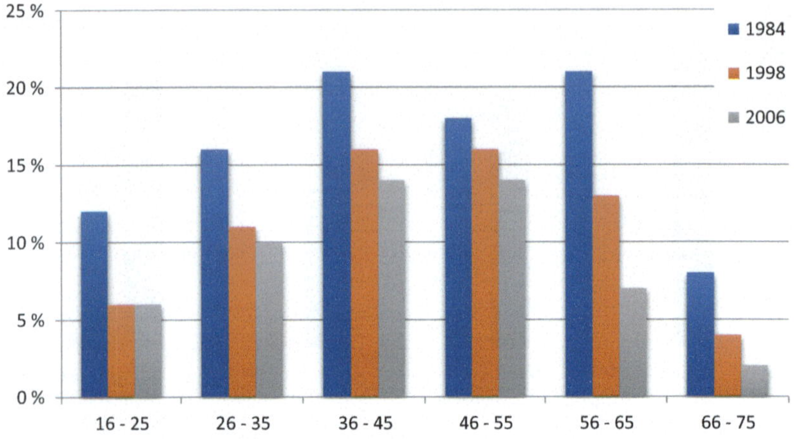

Fig. 7.6 Union density by age in Mexico; 1984, 1998, 2006 (scheme A1) (*Source* Data from 1984 and 1998, Fairris & Levin, 2004; data from 2006, calculated from ENIGH, 2006)

2006; indeed, there were 1,404 children unionized. These figures confirm diverse newspapers reports about children working mainly in the agriculture sector. The states that concentrate the highest number of child labor are Veracruz (111,899), Chiapas (98,444), Jalisco (86,133), and Puebla (68,884). As the data displayed here demonstrate, there has been an overwhelming decline in union density rates across most industries, sectors, and occupations in Mexico over the period 1984–2006; and the exceptions to this trend represent a minority.

Union Density by Sector and Labor Organizations

In contrast to the majority of developed countries, Mexico's official department of labor (STPS) does not provide complete and detailed information on union membership or density by sector, occupation, and the like. The only available data collected and displayed by this office is on union membership in the national private sector; indeed, these statistics derive not from surveys or census, but from the union offices, which report their numbers to the STPS.

It is claimed that labor unions hide their real statistics since membership is a source of political power. The higher the union membership, the more political positions are controlled by union leaders in government. Thus, if low levels of union membership were demonstrated, the political quota for unions would diminish.

The following sections include the analysis and figures of union membership and density in the second quarter of 2006, according to diverse official sources (Scheme B) from the Mexican government. According to several sources (Scheme B1), union density in Mexico decreased during the period 1993–1997. It then displayed stable patterns until 2006. However, one of the most drastic slumps occurred from 1978–1980 to 1986, from 15.5 to 9% in the period. But after that, according to these sources, unionization increased from 9 to 13.8% between 1986 and 1993 (the rate of unionization in the mid-1980s differs from that of Scheme A). It later declined to 11.6% in 2000. At this level it has remained during the 2000s; nevertheless, a negative trend is evident for organized workers in the past decades before an economic and political system, not propitious for their fortification. Previous research (Aguilar, 2005; Zazueta & De la Peña, 1984) which examines statistics on union membership and recent official data collected from the STPS make it possible to perform estimations of union density fluctuations over the three last decades. The trends observed appear to be negative for labor unions in terms of unionization. Evidently, labor organizations have suffered the offensive of neoliberal governments and economic liberalization in the country since 1982, which is still a reality (Tables 7.10 and 7.11).

Findings

Towards the second quarter of 2006, union density in Mexico accounted for 11.4%. This was obtained from the total number of unionized workers regarding the EAP relying on recent official data collected from STPS, ISSSTE and INEGI (Scheme B). Within the conducted analysis, the following outcomes can be summarized:

- While the number of Mexicans included in the EAP was about 43.5 million, union membership represented about 4.8 million. In this sense, the union density rate was at 11.4% regarding the EAP and 19.5% with regard to the waged workers.
- The number of unionized workers was slightly higher in the private than in the public sector. There were about 2.4 million union

Table 7.10 Union density and EAP in Mexico, 1978–2006 (Scheme B1) (Numbers in 000s)

Year	*Total population*	*EAP*	*Occupied Population*	*Unionized workers*	*Union density*
1978~	67,000	22,066*		3,429	15.5%
1986	79,542	26,280	21,640	2,369	9.0
1993	86,613	33,652	32,833	4,644	13.8
1997	94,732	38,095	36,298	4,493	11.7
2000**	99,356	40,307	39,695	4,704	11.6
2006**	104,748	43,584	42,197	4,950+	11.4

Source Aguilar (2005: 145–158)
~Zazueta and De la Peña (1984)
*1980
**INEGI (2007)
+STyPS (2006a)

Table 7.11 Union Membership in Mexico, 2006 (Scheme B)

Category	*Numbers*
Unionized workers from section A; federal jurisdiction (1)	1,409,876
Unionized workers from section A; local jurisdiction (2)	1,115,753
Unionized workers from section B; local and federal jurisdiction (3)	2,424,773
Total union membership	4,950,402

(1) STyPS (2006a)
(2) STyPS (2006b)
(3) ISSSTE (2007)

workers in the public sector, whereas the private sector displayed 2.5 million. Indeed, during recent years, employment growth has been greater in the private than in the public sector.

- Labor organizations in the private sector with the highest union membership were as follows: CTM (557,930 members), independent unions (492,065), FESEBS (138,193), CROC (75,010), among others.
- Within the public sector, membership registered 2,378,257 members, who are affiliated in both FSTSE (800,000) and FEDESSP (1.6 million). Within FEDESSP, the SNTE was the largest labor unions with a membership around 1.2 million.

Union membership among the workers from the private sector of federal jurisdiction was not very representative. According to the sources consulted, in Mexico there were 1,186 union organizations in 2006. These organizations are within 34 national organizations, in which 1,409,876 workers were affiliated. In order to detect the total union membership in the private sector, it was necessary to add to the former figure the number of unionized workers from the local private sector (1,115,753); therefore, the final result was 2,525,629 union members in the private sector both in local and federal jurisdictions. As the data provided by the ENOE survey conducted by INEGI (as well as other similar household surveys) do not provide the total employed labor in the private and public sectors, it is not feasible to calculate union density in these categories.

On the other hand, in terms of union density, the public sector is more unionized than the private sector, because all workers in public sector, according to the legislation, are to be unionized. The total number of unionized workers in the public sector in 2006 was 2,424,773. When union density rates are calculated, regarding the employed labor force in the public sector, the result is almost 100%. But, according to some figures, it is about 90%. The overall union density rate in the second quarter of 2006 was at 11.4%, obtained from the union membership (4,895,439) with regard to the number of workers within the EAP (43,584,461). After examining these figures, we can highlight that union density rate in Mexico is one of the lowest throughout the world. Most workers in the country (9 out of 10) are not unionized.

Union Members by Organization

According to the STPS, the total number of unionized workers in 2006 from federal private sector was 1,409,876. From this figure, about 30% was affiliated to the CTM (557,930); whereas other national organizations such as the FESEBS, which includes STRM and others, registered 138,193 members, which represent about 10% of the overall union membership in the sector. According to these figures, national confederations, and federations of unions such as the CROC (75,010), FENASIB

Table 7.12 Union membership in Mexico by labor organization in 2006. Private and public sectors

Labor organization	*Organizations*	*Union Members*	*Percentage*
Private sector			
CTM	348	557,930	39.6
Independents	256	492,065	
FESEBS	10	138,193	34.9
CROC	168	75,010	9.8
FENASIB	9	36,247	5.3
CROM	150	26,761	2.6
28 labor organizations of minor representation	245	83,670	5.9
Total	**1,186**	**1,409,876**	
Public sector			
FEDESSP	21	1.7 million*	80
FSTSE		700,000*	20
Total			2.4 million

Source DGRA of STPS, ISSSTE, 2007. Database created by the author
*Estimations of the author

(36,247), and CROM (26,761), were also among the most representative labor organizations in the country. On the other hand, official statistics also show that independent national labor unions, according to DGRA classification, some of which belong to the CT, represent 492,065 members on the whole, accounting for 35% of total union membership in this sector. The most important national unions in this category are from sectors such as the mining, social security (health) and railroad sectors. Finally, there are 28 minor labor organizations, which in total represent around 5% of overall union membership in Mexico in this category (Table 7.12).

Union Membership by Sector (Scheme Bi)

The majority of labor unions from the public sector are affiliated with two major umbrella organizations: FSTSE and FEDESSP. All workers from the public sector, both in local and national governments belong to any of these organizations. In 2006, according to data provided by ISSSTE, workers affiliated to this institute were 2.3 million. However, diverse sources consider that about 2 million workers represent the total membership in this sector, since around 15% of the ISSSTE members are not unionized. In 2004, the FSTSE underwent a split from 21 organizations, about 1.6 million workers, which in turn created the FEDESSP (*Federación Democrática de Sindicatos de Servidores Públicos*) controlled by the union of education workers (SNTE). This new organization represented about 80% of total union membership in the public sector (Pastrana, 2004). According to these figures, the overall union membership was around 2 million in that year (2.3 million in 2006). This split was encouraged by the SNTE authentic leader, Elba Esther Gordillo, because of a conflict of interests with the FSTSE leader, Joel Ayala. After diverse procedures, at the end of 2004, the judicial branch decided to grant the right of this organization to obtain the registration and the 'taking of note' (*toma de nota*) provided by labor authorities. However, despite this situation, it has not been clearly determined the role of each one of these organizations in the collective bargaining process with the employers (in this case, the government).

Regarding union membership in the private sector, the majority of unionization is affiliated to CTM, then, other organizations such as the CROM, CROC and other of the CT congregate the union members in this sector. By 2006, in the federal jurisdiction of the private sector, the CTM was the most important labor organizations with 557,930 members. It also is important to consider that the CTM membership in the local sector, which according to other scholars is around 500 thousand. Then, in 2006, the estimated membership of the CTM would be around one million in both the local and federal jurisdictions of the private sector.

Assessing Union Density Decline in Mexico

The only description of union density rates cannot clarify the factors accounting for the decline of labor unions, but it allows us to identify the panorama in terms of union density variations in the country and the sectors more affected. The decline of labor unions may be analyzed from various perspectives, for instance, considering economic performance, unemployment and inflation, employment composition and political-institutional factors. As mentioned in Chapter 6, the economic performance and the employment characteristics prevailing during the last three decades have not been adequate for the expansion of labor union density. The economic performance has been poor, and in some periods, negative; the creation of jobs in the formal sector has not been enough for the available labor force in the country, leading to the informality of labor markets and complicating the organization activities of labor unions. On the other hand, technocratic governments in Mexico since the 1980s withdrew political support from the official labor unions confederations which were major political actors during the second post-war period. Since the 1980s, these governments promoted, in practice, a labor framework more flexible to the conditions imposed by neoliberal globalization. Under these circumstances, the official labor unions began a process of deterioration. Diverse features of the authoritarian political system have determined a deleterious context for labor unions. Indeed, even within a democratic environment, as was the case in the Fox administration, a stagnation of union density in Mexico prevailed during the period 2000–2006. The connections between the economic cycle, the characteristics of the labor markets and the political context are pertinent.

On the other hand, some specific institutional settings have operated against the organization of authentic labor unions. As mentioned in Chapter 5, between 70 and 90% of the contracts in the private sector are false, also known as 'labor contracts of protection' and with 'ghost unions'. This situation may undermine the validity of the official statistics of unionization analyzed here. It is necessary to distinguish between authentic and false union affiliation. However, since there are not exact estimations in this regard, we cannot identify in precise terms the real union membership in the country. We can suggest that a large share of the unionization in the private sector, which is around 50% of the total union membership, is considered as simulated.

Conclusions

As seen in most developed countries, there was a decline in labor union density in Mexico during the last decades. The analysis of previous literature and statistics illustrate a decline in the total union density but also in the disaggregated union density in the vast majority of sectors, occupations and considering diverse socio-demographic characteristics of union members.

Despite all the discrepancies to calculate union membership and density, it is possible to identify several valuable concluding points. The statistical analysis suggests a deeper decline during the first half of the 1990s in comparison to the 1980s and 2000s. This implies that as certain policies were implemented in the country in the early 1990s, in the same way, there was a reduction of unionized workers regarding the employed labor force. In this sense, two major factors must be considered: first, a combination of a group of policies during the Salinas administration period (1988–1994). Second, the economic crisis of 1994–1995 implied heavy repercussions for the working class as unemployment and the informal sector increased. These factors, within a context of authoritarian rule, resulted even more pernicious for the affiliation and maintenance of new union members. The rise of the informal sector, about 50–60% of the labor force, in Mexico in recent years has complicated the organization activities of labor unions. This situation makes the affiliation of new members and the expansion of union membership more difficult.

The large share of unionization in Mexico took place in three main sectors: the public, education and manufacturing sectors. Data analyzed here confirm that these segments of the employed labor force are the most unionized in the country. This situation may be attributed to the labor legislation which states that all the employees in the public sector must be unionized in a compulsory way. In this same logic, the education workers have the largest labor union in the country (SNTE): unionization is also essential to get the job. The high levels of union members in the manufacturing sector is mainly attributable to the employment expansion of this sector in recent decades. In the other industries and sectors union representation is relatively low in all the country.

According to the statistical data displayed in this chapter, it is evident that in terms of labor organizations, the largest centrals in the private sector are found in the official unionism: the Confederation of Mexican Workers (CTM) is still the biggest national labor organization in this area. Similarly, the CROM and CROC along with other less relevant organizations gathered in the Congress of Labor represent the vast majority of union members in the private sector. On the other hand, in the public sector, there have been some reallocations in the top umbrella labor organizations. The FSTSE is not any longer the union federation concentrating the vast majority of unionized workers in the sector; after the split of 2004, the FEDESSP became the labor federation with more union members in the public sector since it has the SNTE affiliation (teachers union), which is the largest labor union in Latin America. In sum, unions affiliated in the CT represent the majority in the private sector, while in the public sector the FEDESSP has the most significant union representation.

Bibliography

Aguilar, J. (2005). *La población trabajadora y sindicalizada en México en el período de la globalización*. Mexico: UNAM, FCE.

Cardoso, A., & Gindin, J. (2009). *Industrial relations and collective bargaining: Argentina, Brazil and Mexico compared* (Working Paper No. 5). Geneva: Industrial and Employment Relations Department International Labor Office.

Commission for Labor Cooperation. (2003). *Recent trends in union density in North America*. Washington, DC: Commission for Labor Cooperation.

De la Garza, E. (2003). La crisis de los modelos sindicales en Mexico y sus opciones. In E. De la Garza & C. Salas (Eds.), *La situación del trabajo en Mexico, 2003* (pp. 349–377). Mexico: Plaza y Valdez.

Encuesta Nacional de Ingresos y Gastos de los Hogares (ENIGH). (2006). México: INEGI.

Fairris, D. (2005). *What do unions do in Mexico* (Working Paper). Riverside: University of California.

Fairris, D., & Levine, E. (2004). Declining union density in Mexico, 1984–2000. *Monthly Labor Review, 127*(9), 10–17.

Herrera, F., & Melgoza, J. (2003). Evolución reciente de la afiliación sindical y la regulación laboral en Mexico. In E. De la Garza & C. Salas (Eds.), *La situación del trabajo en Mexico, 2003* (pp. 323–347). Mexico: Plaza y Valdez.

INEGI. (2006a). *Encuesta Nacional de Ingresos y Gastos de los Hogares (ENIGH) 2006*. Aguascalientes: INEGI.

INEGI. (2006b). *Encuesta Nacional de Ingresos y Gastos de los Hogares (ENIGH) 1984, 1989, 1992, 1994, 1996, 1998, 2000, 2002, 2004*. Aguascalientes: INEGI.

INEGI. (2007). *Encuesta Nacional de Ocupacion y Empleo (ENOE) 2007*. Aguascalientes: INEGI.

International Labor Organization. (1998). *World labor report 1997–1998*. Geneva: ILO.

ISSSTE. (2007). *Anuario Estadístico*. Instituto de seguridad y servicios sociales de los trabajadores del Estado. Available online http://www.issste.gob.mx/, consulted in March 2007.

La Botz, D. (2005). Mexico's labor movement in transition. *Monthly Review, 57*(2), 62–72.

Marshall, A. (2006). *Efectos de la regulación del trabajo sobre la afiliación sindical: estudio comparativo de Argentina, Chile y Mexico*. Argentina: Cuadernos del Instituto de Desarrollo Económico y Social.

OECD. (2004a). *Trade union density and collective bargaining coverage*. OECD, Economic Outlook.

OECD. (2004b). *OECD Employment outlook*. Paris: OECD.

OECD. (2009). *Society at a glance 2009—OECD social indicators*. Statistical annexe, trade union members.

Panagides, A., & Patrinos, H. A. (1994). *Wage differentials in the developing world: a case study of Mexico* (Policy Research Working Paper, No. 1269). Washington, DC: The World Bank.

Pastrana, D. (2004, December 12). La CTM: ¿más viva que nunca? *La Jornada*.

Quintero, C. (1997). *Reestructuración sindical en las maquiladoras mexicanas*. Mexico: COLEF.

STyPS. (2006a). *Dirección General de Registro de Asociaciones (DGRA)*. Secretaria del Trabajo y Prevision Social. Available online www.stps.gob.mx, consulted in May 2006.

STyPS. (2006b). 'Trabajadores Involucrados en las Revisiones Salariales y Contractuales en la Jurisdicción Local por Entidad Federativa, 2006', table IV.8.11. *Secretaria del Trabajo y Prevision Social*. Available online www.stps.gob.mx, consulted in June 2006.

Zapata, F. (1995). *El sindicalismo mexicano frente a la restructuración*. México: El Colegio de México.

Zapata, F. (2005). *Tiempos Neoliberales en México*. México: El Colegio de México.

Zazueta, C., & De la Peña, R. (1984). *La estructura del Congreso del Trabajo*. Mexico: FCE.

Interviews

Alcalde, A. (2007, September). *Labor lawyer and advisor of independent labor unions (FAT, UNT and others)*. Mexico City.

Bouzas, A. (2007, September). *Labor lawyer and academic scholar*. UNAM, Mexico City.

De Buen, N. (2007, September). *Labor lawyer and union advisor (SNTMM and others)*. Mexico City.

Mirón, L. (2007, November). *Ministry of labor, government of Distrito Federal*. Mexico City.

CHAPTER 8

Conclusions

Union Density

Union density is one of the most widely used indicators to assess the relevance of labor unions during a certain period, through different sectors and industries in the employed labor force and also in individual or among groups of countries. The significance of union density was corroborated in the recent reports and databases on union density generated by international bodies, such as the ILO and OECD. Union representation in the labor force, measured through union membership and union density, has attracted the attention of international bodies and academic scholars assessing the changing situation of labor unions considering the political and economic transformations over the last decades.

This study has analyzed not only union density variations since the 1980s but also the factors accounting for these trends. No universal pattern emerged, as some countries saw a decline, whereas others an expansion. However, labor unions have experienced a decline in terms of union membership in the labor force in most countries examined here. Despite the decline of labor union density during the last decades, it should be pointed out that labor unions are still important institutions representing workers' interests with a crucial role in the political regime in many countries; they have not disappeared even though they have lost members and political influence.

R. Zepeda, *The Decline of Labor Unions in Mexico during the Neoliberal Period*, Governance, Development, and Social Inclusion in Latin America, https://doi.org/10.1007/978-3-030-65710-9_8

A decline of union density rates occurred in the majority of OECD and Latin American countries during the last two decades of the twentieth century, but it has been stable in the first two decades of the twenty-first century. This suggests that union organizations have entered a period of stabilization in which most have not been able to revitalize and increase their presence in the employed labor force. One of the main issues is related to the revitalization or growth of unions in the new economic and political circumstances (which was not assessed in this study). According to statistics analyzed here, provided by the OECD, the ILO and official bodies, labor movements in a reduced number of countries have been able to revitalize (considering union density rates) since the 1980s amidst a general environment of declining union density. For instance, various countries, such as Sweden, Spain, Belgium, Finland, and Iceland, have seen an increase of labor union representation during the last three decades.

Union Density in Mexico

In terms of unionization, union density levels in Mexico were lower than average not only in North America and Latin America but also within the OECD countries during the neoliberal period. As noted in Chapter 2, union density decline took place in the last two decades of the twentieth century in many developed and developing countries. This was also the case of Mexico, but with diverse fluctuations. Official statistical data reveal that while unionization rates in Mexico improved in the second half of the 1980s, a notable decline took place in the 1990s. The reduction of union density was from 17.8% in 1989 to 10.1% in 1996 but it has remained around 10% in the period 1996-2016. This level of unionization in Mexico is very similar to that of France and the United States, and the magnitude of the decline in the period 1980–2000 is very similar to those of Germany and Japan.

Nevertheless, not only the decline of union density took place in Mexico, but also the decline of labor unionism (that is, the debacle of its corporatist power). In other words, the decline of unionization in Mexico was not as important as it was in other countries (United States, United Kingdom, France, among others), but rather it can be suggested that labor unionism lost influence in the political and labor spheres, partly as a consequence of the transformation in the economic model and the conversion of labor unions—state relations within a more democratic political environment.

As noted in Chapter 4, the support of labor unions in Mexico during most of the past century (1940–1980), on the one hand its corporatist relation with the state and, on the other hand, its relevance in the economic model (ISI), modified since the 1980s with the advent of neoliberalism. As a result of the turn in the guiding principles of the political economy and the process of political democratization, the state redefined elements of the corporatist framework initiated in the 1920s-1930s, which implied the existence of strong official labor confederations, public policies that encouraged employment and wide social benefits for unionized workers. During the transformation of the political economy in the 1980s, certain policies impacted on workers and labor unions and were important in the adjustment of labor—state relations. For instance, the structural adjustment program which comprised the reduction of social spending and subsidies, the social pacts to reduce and control inflation, via the constraint of wages and prices and the lack of an adequate industrial policy to generate employment. These policies contributed to the deterioration of wages and labor benefits, but also the reduction of union membership and density regarding the labor force.

However, political democratization also contributed to the decline of unions in the neoliberal period. Political democratization and neoliberal policies are not isolated processes in Mexico and have to be assessed in context or as a sequence of events. The undermining of the official party (PRI) by means of more democratic practices made the official unions weaker organizations not only in the official party but also regarding its position towards the state. The debt crisis of 1982 led the government to implement a group of policies more identified with neoliberal prescriptions as mentioned above. This generated discontent among workers, while labor organizations supported these unpopular governmental policies. In 1988, citizens punished the PRI in the presidential elections. Labor confederations were not capable of providing votes for the party and lost privileges during the Salinas period. Organized labor was divided by the Salinas government and became even weaker before the state and employers. In this context, union membership occurred, as can be seen in the official statistics analyzed in Chapter 7.

The specific period of union density decline in Mexico occurred between 1989 and 1996. It can be suggested that such a decline is related to specific policies implemented in the Salinas administration as well as because of the negative effects of the economic crisis of 1994–1995 (the peso crisis) which impacted employment and quality of jobs. Conversely, the period 1984-1989 was negative for workers in terms of real wages and living standards, but surprisingly there was not a negative tendency on union density levels as can be seen in the union membership figures. Between 1984 and 1989, the number of union members increased in a context of a stagnate economy and high rates of inflation. The aforementioned contradicts the cyclical approach regarding the relation between economic performance and union density, but partly coincides with regard to the relation between inflation and unionization.

The decline of union density is linked to the redefinition of labor unions—state relations. As mentioned in Chapter 4, Salinas encouraged a new kind of relations with the official labor unions, promoting not only their debilitation by restraining their access to public resources, but also their fragmentation by creating new top labor organizations. Therefore, there were more labor organizations but not more union members in the country during the 1990s. There was more activism of labor unions, mobilizations in the streets and public demonstrations and forums, but there was not more union affiliation. The weakening of unions was done by reducing their public resources and encouraging their fragmentation and division among labor confederations. It is not a coincidence that the decline of unions occurred during the Salinas government which has been identified as the most important in terms of the economic transformation and the one that promoted a different kind of government relations with the organized sectors of the official party, such as labor organizations.

The decline of labor union density is also related to the stagnation of formal employment in the private sector, especially in the 1990s, as observed in Chapter 6. Between 1990 and 1995 the number of jobs in the formal private sector hardly increased from 9.3 million to 9.4 million (that is, less than 100 thousand in 5 years). This could be considered a negative factor that affected the union affiliation of workers in this period. It is also remarkable that the period 1989-1994, featured by relative high rates of economic growth; it, however, was not accompanied by the expansion of formal jobs in the private sector. In this way, structural factors played a significant role in union density decline. Furthermore, the peso crisis of 1994–1995 generated effects that were negative for union affiliation. For instance: the slowdown of employment creation and the expansion of the informal sector. The aforementioned can be confirmed with the analysis of the employed labor force and other indicators.

By the early twenty-first century, there was a diminished labor movement in comparison with previous decades, from many perspectives: in terms of its influence on policy-making and favorable official policies, in terms of its relation and alliances with political parties and the state and in terms of its representation within the employed labor force. Furthermore, as mentioned in Chapter 5, the fragmentation of the labor movement in Mexico prevented an effective strategy to negotiate with the state the attenuation of the repercussions of the dual transition, in aspects such as privatization and the reduction of public resources and economic and social policies impacting the working class. However, at the same time, the official unions have survived the neoliberal transition. As mentioned in Chapter 7, the CTM affiliated unions represent most unionized workers in the manufacturing sector and in the electricity and oil industries. Other independent organizations, like the UNT, play an important role in the labor movement and represent workers in the telecommunications sector, and employees in university and health care sectors.

Drawing on previous research in the field, original figures were calculated corresponding to primary data from household surveys conducted by the Mexican government, every ENIGH survey conducted between 1984 and 2006. Diverse official sources were consulted to estimate union membership in Mexico. Schemes A1 (based on ENIGH micro-data) and B1 (based on STPS, ISSSTE data) were used to estimate the overall union membership in 2006. The figures obtained from these schemes represented useful indicators to assess the levels of union representation in Mexico.

In terms of union density in Mexico, this research found the following results. With respect to union density by gender in Mexico, it was higher among female than male workers in 2006. However, as illustrated in Chapter 7, unionized male workers had more representation in the employed labor force. In 2006, union density in female workers was about 10.5%; in contrast, males registered a rate of 9.2%. On the other hand, union membership among male workers was higher than female workers that year: male union members accounted for 2.4 million in contrast to 1.8 million in the case of women. Moreover, during the period 1984–2006, as observed in Chapter 2, these figures appear similar to the trends in Canada, the United States, and the UK, where the gap among men and women in terms of union density has shortened in recent years. This also indicates the expansion of female workers both in the employed labor force and labor union membership.

As mentioned in Chapter 7, union density by age in Mexico in 2006 reached the highest levels among workers between 36 and 45 years old (14%) and 46–55 (13.9%). On the other hand, the lowest rates were in the groups of 16–25 (6%) and of 26–35 (10%). Thus, union density rates tend to gradually increase from the age 18 to 45, but then it falls until the age 65. Compared to the international landscape, as assessed in Chapter 2, these figures resemble those displayed in developed countries (for instance, U.S., Canada), where unionization rates appear higher in workers aged between 30 and 50, while lower density rates are found in younger workers, mainly those aged between 18 and 30 years. This panorama also suggests the slowdown of union affiliation in recent years, which is not as significant as in past decades. Similarly, unionization increasingly represents a small fraction in the new kind of employment, as suggested by data. The forthcoming scenario for unions suggests that union density decline will persist, since the largest part of union membership is on the brink of abandoning the employed labor force.

With regard to union density fluctuations by industrial branches in the period 1984-2006, the most striking declines were in the following categories. The branch of 'transportation, communications, post and warehousing' suffered a drastic decline. It passed from 50% in 1984 to 12% in 2006. Similarly, the sector 'mining, electricity, and water and gas transmission' faced notable declining trends. In addition, the manufacturing sector decreased from 29% in 1984 to 14% in 2006. The vast majority of industries and sectors experienced a decline in terms of unionization with respect to labor force in the period 1984–1998, and this tendency was corroborated with generated data of 2006.

In terms of union membership by region in Mexico, it was notably concentrated in a few geographical states. For instance, the majority of the unionized workforce was located in the state of Mexico, Mexico City (D.F.), Nuevo Leon and Veracruz. At the same time, these regions contribute significantly to the economic production in the country. This panorama suggests that unionization is conditioned by various factors. First, a big share of production is found in these states, which means that union members are located in regions with more economic production in industry and services. Second, the majority of jobs in the public sector are in Mexico City, since it is not only the biggest metropolitan area in the country, but also the base of the federal governments and most of its official branches. In summary, the distribution of unionized workers in Mexico is determined by the relevance of economic activities in the region and the magnitude of employed labor force.

However, the existence of labor contracts of protection also has to be taken into account. As mentioned in Chapter 5, a large share of labor unions in the private sector are considered 'ghost unions' with labor contracts of protection. In this way, the official statistics may overestimate the real and authentic union membership in the country. Many suggest that the between 70 and 90% of the collective contracts in the private sector are 'labor contracts of protection' which automatically create 'ghost unions', which are labor unions created by corporations and official unions to prevent the authentic union representation. However, there are not exact figures about the number of workers included within the 70%-90% of labor contracts of protection in the private sector. In Chapter 7, we found that union membership in the private sector in 2006 was around 2.5 million whereas in the public sector it was 2.4 million. That is, around 50% of union membership is in the private sector. Then, if we consider that a large share of union membership in this sector is false, we would have to reduce the overall union density rate. In this way, the authentic unionization in Mexico may be calculated considering the total union membership in the public sector and a fraction of union membership in the private sector. The final results can thus produce a union density rate ranging from 5 to 8%.

The Contexts of Transformation

The decline of labor unions in Mexico took place during the period 1984–2006 within two major dimensions. First, the political liberalization and democratization in Mexico which meant not only the PRI debacle but also the redefinition of some aspects of the corporatist structure in which labor unions occupied a privileged position. This led to the deterioration of the official labor organizations and to the fragmentation of organized labor. Second, the political economy, promoted since the 1980s, which marked the transition from the Import-Substitution-Industrialization model to the neoliberal export-oriented model. It comprised a group of policies that affected the workers' wages and real incomes.

The case of Mexico could be considered as a country where the democratization process, materialized in 2000, did not comprise the labor sphere and consequently, it had limited effects on the revitalization of the labor movement. Once more Mexico appears as a unique case in

Latin America. Between 1930 and 1980, Mexico represented an exception in terms of political stability in comparison with Brazil, Argentina, and Chile, among other countries featured by political instability, military coups, and repressive dictatorships. Although the PRI regime was not precisely a democratic regime and political conflicts and social movements were not absent, it had relatively less political turbulence during this period. The political machinery of the PRI regime was effective at least to guarantee certain levels of political stability by incorporating wide social sectors into the party and allocating diverse resources to workers, peasants, and other organized groups. Thus, the outcomes of democratization in Mexico were different regarding other Latin American countries. Between 1980 and 2000 the corporatist framework that sustained the PRI-dominated political regime, started to collapse. While many Latin American countries became democratic leaving behind the authoritarian practices of earlier decades, Mexico remained with undemocratic practices amidst the third wave of democratization. This was also reflected in the labor sphere. Chile, Argentina, and Brazil saw a recovering of labor rights and the reactivation of the labor movements which had wider opportunities to organize the labor force and deploy mobilizations to oppose neoliberal policies and advocate for more democratic regimes. Whereas Mexico's organized labor remained tied to the authoritarian PRI regime and even when democratization arrived, labor unions have not been able to revitalize.

The positive relation between political democratization and union density variations (that is, the more democratic a country, the more unionized and vice versa) is not very clear in many cases. As mentioned in Chapter 3, countries with high levels of union density over the last few decades have been considered to be full democracies (Sweden, Finland, Belgium) but also countries with authoritarian or antidemocratic attributes (USSR/Russia and China) are among the most unionized in the world. Labor organizations with high levels of unionization inhabit both in democratic and undemocratic environments. However, unionization does not reflect the whole picture of labor unions. For instance, the roles and activities of labor unions but also the opportunities for the creation of authentic and independent union organizations, representing genuinely the workers' interests, are shaped by the political context. Certainly, features such as employment composition and economic performance cannot be overlooked, but even when these factors create an adequate context for union affiliation, the political regime and its institutions become the most determining factors for unionization and the operation of authentic labor unions. In other words, if good economic performance and labor composition more likely to be unionized (for example, industrial jobs) are not accompanied by propitious political and institutional conditions that guarantee the organization of genuine unions, then it is possible that unions would continue facing difficult circumstances.

In the case of Mexico, the political democratization process does not explain thoroughly the deterioration or influence of labor organizations in the political sphere. As mentioned before, it is evident that the most severe period faced by labor organizations was between 1989 and 1996 during the government of President Salinas (1988–1994) and the early years of the Zedillo (1994–2000) administration. The decline of labor unions and the erosion of power and influence in the Salinas government are explained by the policies promoted in this administration and the transformation of the hegemonic party system. In the Zedillo *sexenio*, the decline of labor unions is related to the effects brought by the peso crisis. Nonetheless, it is important to highlight, these years were not entirely featured by democratic conditions.

It is suggested here that a radical change took place in Mexico after 1982, which represents a watershed in many respects. As opposed to other Latin American countries, there was not a democratization, but there was a reallocation of power within the PRI's ruling elite, in which a technocratic group took over the main sources of political power and implemented a gradual change in the economic model spreading to the political realm. This political group or *camarilla* in the PRI, headed by de la Madrid, Salinas, and Zedillo between 1982 and until 2000 redefined the alliances of the state with organized groups that sustained the post-revolutionary corporatist framework. Yet the deterioration of labor unions, considering its membership in the labor force and the split within the official unionism, took place more clearly during the government of Salinas and the beginning of Zedillo's. This trend also coincides with the deterioration of Mexican workers' real wages in that period. Therefore, it is important to analyze the connections between these two developments in further research.

In the case of Mexico, the most important labor confederations and national unions, as mentioned in Chapter 4, were instituted and developed within an authoritarian regime which molded their features, leaderships, internal life and forms of operation in the social, labor and political realms for many decades. The scope of actions of labor organizations was limited by the state through the corporatist framework to preserve and maintain the characteristics of such an authoritarian regime. Labor unions and other social organizations that did not fulfil the state policies were either co-opted or repressed, as has been widely documented in the case of labor protests during the PRI era (see Chapters 4 and 5). Therefore, during this regime the majority of union organizations were within the official wing of unionism. The access to political resources and political position for union leaders that favored the working class with social benefits, were obtained in most cases by labor organizations through negotiations with the state rather than mobilizations and protests. This explains the fact that the official unions were incapable of reacting effectively during the 1980s when the state opted for breaking the alliance with labor organizations. Labor unions in Mexico lacked a democratic tradition because they were products of an authoritarian regime where previous labor protests had been repressed and the state had also opened spaces of negotiation; thus, official unions, especially the CTM, were not accustomed to dealing with a different kind of negotiations with the state, such as relying on wide and long mobilizations and strikes.

In order to explain the acquiescence of organized labor in light of the change in economic and social policies adopted by the state in the 1980s and 1990s, the corporatist framework with regard to the relations between unions and the state becomes the crucial factor. As highlighted in Chapter 2, corporatism is an important factor defining the role of labor unions as it was detected that the countries with varied corporatist structures of government have the highest levels of union density. Another aspect is that the countries with more pluralist systems are less unionized (for example, France and the United States). Within corporatist schemes, the alliance between labor unions and the state determines to a great extent the existence of strong unions in various spheres such as the representation of labor unions in the employed labor force. This leads to high levels of union density in the workforce.

In the case of Mexico, corporatism was also an important factor within the political and institutional realm to account for the strength of organized labor. The kind of corporatism in this country was a peculiar corporatism shaped by the existence of a hegemonic political party (PRI) ruling the country for more than 70 years. The authoritarian political regime also constrained the operation of labor unions to its own agenda. In this context, the close relationship with the state marked the fate of labor organizations. During the PRI era, a particular corporatist framework prevailed with different gradations of intensity. But what is clear is that the more evident the corporatist framework was in the political regime, the more relevant labor organizations were in the employed labor force. From the 1940s to the 1970s, the corporatist structure shaped by the hegemonic political party saw its preponderance in the political system. In addition, during such a period, labor unions were important actors in the political arena and, therefore, occupied an important position in the employed labor force, with substantial levels of union membership. However, as corporatism lost predominance along with the hegemonic party system, labor unions also saw a reduction in their political influence and of union members in the labor force. It is clear that the alliance between organized labor and the state was crucial to sustain high levels of union membership and other aspects such as the influence in policymaking and the access of labor unions to political positions and public resources.

It is also remarkable that President Salinas utilized and relied on the corporatist structure headed by the state, integrated by organized groups such as national labor organizations and employer confederations, in order to implement neoliberal policies, such as the control of inflation through establishing limits on wages and prices. The abovementioned can be corroborated in the diverse *Pactos* signed by the government, unions, and employers' organizations between 1987 and 1995. In this way, the corporatist structure, although diminished, regained preponderance in the Mexican case as it was used by the government during the late 1980s and early 1990s to implement unpopular policies for the working class. Moreover, after the democratization process, corporatist arrangements were preserved to guarantee a docile and collaborative labor movement, especially from the CTM and CT affiliated labor organizations towards the Fox administration.

The implementation of neoliberal policies to face the negative effects of the debt crisis, were followed by mobilizations and protests of labor unions and other organized groups. In the cases of Argentina and Venezuela, for instance, there was opposition to neoliberal reforms. In various Latin American countries, such as Argentina, Brazil, also Spain, where the military and authoritarian regimes subjugated labor unions and suppressed their guarantees, the arrival of democratization brought about the revitalization of labor unions and in some cases the increase of union membership as in Spain. In contrast, democratization, in the case of Mexico, was not a crucial factor of labor renovation or a development that facilitated the strengthening of labor unions. Especially because the majority of unionized workers were in official organizations tied to the authoritarian government sustained by the hegemonic party and the corporatist framework.

In this way, the official labor organizations pursued a practical strategy that consisted of supporting the PRI authoritarian regime as their privileged conditions stem from that regime. Democratization in Mexico undermined the corporatist framework and the hegemonic party system that guaranteed political stability during previous decades. However, the democratic regime emerging in the 2000s has not created opportunities for the strengthening of labor unions. As opposed to other democratization processes, in the case of Mexico there has not been an effective transition, as was the case in Spain, for instance. There has not been a common agenda between the government and the PRI, the most important opposition party. In Spain the demise of the authoritarian regime was followed by an agreed transition among the most important political parties which created conditions for the strengthening of labor unions. In Spain, as a result of democratization, labor unions recovered from illegality and persecution, which was certainly not the case in Mexico.

The role of neoliberalism was not very clear in terms of its impacts on labor union density. Some features of neoliberalism such as economic globalization, *flexibilization*, privatization and the adjustment of macroeconomic indicators (inflation), were observed. As mentioned in Chapter 6, a structural adjustment program was implemented after 1982, which consisted of policies to stabilize macroeconomic indicators. For example, the contention of inflation affected Mexican workers' living standards as it was achieved through the limitation of wage increases and price controls. As figures on unionization suggest, these policies did not generate the decline of union density. Other neoliberal policies were crucial in this regard. The privatization of state companies resulted in the reduction of employees in the public sector, one of the bastions of organized labor. It also implied the *flexibilization* of collective agreements, deleting previous benefits for unionized workers. Nevertheless, the outcomes of the privatization process were diverse; in some cases, unionized workers were dismissed (e.g., SICARTSA and Cananea; see Chapter 6). However, in other cases the privatization process included the participation of the union in the negotiation of the collective contract providing benefits during the process, for example, the privatization of TELMEX permitted a favorable contract for the workers of the STRM.

As mentioned in Chapter 6, the erroneous control and mismanagement of macroeconomic policies by the government in the 1970s and in the early 1990s generated economic shocks. For instance, in the late 1970s, the economy was sustained by the high oil prices and the low interest rates. In the early 1990s, the economy benefitted from foreign investment, mostly volatile capital flows, while it maintained a pegged exchange rate regime. Therefore, the main cause of the decline of union density and union influence in the political realm is more linked to the economic crises of 1982 and 1994–1995, rather than considering the effects of neoliberal policies in this regard.

On the other hand, neoliberalism promoted economic globalization, opening the national economy to international markets and depending on free trade and transnational financial capital as the main tool for domestic economic development. In order to attract foreign capital, neoliberal governments in the country maintained low labor costs and, at the same time, consented to the creation of "ghost unions" with labor contracts of protection. Nevertheless, economic liberalization was not strongly related to the union density decline as was the case in many developed countries. In the case of Mexico, there was not a strong relation between economic globalization and labor union density. Most of the decline of union density occurred between 1989 and 1994 (only a small fraction of the decline took place after 1994) when NAFTA initiated.

The most important labor confederations in Mexico have survived the neoliberal reforms and the wave of political democratization and adapted to these conditions. Although it opposed in some cases, in general, the CTM endorsed the implementation of neoliberal policies in the 1980s and 1990s. Despite the fact that it has lost members in some areas, the CTM-affiliated unions are still powerful, especially in some sectors such as the electricity power generation (SUTERM), energy and oil (STPRM), and other regional affiliated federations in provincial states represent significant shares of the employed labor force in key sectors of the economy.

The administration of President Andrés Manuel López Obrador represents an opportunity for the expansion of union membership and the revitalization of the labor movement. A change in the structure of corporatism that regulates relations between the state and the unions is feasible.

Finally, it is possible that workers' working conditions will improve in terms of their earnings and wages, which in turn will lead to the reduction of inequality.

Index

R. Zepeda, *The Decline of Labor Unions in Mexico during the Neoliberal Period*, Governance, Development, and Social Inclusion in Latin America, https://doi.org/10.1007/978-3-030-65710-9

The manufacturer's authorised representative in the EU is Springer Nature Customer Service Centre GmbH, Europaplatz 3, 69115 Heidelberg, Germany. If you have any concerns regarding our products, please contact ProductSafety@springernature.com

Printed and bound by CPI Group (UK) Ltd, Croydon, CR0 4YY
30/09/2026
02225700-0004